God's Call to
Women

God's Call to Women

Twelve Spiritual Memoirs

EDITED BY
CHRISTINE ANNE MUGRIDGE

CHARIS

SERVANT PUBLICATIONS
ANN ARBOR, MICHIGAN

Charis Books is an imprint of Servant Publications especially designed to serve Roman Catholics.

Servant Publications—Mission Statement

We are dedicated to publishing books that spread the gospel of Jesus Christ, help Christians to live in accordance with that gospel, promote renewal in the church, and bear witness to Christian unity.

Previously published by Hermitage Press as *The Gift of Femininity,* ISBN: 0-9715985-2-5

This edition published by:
Servant Publications
P.O. Box 8617
Ann Arbor, MI 48107
www.servantpub.com

Cover design: Noah Pudgil Design Professionals

03 04 05 06 10 9 8 7 6 5 4 3 2 1

Printed in the United States of America
ISBN 1-56955-383-1

Library of Congress Cataloging-in-Publication Data

  God's call to women : twelve spiritual memoirs / edited by Christine
Anne Mugridge.
      p. cm.
Originally published: The gift of femininity. [S.l.] : Hermitage Press,
2002.
  ISBN 1-56955-383-1 (alk. paper)
  1. Catholic women--Religious life. I. Mugridge, Christine Anne. II.
Title.
  BX2353.G54 2003
  282'.092'2--dc21
                                          2003010627

Acknowledgements

This book is dedicated to Our Lady, the Star of the New Evangelization, the Mother of Hope, and the Delightful Tabernacle of the Most Holy Trinity, and to Pope John Paul II, whose priesthood, having been formed in the heart of the Blessed Mother, is a great gift to humanity, and in particular to the women of the world.

I thank God for my parents, Dr. Harry Raymond and Elizabeth Mary Mugridge; the heritage of faith with which they provided me is their greatest legacy. Likewise, I wish to thank my immediate family for their love and encouragement during this project. Mike and Chris, Lynne and Candace, your help has been invaluable.

Most especially, I wish to thank the contributing authors of this anthology. You are my heroes in faith. Your witness to the love of God is profound and your generosity in sharing your personal testimonies is greatly appreciated. May your ministries and lives continue to be blessed.

Thank you also to my friends Shawnda Draeger, Jennifer Balster, Susan Coons, David and Cindy Claeys, Stephen and Sheila Warner, Sisters Michael and Mary, Shari Rose Antol, Denise Leach, Jerry Usher, and John and Mary Klein, whose support throughout the years during the unfolding of this work was consistent and untiring.

Finally, thank you to my spiritual fathers who have guided me during the most crucial times in my life and brought me closer to God: Fr. Abbot Joseph, Fr. Ray Ryland, Fr. Charles Kubsz, Msgr. George Monaghan, Fr. Gary Sumpter, Fr. John Corapi, and Fr. James Flanagan. God love you!

Contents

W e give thanks as a family of Our Father for each and every woman, and the mothers, sisters, and wives in this book and all women who have come forth from the heart of God as they have been embraced by his eternal love. They gift themselves to the human family from the bosom of the Holy Trinity.

We are ever so grateful for the genius of women in the midst of all peoples and nations. We give thanks to the Holy Spirit for all his gifts bestowed on them. We pray that the fruits of this book will bring all those who read this book to the holiness to which the Triune God has called us all.

We are grateful as well for the inspirations given the compiler of this book and her tenacity in the work of its publication.

Father James H. Flanagan, SOLT
August 23, 2001
Feast of Saint Rose of Lima

Twelve lives ...
A Spiritual Bouquet ...
One dozen roses for Our Lady ...

*L*isten, my faithful children; open up your petals, like roses planted near running waters; send up the sweet odor of incense, break forth in blossoms like the lily. Send up the sweet odor of your hymn of praise; bless the Lord for all he has done (Sir 39:13-14).

The concept for this collection was formulated while on retreat in northern California shortly after a life-changing mission trip to Russia. In the last twelve years I have had the opportunity to travel to many countries and witness firsthand the astounding growth of existing apostolates and societies as well as the formation of numerous new ecclesial groups and communities. From these groups, the lives of various individuals both living and deceased radiated the light of Christ in ways that were heroic and inspiring. I've met many men and women who are gifted leaders, modern "saints in the making," whose lives have touched not only mine but thousands of others' as well. It amazed me how many women were in leadership positions, or as they would prefer to say it, called by God into "service." The thought occurred to me, "Why not bring a collection of women together who can share their personal testimony and in so doing offer a positive witness to the universal truths of our faith?"

Work began and later developed primarily as a twofold "response" to a movement of the Holy Spirit deep within my heart. First of all, during a time when the doctrines of the Church, the Magisterium, and the Holy Father are coming under great criticism, I felt it important to reflect upon what is good and true about the Catholic faith. Too often a negative, critical voice is heard throughout the media while the truth once again stands as Christ did: alone, condemned in silence, crowned with thorns. I have had the opportunity to study the teachings of Christ as established in Catholic doctrine. So many of the arguments I have heard against the Church are based on false premises and misunderstanding. Granted, due to human sinfulness there have been many men and women wounded in the process of the gospel message being proclaimed. However, the message of the gospel needs to be proclaimed, in a forward-moving spirit of truth, as opposed to a stand of defense. It is the obligation of each Christian to follow the command of Christ and "Preach the Gospel to all creation" (Mk 16:15). What better way to clarify the truth than through living personal testimony? We witness a striking example of this in the woman at the well with Christ (see Jn 4). As the woman ran back from the well after her encounter with the Messiah, the whole town came out to discover for themselves the truth of her story.

Especially today, the testimony of women is important. Sadly, many of the loudest voices raised in angry opposition to the Church are those of women. However, this book, being a collection of testimony, is not rooted in response to this social phenomenon. It finds its origin once again in the choice of Christ, for it was to the women first that Our Savior chose to appear after his resurrection. The women who stood so faithfully by him at his crucifixion were asked by him to go and proclaim to his followers that indeed he had risen from the dead. The women in his life became the apostles to the apostles!

The second element of my response to the Holy Spirit occurred in a more personal manner. I have had the joy and blessing of meeting the Holy Father, Pope John Paul II. On one occasion, I was able to attend Mass in his private chapel in Rome. It was during the reception of Holy Communion, as I knelt, that John Paul then placed his hands over my head. He prayed over me aloud, hands extended, in his native tongue. I was at first surprised, but I did not move! As I looked up at him, I realized a moment of profound communion and anointing. This moment of prayer gave me great strength, and continues to do so. After the Mass, those in attendance prayed quietly together in the chapel with the Holy Father. The room was silent save for the slight "groaning in the Spirit" that could be heard from John Paul. Immediately following, we were led to a brief meeting with the Holy Father in a receiving room. Each of us had the opportunity to speak with him personally. The words exchanged with him further sealed my sense of solidarity and mission. This mission is exactly the gospel mandate and is united with my identity as a daughter of the Church. Particularly it is based on the personal response each Catholic has been asked to give to the Holy Father's Apostolic Exhortation, *Ecclesia in America*. Avanti!

My childhood was spent in the 1960s and 1970s. These decades saw great changes in social structures as well as in the Church. The thirty-plus years since the closing of the Second Vatican Council have been somewhat tumultuous, to say the least. The Holy Father quotes from the Closing Message of the council in his encyclical "On the Dignity and Vocation of Women," saying, "The hour is coming, in fact has come, when the vocation of women is being acknowledged in its fullness, the hour in which women acquire in the world an influence, an effect and a power never hitherto achieved. That is why, at this moment when the human race is undergoing so deep a transformation, women imbued with a spirit of the Gospel can do so much to aid humanity in not falling."[1] Pope John Paul himself is encouraging women from all areas of life to take up the great commissioning call of Christ, utilizing the gifts unique to their gender. Special emphasis, in truth, is being placed upon women and the importance of their active role within the Church and society. In his Post-Synodal Apostolic Exhortation, *Ecclesia in America,* John Paul notes:

Particular attention needs to be given to the vocation of women. On other occasions I have expressed my esteem for the specific contribution of women to the progress of humanity and recognized the legitimacy of their aspiration to take part fully in ecclesial, cultural, social and economic life. (167) Without this contribution, we would miss the enrichment which only the "feminine genius" (168) can bring to the life of the Church and to society. To fail to recognize this would be an historic injustice, especially in America, if we consider the contribution which women have made to the material and cultural development of the continent, just as they have in handing down and preserving the faith. Indeed, "their role was decisive...."[2]

If this is the age where women will have an influence in the world "never hitherto achieved," and I believe it is, then Catholic women especially should feel the weight of responsibility upon their shoulders and *respond with courage* to the call of Christ. The Holy Father in a manner both traditional and fresh has lifted up as model and exemplar that "woman" from Scripture, Mary. Through the pope's leading, we have entered into an extraordinary period of reflection upon the Mother of God. He urges us along, to cross with him the "threshold of hope," speaking of a time of "New Pentecost." The Blessed Virgin Mary is key to this time of New Evangelization. The Holy Father has given her the title "Star of the New Evangelization," and as such she is a Mother of Hope for all people.

The original title of this book, *The Gift of Femininity,* was inspired by the witness of the Blessed Mother and those women immediately closest to Christ during his life, death, and resurrection. In Christ, who was sent by the Father, a new and everlasting covenant is established; one that can never be broken by human sin, as in the past. Through the paschal mystery of Christ, we are grafted into the heart of God himself. We celebrate and renew this covenant with each Holy

Eucharist. In this covenant relationship with God, the sting of death is not only wiped away and Eden is not merely restored. The hope of glory is fulfilled in Christ and the kingdom of God is immediately at hand!

The first person to receive the salvific merits of everlasting life through Christ was Mary. She, being "pre-redeemed," was prepared to give of herself completely as a woman who was free from the stain of original sin, in fulfillment of the plan of God the Father. In Mary, we see a reversal of the first garden scenario where Eve was taken from Adam. Now the "new Adam" was formed within the "new Eve" by the power of the Holy Spirit. Mary herself, upon uttering her "Fiat," became the mother of "all the living," and within her existed the eternally new garden. She is the sacred vessel of grace and mercy for all humanity. As the angels breathed a sigh of relief upon hearing her reply, the Creator of the universe came to dwell within the womb of the Virgin. Mary realizes the great fulfillment, not only of her own life, but also of generations past, present, and still to come!

Being of the House of David, she was a chosen daughter of a chosen people. She proclaimed the sacred and historical covenant lineage she shared with Abraham in her Magnificat: "He has come to the help of his servant Israel for he has remembered his promise of mercy, the promise he made to our fathers, to Abraham and his children for ever."

Mary's lineage then becomes the lineage of *all* the children of God; a lineage formed by the breath of the Father to prepare for and be receptive to the arrival of the Messiah at the "fullness of time." We don't need to be preoccupied with the scientific search for the so-called missing link. Salvation history includes the important "missing link," and it is Mary!

Mary, then, in offering the gift of herself, demonstrates the profound gift of femininity as God intended it to be realized. This gift is a model and a blessing to all humanity. As it was with Mary, the gift of femininity is meant to be fruitful in the church and the world, today and tomorrow. *We need to see and hear of the heroic witnesses of faith among us.*

This book, then, consists of a collection of shared personal thoughts and testimony on the Church and the Catholic faith to demonstrate the unique feminine presence and contribution active today. The chapters herein are written by women, each of which, like Our Blessed Lady, is "blessed because she believed." These are the stories of the development of faith and ministries through trial and conversion.

I wanted to call upon women who had a deep love for God and who were active in a ministry within the Church. The authors are not only "content" to be members of the Catholic Church. These women have found solace, consolation, inspiration, and salvation through the teachings and sacraments of their Catholic faith. Their lives have not been without pain. Their walk with Christ at times has been quite challenging. Throughout these pages, they witness to the saving power of grace and the mystery of man's free will to cooperate with that grace. The women who have taken the time to share their thoughts and inspirations with you would not consider themselves to be out of the ordinary. Yet it is precisely in the "ordinary" that the action of the Holy Spirit is seen most clearly. "Grace builds upon nature," and thus a life that is merely human becomes in the hands of God quite holy.

In the history of the Church, even from earliest times, there were side-by-side with men *a number of women,* for whom the response of the Bride to the Bridegroom's redemptive love acquired full expressive force.... The same thing is repeated down the centuries, from one generation to the next, as *the history of the Church* demonstrates. By defending the dignity of women and their vocation, the Church has shown honor and gratitude for those women who—faithful to the Gospel—have shared in every age in the apostolic mission of the whole People of God. They are the holy martyrs, virgins and mothers of families, who bravely bore witness to their faith and passed on the Church's faith and tradition by bringing up their children in the spirit of the Gospel. In every age and in every country we find many "perfect" women (Cf. Prov. 31:10) who, despite persecution, difficulties and discrimination, have shared in the Church's mission.... The witness and the achievements of Christian women have had a significant impact on the life of the Church as well as of society. Even in the face of serious social discrimination, holy women have acted "freely," strengthened by their union with Christ.... In our own days too the Church is constantly enriched by the witness of the many women who fulfill their vocation to holiness. Holy women are an incarnation of the feminine ideal; they are also a model for all Christians, a model of the "sequela Christi," an example of how the Bride must respond with love to the love of the Bridegroom.[3]

In the shared experiences within this book I hope you will see the living witness of the faith of various women who are given to Christ, and in their witness a testimony also to the gift of femininity in the Church. What I sense after reading this collection is the evidence not of a new "ism" but of what I prefer to call the *authentic femininity* already existing within the Church. Authentic femininity has its foundations in the God-given "dignity and vocation" of women which John Paul II clarified for us in his encyclical of the same title. This is a subject that is only just beginning to be explored. At this stage, the gift of femininity is much like the budding of a mystical rose in the heart of the Church. As time passes, it will open with greater beauty to glorify God.

What is needed in our day is encouragement and hope. It is time for a joyful word of thanks from women who love the Church and are blessed by their Holy Father. For it is in and through the Church that *hope* comes to the world, making our daily lives more than just tolerable ... making our lives, in fact, living icons of Christ's presence in the world, a foreshadowing of the glory that is to come. The very breath of God is poured out upon humanity in a sweet and ever-creative manner through the Church. There are those within this "pilgrim people" that would say the foundational points of our faith need to change in order for it to continue. Not so. The Church herself proves that her unchanging foundation is divinely instituted, by the children she bears. In the history of the Church there have blossomed many great saints. Cooperating in this bringing forth of fruit is John Paul II. Far from being against women, this present Holy Father has canonized more women saints than any of his predecessors! This collection of stories serves to demonstrate the fact that the daughters of Abraham are thriving and well.

The Holy Father has requested on numerous occasions that the Church universal reflect upon the contribution of women, encouraging us to ask ourselves, "What exactly constitutes the full measure of a woman's feminine dignity?" He has held Mary up to us as a model of the "ideal." As we read the testimonies chronicled in this book, let us reflect also upon Our Lady's *Magnificat*. In so doing we will gain insight into this God-given dignity. We are called to rejoice in the marvels of God, which he has worked through this woman of the gospel and will continue to manifest through all women throughout salvation history.

The chapters in this book reveal also the desires of the hearts of individual Catholic women from around the world, who represent countless unknown women like them. May their voices be heard, may the truth of Christ be revealed to the world through them, and may your life be enhanced as you encounter their gift of femininity.

I pray the reading of this book will bless you as it has me and that it will inspire you to even greater faith in Christ and his Church. Finally, may our Lady, who is that "feminine genius" personified, bring to birth in your hearts and lives the indwelling of the Holy Trinity to whom she is united as our Advocate. I commend this work to her:

Woman of the New and Everlasting Covenant; Daughter of Abraham

O Blessed Woman,
Mother of the New and Everlasting Covenant
who is Jesus Christ himself,
bear Grace and Mercy to the People of God
who lift their supplications to you.
Dear Lady, we love you and
we entrust ourselves to you.
Virgin Daughter of Abraham,
assist us in the living out of our Fiat
so that we too may experience the joy
of our heavenly inheritance
and once more know
the loving embrace of our Abba, Father.
You who are the Star of the New Evangelization,
Heavenly Prophetess
of the Triumphant coming of Christ;
take us into your Heart Full of Grace and
there shine upon us the
Light of the Dawning of the New Pentecost.
Mother of Hope, unite us to your Heavenly Spouse
so that we, your children, may
proclaim with you eternally, all
Glory to the Father, and to the Son,
and to the Holy Spirit,
now and forever. Amen

Christine Anne Mugridge
February 14, 2002
Santa Rosa, California

PART ONE

Receptivity: Encounter With the Divine

*"My soul proclaims the greatness of the Lord,
my spirit rejoices in God my Savior
for he has looked with favor on his lowly servant."*

*G*od, the Most Holy Trinity, our Creator, calls us into union with himself. How we respond to God's initiative of love is crucial in determining our eternal destiny:

> *"Woman—Mother of God"* ... This reality also determines the essential horizon of reflection on the dignity and vocation of women. In anything we think, say or do concerning the dignity and the vocation of women, our thoughts, hearts and actions must not become detached from this horizon. The dignity of every human being and the vocation corresponding to that dignity find their definitive measure in *union with God.* Mary, the woman of the Bible, is the most complete expression of this dignity and vocation. For no human being, male or female, created in the image and likeness of God, can *in any* way attain fulfillment apart from this image and likeness.[1]

Women are naturally gifted with an interior awareness of the voice of God; that is to say, they possess a natural "receptivity." This grace-filled sensitivity predisposes them to be more responsive to the *encounter with the divine.* The personal encounter with each person of the Trinity is the first step toward personal conversion and union with God. The witness of this union is a powerful testimony for humanity; however, this witness takes on a unique importance in the woman, Mary:

> Mary ... conceived the Incarnate Word by the power of the Holy Spirit and then in the whole of her life allowed herself to be guided by his interior activity ... as the woman who was docile to the voice of the Spirit, a woman of silence and attentiveness, a woman of hope who, like Abraham, accepted God's will "hoping against hope" (cf. Romans 4:18). Mary gave full expression

to the longing of the poor of Yahweh and is a radiant model for those who entrust themselves with all their hearts to the promises of God.[2]

The faith of the Blessed Virgin Mary is the perfect response to God's love and a model for the Church throughout the centuries. Mary seeks the face of God daily in prayer and is open to his inspirations. Therefore, upon hearing the Word of God, she does not hesitate to respond with her "Fiat"—that is, with her total free-will offering of herself back to God. She is the "loftiest model" of woman's cooperation with the plan of God. Her faith sets the precedence for the Church itself in all its activities for the salvation of souls:

> In the faith which Mary professed at the Annunciation as the "handmaid of the Lord" and in which she constantly "precedes" the pilgrim People of God throughout the earth, the Church strives energetically and constantly to bring all humanity ... back to Christ its head in the unity of his Spirit.[3]

Thus, Mary sheds light on the role of women in salvation history, while demonstrating God's respect for women. Her life emphasizes the truth that free-will cooperation with God quickly moves a person into a position of collaboration with the divine plan of salvation. Her proximity to her Savior elevates her great gift of service and crowns her with the title "Queen":

> From the first moment of her divine motherhood, of her union with the Son whom "the Father sent into the world, that the world might be saved through him" (cf. John 3:17), *Mary takes her place within Christ's messianic service.* It is precisely this service which constitutes the very foundation of that Kingdom in which "to serve ... means to reign." Christ, the "Servant of the Lord," will show all people the royal dignity of service, the

dignity which is joined in the closest possible way to the vocation of every person.[4]

Mary is addressed by the angel Gabriel at the Annunciation as "full of grace." In her discourse with him, she makes no demands, nor does she imply any personal ambition. With total trusting acceptance of the will of God, she offers her humble service. One could say that she is "full of divine love" and becomes immediately a mediatrix of this grace and love to all. At the moment of the Annunciation, Mary exhibits a union with God first in her heart, and sets into motion a new collaboration with God in the work of salvation:

> In the language of the Bible "grace" means a special gift, which according to the New Testament has its source precisely in the Trinitarian life of God himself, God who is love (cf. 1 Jn 4:8).[5] The history of "fairest love" begins, ... in those wondrous words which the angel spoke to Mary, called to become the Mother of the Son of God. With Mary's "yes," the One who is "God from God and Light from Light becomes a son of man. Mary is his Mother,... the *Mother of fairest love.*"[6]

With her whole being, Mary rejoices at the long-awaited gift of her Savior, now growing within her. Her soul magnifies God's greatness. She will point to him throughout her life, continuing to use all of her gifts to "magnify" *him.* In her words, we glimpse a profound "soul to soul" relationship between Our Lady and the Most Holy Trinity. Her spirit, a spirit of rejoicing, delights in the salvation that the conception of the Christ-child initiates. Therefore, she *desires to serve* all those generations who came before her and will follow until the end of time. While not losing sight of her own "creatureliness," she courageously cooperates in God's salvific plan. In this work, it is her humility that compels the Almighty to become man.

The Blessed One's acceptance of the will of God, while far from being passive, demonstrates the high capacity for personal self-giving that is a hallmark of women. Here we see exemplified a particular sensitivity to what the Holy Father refers to as the "values of the heart." This understanding of self-donation is integral to understanding the very nature of God himself. It is in this manner that the love of God is potentially reflected through women. Often this gift of the feminine genius is mocked and misunderstood, even taken advantage of to the point where, as a result, women become hardened to their own nature. There is however, a special bond with Mary that all women have, which, when realized, can bring tremendous healing and graces. Their interior sentiment of "forgetfulness of self," when made perfect by grace, translates into an *attitude of mercy*. It is this attitude of mercy, patterned after the heart of the Most Holy Trinity, that the world needs so desperately today. Mankind, wounded by hatred and sin, has often experienced cruelty upon cruelty. Antithetical to this is the reality that the "development of the feminine personality calls for a commitment to charity."7 This commitment to charity begins, of course, in the heart, whereby women are able to "sow the seeds of the 'civilization of love.'"8 This attitude of mercy bespeaks an interior predisposition strengthened by the indwelling presence of God.

The next three chapters exemplify the commitment to charity. The women herein demonstrate that particularly feminine *attitude of mercy*. Through their intimate union with God, the authors remain open to his inspirations. Through the course of their lives, they manifest the will of God. As they reflect upon this relationship, they testify to his blessings. Here we read of the Divine Initiative being presented and *responded to*. So, much like Mary, through their example the "greatness of the Lord" is proclaimed. Let us read about these women who understand the importance of being a servant *and* rejoicing in God their Savior.

Chapter 1

The Grace of a Call

CHIARA LUBICH

A pen does not know what it is going to print. The chisel does not know what it is going to sculpt. Similarly, when God takes a person in hand, to create one of his works, the person concerned does not know what he or she will have to do. He or she is God's instrument, and God's instruments, generally speaking, have one characteristic: littleness, weakness. As the apostle Paul says, "God chose those who by human standards are weak. God chose ... those who count for nothing ... so that no human being may boast before God" (1 Cor 1:27-29). I think this description fits me as well.

The Grace of a Call

I first realized the grace of a special call in Loreto, in Mary's shrine. I had gone to that city for a convention of female Catholic students. It was the year 1939. As yet, I did not know what the Lord wanted from me, and I was not giving much thought to it.

The first time I entered the "little house," preserved in the fortress-like church that was built around it, I was seized by a great emotion. I did not even have the time to ask myself whether history could objectively prove that the house was truly the dwelling that had given shelter to the Holy Family. I felt collected all by myself, caught up in that great mystery. As a steady stream of tears rolled down my face—quite an unusual experience for me—I began to reflect on everything that might have taken place in that house: the angel's annunciation to Mary, the life of the three persons there—Jesus, Mary, and Joseph.

In deep veneration, I was touching those stones and wooden boards, while envisioning in my imagination the house built by Joseph. I was almost hearing the voice of the infant Jesus, seeing him run across the room; I was looking at those walls made holy by the voice of Mary singing hymns.

While my companions remained in the school building where we were lodging, I, personally, though taking part in the convention, did not let a single day pass by without rushing to the "little house." While there, I went through the same experience and the same deep emotion each time, as if a special grace of God would envelop me, as if God's presence would crush me. It was contemplation, for sure; it was prayer, in a way; and it was a living together with the three holy people there.

The seminar came to an end with a Mass celebrated precisely in the larger Basilica, filled with people. I took part in it wholeheartedly. *Quite suddenly, a light came upon me: I had found my "way," and many, many others would follow along in it also.*

After the experience at Loreto, I went back to Trent full of joy. I did not possess any other significant elements about my future but those just given here. At any rate, to a priest who asked me what had taken place in Loreto, I replied: "I found my way."

"Which one?" he continued. "Marriage?"

"No," I replied.

"A life of virginity in the world?"

"No."

"A life in the convent?"

"No."

The little house of Loreto had unveiled to me something rather mysterious, yet quite certain; it was *a fourth way,* which would later be put into practice, a way after the likeness of the Holy Family, namely a living together of virgins and married people—men and women, all of them offered up in oblation to God, although in a diversified manner; it would become the "Focolare."

The Gift of Unity

Every time I have been asked to define the spirituality of the Focolare Movement and what difference there might be between God's gift to our Movement and the gifts whereby he has endowed others in the Church both in our days and throughout the centuries, we have no hesitation to say that it is the gift of unity. Unity is our distinctive calling.

The year was 1944. The Second World War was raging, even in Trent, my hometown, in northern Italy. There were bombs, rubble, and death.

It happened, one day during the war, that while taking shelter from the bombings my friends and I met in a dark basement. In the light of a single candle, we opened the Gospel. Our eyes fell on the prayer that Jesus addressed to his Father before he went to die: "May they all be one. Father, may they be one in us, as you are in me and I in you" (Jn 17:21). We had some difficulty understanding this text. Yet in our hearts we felt a certain perception that we had been created precisely for the fulfillment of those words, that in them was to be found the magna charta of the Movement that was coming into being. We perceived that we were called to give a contribution to the attainment of the unity, which Jesus mentions in his prayer.

The bombing continued, and they took from us the people or things that had been the goals, the ideals of our young hearts. One of us was waiting to get married; her fiancée did not come back from the front. Another loved her home; it was damaged. My ideal was the study of philosophy; the war prevented me from attending the university.

All that happened affected us deeply. The lesson that God was offering us through these circumstances was clear; everything is "vanity of vanities" (Eccl 1:2; 12:8). Everything passes away. At the same time,

God put a question in my heart and with it, the answer: is there an ideal that will not die, that no bomb can destroy, to which we can give the whole of ourselves? Yes, there is. It is God. We decided to make God the ideal of our lives.

Our parents were evacuated into the valleys far from the city. We remained in Trent. Some stayed for work or study. I stayed above all to look after the movement that was coming to life. We lived together in a small apartment. It was the first "Focolare." We ran to the air-raid shelters night and day, and could take only a small Gospel with us.

We had found the ideal to live for: God.

But how could we do this?

Jesus taught: "Not everyone who says to me, 'Lord, Lord,' will enter the kingdom of heaven, but only the one who does the will of my Father in heaven" (Mt 7:21). So it was not a matter of feelings or trying to be pious. To do God's will; that was what mattered.

The air-raid shelters offered little protection; death could have come at any time. So another pressing question arose: "Is there something God especially wants us to do, something particularly dear to his heart?" If we were going to die, we wanted to be able to put that very thing into practice, at least in our last moments.

The Gospels gave us the answer, telling us of Jesus' "new commandment": "This is my commandment: Love one another as I have loved you. No one has greater love than this, to lay down one's life for one's friends" (Jn 15:12-13).

We looked one another in the eye and declared:

"I am ready to give my life for you."

"And I for you."

"And I for you."

Every one of us for each of the others.

This solemn promise helped us to do willingly the thousand and one little things that love demands of us each day. For we were not usually asked to die for one another, but in the meantime we could share everything—worries, joys, sufferings, our few belongings, our small spiritual treasures.

Jesus in Our Midst

We noticed that, because of this mutual love put into practice, the quality of our lives changed significantly. Our hearts experienced new confidence, joy, and peace we had never known before, a new fullness of life, and a new understanding, totally unlike any other. Someone, very quietly, had joined our group—our invisible Brother, Jesus. Because of our mutual love, his words had been fulfilled among us: "For where two or three are gathered in my name, [which means in my love], there am I in the midst of them" (Mt 18:20). We never wanted to lose his presence again.

After beginning this new way of life with Jesus in our midst, I experienced that his presence becomes a light that enlightens and makes Scripture and even the mysteries of our faith, to a certain extent, comprehensible to us in a new manner.

Moreover, we always felt that if we loved one another as he loved us, he would become in our midst the Saint communicating his holiness to us. Of course, all the holy men and women of the Church, as brothers and sisters, have enlightened and strengthened us also during all these years. If we wish to learn the way to meditate, we must have recourse to the contemplative saints, such as Teresa of Avila and John of the Cross. If we wish to make the spiritual exercises, we cannot ignore Saint Ignatius, who is the master, just as Saint Francis will always reveal to us what poverty truly is, and Saint Thérèse of the Infant Jesus will always inspire whoever desires to attain holiness in a short time.

God was teaching us a new way, as yet unknown to us—that of going to holiness together, with Christ, the Saint, in our midst. Another immediate effect of his presence was that hearts were touched around us.

Christ had said, "May they be one in us, so that the world may believe" (Jn 17:21). If there is unity, the world around us believes. And this is what happened. Many people radically changed their way of life and others found the strength to respond to God's call or to be faithful to their decision to live for him. In just a few months, about five hundred people of all ages and social backgrounds had decided to share our Ideal. We held everything in common among us, like the first Christian community.

The Eucharist—Bond of Unity

Without excluding the importance of all the sacraments, I would like to speak briefly of the very close tie existing between our movement and the Eucharist. Why is the Eucharist so primary in my life and the Focolare? We learned this truth early on.

Since our ideal is unity, we thought it very indicative that Jesus, turning to the Father in the well-known prayer, pleads for unity among his own and among those who would follow them immediately after the institution of the Eucharist that made that unity possible.

Indeed, in order to make us achieve unity, the Lord had prompted us first of all to live that Word in which the entire law and the prophets are summed up, namely to practice love, Christian love indeed as illustrated in the Scriptures, the gospel in particular, a love that appeared to us totally new and demanding in all its requirements. Most certainly, as the members of the movement practiced his love, Jesus, who was already present in them on account of baptism, began to grow within their hearts to make them become each another Jesus walking in this world. Yet it was the Eucharist that gave and continues to give greater solidity to the image of Jesus in each one of us. Moreover, the Eucharist brings about full communion among the brethren; it binds the believers in the unity of the mystical Body of Christ, and makes them more deeply participants in Christ's life, both as a group and as individuals. It prompts them to be "living Church," in the deepest sense of the word.

Thus we may now understand why, from the beginning of the movement, we were motivated to receive the Eucharist daily. The Holy Spirit knew that this sacrament would be indispensable to our movement to carry out the task assigned to it, namely to bring unity to the world. Just like the newborn baby, who, even without realizing it, turns instinctively to the mother's breast to feed on her milk, so also the members of our movement, compelled by a supernatural instinct, the instinct of the Holy Spirit, from the very beginning turned to the breast of Holy Mother Church at all times, to feed on what she holds as her most precious possession for the life of her children. Endowed with this deep personal and collective unity, brought about and made stable by the Eucharist, as children of the Catholic Church, we are made capable to undertake and carry on the various encounters, the "dialogues" with others to which we are called.

A Spirituality for All

When the war ended, those who belonged to the movement were able to move about the country to study, to find work, or to take this life to others. In fact, they were invited to many cities and towns to talk about what they had lived and witnessed.

Meanwhile, in addition to the several women's Focolares, the first men's Focolares began. And something very new happened—married people wanting to give themselves completely to God, to the fullest extent possible, were welcomed as members of these Focolare households.

Up and down Italy, in a quiet way, Christian communities grew up along the lines of the first one in Trent. The Church of Rome, with its centuries of experience and wisdom, carefully studied the new movement and, later on, approved it.

The Role of Women

I have often been asked about the role of women in the Church and in society, especially taking into consideration that the first Focolare households were comprised entirely of women. I would say that women have a special inclination toward love and, as such, they are particularly gifted in being builders of the peace and unity so sorely needed in our age.

In fact, women are *especially called to love.* This does not mean that men are not. History offers countless examples of men who were giant figures of love, of divine charity. However, this does not negate the fact that women are particularly inclined.

Yet, in our times, where can women find the possibility of a new encounter with Jesus and his message? And how are they to manifest a response to this encounter with the divine? We know that the question of women today is a sign of the times. This also indicates the will of God. Yet God, who is Love, who is Providence, does not stop at giving evidence. He opens ways, gives answers, offers possibilities—and he does this above all in his Church. The Church, in fact, through her highest authorities, has set out to give an answer to this timely question. The Church continues to supply divine evidence in this regard. Bishops of every country are earnestly committed so that women's rights may be fully recognized. Furthermore, we know that entire Episcopal Conferences work, offer ideas, and are concerned with obtaining results.

A luminous example of the Church's response to the concerns of women today is found in the person and writings of the Holy Father. In his Apostolic Letter *Mulieris Dignitatem* (On the dignity and vocation of women), is revealed his pastoral concern and ardent desire to give a contribution of justice to the question.[1]

In this letter, today the most significant and authoritative documentation on the dignity and vocation of women, John Paul II emphasizes the reality and role of women, as I believe no one has done since Jesus. Indeed, through the centuries, no other document, after the gospel, contains such lofty praises of the dignity of woman.

I share the pope's view about women as he expounds upon it in *Mulieris Dignitatem*. I would like, therefore, to offer some considerations and call to mind some passages that affected me the most. The pope's view is a new outlook that opens our hearts to hope for a future more considerate of the dignity of women and of the specific role of women in both civil and religious society.

The pope begins by recalling the figure of Mary, the Mother of God, "Theotókos," and he shows us the extraordinary dignity to which God has elevated women in her. Thus he puts into evidence how union with God, to which every person is called, is realized in Mary in the most eminent manner, and for this reason, Mary, the "woman," is the representative of the whole human race, the archetype of every man and woman.

On the other hand, in the "Theotókos" there is "a form of union with the living God which can *only belong to the 'woman,'* Mary."[2] This union "fulfills in the most eminent manner the supernatural predestination to union with the Father which is granted to every human being."[3] In the order of grace, we witness the Virgin of Nazareth as "Theotókos" receiving a superabundance of grace. "Therefore the *fullness of grace* that was granted to the Virgin of Nazareth, with a view to the fact that she would become '*Theotókos' also signifies the fullness of the perfection of 'what is characteristic of woman,'* of '*what is feminine.'* Here we find ourselves, in a sense, at the culminating point, the archetype, of the personal dignity of women."[4] The pope affirms that it is in the light of this reality, "Woman—Mother of God," that every reflection on women should be made.

Beginning with the texts of Genesis on the origins of humanity, the basis of all Christian anthropology, the Holy Father next presents God's plan for man and woman in all its greatness. God created both in his image, not only as individuals, but in their common humanity, as a *unity of the two*. Therefore, woman and man are essentially equal.

They are both persons and as such they are called to participate in the intimate life of God. They "are called to live in a communion of love," in the likeness of God who is Love, who is the unity of the Trinity, and to "mirror in the world the communion of love that is in God." In the "unity of the two," man and woman are "called to exist mutually 'one for the other.'"[5]

The pope manifests an extraordinary insight into what women are within God's plan unfolding through history and within the unity to which God has called all men. Hence the pope emphasizes those truly fundamental values that do away with all discriminations of women and give back to God's creation all its pristine splendor.

Mary as the Model

It is quite heartening to see how the Holy Father likens women to Mary, outlining the exceptional role of Mary, the woman par excellence, in the whole history of salvation. Some may object that Mary is so distant a model as to be almost unattainable. Although we may be quite aware that Mary constitutes the ideal we must achieve, and that we must imitate, reproduce, and re-enact Mary in our lives, as it were, we are also conscious of the distance existing between us and her, who is the Immaculate Conception. The Apostolic Letter *Mulieris Dignitatem* helps us bridge, in a way, this distance by showing Mary as the model not just for men and women, but for women in particular, because Mary has fully achieved God's purpose for human creation even in her femininity, namely in what is most characteristic of a woman.

In the letter, the pope dwells also on the value of maternity and virginity, dealing with these topics at length and explaining how they co-exist in Mary, the Virgin Mother, in a special manner. It is precisely maternity—and these are some of his words—it is precisely carrying the child in the womb that moves women to be open to others. The same is not true of men, who are not subject to this experience. On account of this, even after maternity, in real life, that is, in human and social relationships, women are made to love others in a concrete fashion. They are created by God precisely for this purpose.

There is another important observation about virginity, which is not to be understood as giving up something. The pope explains, in a very convincing manner, that virginity includes being spouses and mothers of souls for the kingdom of God. It is not the utterance of a *no,* but of a fundamental *yes;* it is total surrender to the Bridegroom, to God, as a response to his love.

Jesus and Women

There is a passage in *Mulieris Dignitatem* that touched me in a special manner. It is the chapter dedicated to Jesus' dealings with women, which I consider one of the most fascinating. The pope succeeds in showing us how Jesus encounters, deals with, and talks to the women of his time; his behavior stands out for its extraordinary timeliness even in our own day. Jesus speaks to women, even sinful women, about the mystery of the kingdom of God and its most profound truths with such immediacy and simplicity that the apostles consider it a scandal. His conduct is truly revolutionary and unique. Never do we perceive in his behavior toward women, as the pope underlines, any trace of discrimination; rather, we detect respect and love.

For the first time in the Bible, Jesus calls women—any woman—daughters of Abraham, while in the Scriptures the designation "son of Abraham" is reserved only to men. Many are the women who follow Jesus as disciples.

The pope notes that "Jesus' attitude is a continuous protest against whatever violates women's dignity." This is particularly evident in his conversations with sinful women. In the episode of the forgiven adulterous woman, Jesus denounces a male chauvinistic distortion—as we might call it today—and, by way of the power of truth that he possesses, he arouses even in her accusers the consciousness of their own sinfulness and responsibility. This is an episode that reveals the timeliness of Jesus' teaching for all generations.

The document, moreover, contains a powerful emphasis on the innate capacity of women to discern God's truths and to attain a profound and lively understanding of the mystery of Christ to the point that they follow him even to Mount Calvary, with a courage not exhibited by men. On the day of Pentecost, the Spirit descends on everyone, man and woman. Thus the words of the prophet are fulfilled: "Your sons and daughters shall prophesy" (Acts 2:17). From the manner with which Jesus dealt with women there emerges the fundamental equality of man and woman as part of the Christian ethos.

Leading Figures in the Church

Jesus is present and manifests his concern for all, and in our times especially for women, not only through the channels of the Church's hierarchy. He also lives and can be found, for example, in the numerous ecclesial realities that have been founded down throughout the centuries, renewed and updated after the Second Vatican Council. We know that in the present, as in the past, he enriches the Church with new drive in order to meet the needs of our times.

When traveling and visiting people and groups in different continents, it is easy to note how he is working also in favor of women. One cannot help but notice something new about women. Indeed, one gets the impression that in our world, today, a new type of woman is emerging. It is possible to meet her in the movements, groups, associations, and new religious families that have arisen before or after the Second Vatican Council, in Italy and abroad, all expressions of the Church, in which we cannot help but recognize the action of the Holy Spirit.

These women are present everywhere: in families, offices, schools, parliaments, theaters, hospitals, and church organizations. They are single, married, mothers, young women, and adults.

What is particularly evident today is the emergence of new ecclesial groups and their charism and fresh spirituality. Some have certain elements in common to which women are particularly sensitive. Undoubtedly, they are of interest to everyone, men and women alike, indeed to every social class and vocation, but they are particularly suitable to the laity, and in a special way, to women. One common uniting element is the Marian background that characterizes the spirituality of the new ecclesial groups. This Marian spirituality encourages people to share their faith by communicating their experience, as Mary did with Elizabeth. Moved by the Holy Spirit, Mary communicated, with feminine exuberance, her great and divine experience in the Magnificat. These spiritualities give life to the community, small or large examples of what the great family of God should be, in which the unifying capacity of women, already manifest in the natural family, obtains marvelous results. Above all, these spiritualities are based on the "porro unum" of Christianity, love, the "fulfillment of the law" (see Rom 13:10). Women have found in this love "the hidden treasure" for themselves and for every woman. They know that widespread efforts are being made in the world to guarantee women's rights, and they are involved in this work when necessary. Yet they are neither overly distressed nor complacent. They know that there are cultures in which women are even in a state of slavery, so that there is still much to be done. Yet it is not primarily in "doing" that they place their hopes. Women cannot in this way be fully happy: The way is Another.

Having come into contact with a work of the Church, they have encountered Jesus, a *living Jesus*. Furthermore, just as when he was physically present, now, too, they feel that his love and message give them what is most important. They live this message in a new way, meeting the challenges of the Church today, supported by those sources of God that the Church offers and suggests: the sacraments, the Word of God, and prayer. They have great faith in God's love, and often they want to respond to his love by loving him in their brothers and sisters. This is not, I repeat, a privilege only of women, yet they are more inclined, and bring to this endeavor all the wealth of their femininity. Like springs of pure water in a world dried up by secularism and materialism, they quench the thirst of many by offering peace, serenity, and solutions to problems and anguish. Their love and light overflows onto many. They are not lacking in wisdom, because whoever loves is enlightened: "I will manifest myself to the one who loves me" (Jn 14:21), says Jesus. Their joy spreads to others, and many learn how to love as a result.

Yes, women in the Church have opportunities, as they did in the past. They have opportunities to experience anew the interest that Jesus had for them, to hear the echo of his words, to be touched by a ray of his love; in brief, to meet him again so as to better understand themselves, both who they are and who they should be.

The Charism of Peter

I consider it a great privilege to have had the opportunity to know the pope personally and to meet him at various occasions—private audiences, working repasts, and dinners when he participated in important assemblies of the movement or when he visited our centers.

Ever since my first audience, I have derived the joyful impression of a pope who listens, who is attentive and sensitive, who is not satisfied with a superficial knowledge. He asked questions, wanted to have a thorough understanding of our spirituality, and wanted to know about the expansion of our movement in the world. Yet he did not need many words; a simple sentence or a hint was sufficient, and I felt totally understood, as no other person in the world could understand me. I perceived the charism of Peter in a tangible, unique manner. Then he spoke of my charism and presented it within the framework, as it were, of God's plan of salvation for the world today.

My first impression was later confirmed and strengthened, as, over the course of the years, I admired the marvelous manner with which he gave himself to the Church and to each individual. He behaved in the same manner with us. In the Nervi Hall or in Castel Gandolfo, in hundreds of public and private audiences, those who have attended have had a common experience: they have felt loved by him personally as individuals, namely as human beings, as Christians and—I must also add—as members of the Focolare Movement. Many times he himself told me that he had seen our Focolare or Gen groups everywhere in the world. "You can easily identify them," he commented with a smile.

A Special Visit

The pope has often visited our Focolare centers, and has attended some of our events. The most appreciated visit of all, however, was his unexpected and extraordinary visit to the Rocca di Papa Center. Despite the fact that our international center is located next to Castel Gandolfo, we had always refrained from inviting the pope there, so as not to deprive him of any moment of his rare opportunities of relaxation. Yet he invited himself on August 19, 1984, a day we consider among the most beautiful for our movement.

It was a memorable day, not just for him, since he did so describe it, but extraordinary and unforgettable above all for us because of what the pope told us concerning our ecclesial identity and spiritual personality. Three thousand of us were there to receive him on the spacious lawn in front of the center; it was a great festive event that lasted several hours.

Afterward, there would be no important manifestation of the movement that he failed to attend. And every time, not only did he have words of encouragement or guidance for us, but, over and beyond any rule of protocol, he manifested his personal appreciation and love for each one of those present. As expected, he was repaid with spontaneous enthusiasm from thousands of young and old alike.

From the moment that the Castel Gandolfo audience hall was transformed into the Mariapolis Center through his personal initiative, the pope's visits have taken on a characteristic of special intimacy, on account of the center's proximity to his residence and of the warmth displayed in his words.

I recall with joy some of the most meaningful passages from his speeches addressed to the Focolare members. We were particularly touched by the words he addressed to us during his visit to the International Center of Rocca di Papa. He uttered those words unrehearsed, after listening attentively to a summary presentation of the spirit of the movement and its structure done by a few of us from the central office. The words remain for us a point of continuous reference: "Yours is a new charism," he said, "a charism for our times. It is a very simple and attractive charism. Indeed, love is what is most simple and beautiful in our faith; it is the essence of Christianity and the Gospel. But this charity is not an easy virtue. Indeed, it is most difficult and demanding."

In addition, concerning our ecumenical contacts with many Christian churches and the dialogues we had initiated with non-Christians and nonbelievers, the pope added, "In the very structure of the Movement, the vision and ecclesiology of the Second Ecumenical Council is reflected, as it were. It is Vatican II as interpreted in the light of your experience and your apostolate, with the vital principle that is the charism of your Movement."

At the closing of the meeting he could truly say,

I have seen how the Movement lives and grows all over the world, how it achieves its mission.... In today's world, in the life of nations and societies, of various environs and persons, hate and strife are very fiercely present and well organized. Hence we need love, indeed a program of love.... This is your faith; it is the spark motivating everything that you do in the name of the Focolare.... I urge you to carry on along the same path. In the fullness of love that has its source in God himself, in the Holy Spirit, you already have a very clear purpose, a very deeply marked and singular charism.... It is the radical demand of the Gospel for love, which you strive to bring into the lives of today's men and women everywhere in the world ... by giving witness to God who is love.[6]

As one can easily understand, these words of the pope are forever engraved in our hearts. Every time we listen to him, we spontaneously feel that we must give thanks to God for having endowed the Holy Father with an extraordinary charism of discernment and for the service of love he performs in "strengthening his brothers."

The Marian Principle

As concerns the teaching of John Paul II, there is a special aspect of his doctrine that I would like to highlight because it seems to me to be his original and distinct characteristic.

Everyone knows his modern outlook, his openness to old and new problems of the world, his personal deep expertise in the field of doctrinal and moral questions. However, in my estimation, he is bringing about an authentic revolution in the field of ecclesiology. Everyone is aware, for instance, of his frequent emphasis on the necessity of transforming the sacramental and juridical aspects of communion among the faithful into a vital reality, as when, addressing the many bishops who are friends of the movement, he invited them to transform the objective (juridical) collegiality into a collegiality of love, since love is the beginning of the Blessed Trinity's communion, in whose image the Church is fashioned.

Furthermore, the great novelty proclaimed by the pope during his pontificate, both based on Holy Scripture and prompted by the Second Vatican Council, is a new self-awareness of the Church as perceived in her mutually complementing dimensions, namely the Marian and the Petrine dimensions.

An overwhelming emotion seized me when I read the words he addressed some years ago to the Roman Curia whereby he stressed the Marian characteristic of the Church, defining it as just as fundamental and distinctive as the apostolic and Petrine feature, if not more so.

He stated, in fact, that the "Marian dimension of the Church precedes the Petrine dimension, although it is strictly bound to and complementary with it." He also affirmed that "this Marian feature is first both in God's design as well as in its unfolding in history, being also more noble and preeminent, as well as richer with its implications for the individual and the community."[7]

I remember I wrote many years ago that "only Mary understands the Church, and only the Church understands Mary." The expression *totus tuus* (entirely yours) uttered by the pope to Mary is not just a formula; it is the living truth that confers on him the Marian seal capable of making him so lofty yet so keenly human, so elevated and at once so ordinary among men, a veritable "servant of the servants of God," just as aware of his Petrine prerogative as he is free from any form of clericalism.

Uplifting Encounters

Even from a strictly personal point of view, I owe a great deal to John Paul II. I can attest that, in his presence, one feels wholly oneself, because he loves you as you are, for the charism you possess, for the work of service you carry out in the Church. Furthermore, he loves the movement originated from this charism for what it is and what it accomplishes. He makes you feel as if you are the heart of humanity as a woman; you are his daughter, indeed, but also his collaborator to grow in communion together with the Church.

Such is the experience I have had my encounters with him, and this is also the reason why I consider him a great man. John Paul II does not discriminate between man and woman: he loves, recognizes, and brings to light the charisms of both. In women he perceives Mary, the masterpiece of creation; but he also knows that a woman, too, is a masterpiece if she is a real woman. What I mean is that he does not perceive the Marian profile in the Church simply as a spiritual or mystical reality, but also as a historical reality, and he gives witness to it with his deeds. He knows, for instance, that our movement has been also defined as the "Work of Mary," and he never fails to highlight its Marian presence in the Church.

I must add something else as well, even if of a very personal, inner nature. The pope is my religious superior. In my conversations with him, I endeavor to practice to the highest degree my personal unity, and the unity of the entire movement, with the one who represents God and the Church to us, so that we might be called and be in reality a "church" within the Church. I could not fully live and represent unity within the movement without this personal unity with the Holy Father.

After my encounters with him, something very unusual takes place within me, the likes of which does not happen in my contacts with any other person. I experience a deep sense of union with God, quite unique in its kind. It is a feeling that may linger on for a shorter or a longer period of time, but it gives me strength, joy, and comfort, enabling me to face my task in the movement with greater dedication.

John Paul II and the Ecclesial Movements

I don't think it is inappropriate to speak briefly of John Paul II's openness to all new movements within the Church and to their role in her.

It is a well-known fact that John Paul II holds in high esteem the movements, because—according to the words of his speech on this subject—"they are based on those charismatic gifts which, along with the hierarchical gifts, are part of those graces whereby the Holy Spirit enriches the Church, the Bride of Christ."[8]

These gifts differ from one another, he affirms, "but they are also mutually complementary." Out of concern that he might not have spoken with sufficient clarity, he adds that "in the Church, both from the institutional and the charismatic point of view, hierarchy and associations of faithful as well as Movements of believers are co-essential and contribute to the life, renewal and sanctification of the Church." Since the movements strive to live the Word of God objectively in concrete circumstances, "by their own witness they give evangelical life to temporal realities and human values, and enrich the Church with an infinite and never ending variety of enterprises in the field of charity and holiness."

The Holy Father is convinced that the phenomenon of the movements "has and will continue to have considerable relevance in the future of the Church," precisely because he sees "in the new *lay charisms* the key for the vital penetration of the Church in today's real world," and a "privileged channel for the formation and development of lay people who are active and aware of their own role in the Church and in the world."[9]

"Be an Instrument of the Holy Spirit"

I recall one of the Holy Father's most powerful statements, which he spoke to me when, on my knees before him in front of Saint Peter's Basilica, I was presenting to him the Focolare youth of Genfest that filled the spacious square: "Be always an instrument of the Holy Spirit!" Those words became engraved in my heart; they gave me the gift of the fear of God and the courage to believe in our charism and to persevere in our spiritual journey.

It goes without saying that the high teaching ministry of the pope, his doctrinal guidance and pastoral actions, are a light and a stimulus for us. At this particular point I am speaking for all of us and in particular on behalf of the youth from Gen, the new generation of our movement.

They have felt inspired and encouraged by all the words he has addressed to young people, who no doubt occupy a special place of predilection in the heart of the pope. "On you the future depends," he wrote in his letter addressed to the youth of the world on the occasion of the International Year of the Young, "on you the closing of this millennium and the beginning of the new one depend. Do not be simply acquiescent, therefore. Take on your responsibilities in all areas which the world offers you!" It is a world that is in need "of a deep spiritual revival."[10]

Our Gen had an intuition of the trust the pope was placing in them and perceived that in him there beats a youthful heart, not prone to a conventional pessimism, when they declared him their leader.

Our young—and this is a sure guarantee of hope for the future—sense a deep similarity between their lives and the teaching of the pope. They have often experienced that, by embracing even a single one of his desires, their very unity becomes more real, more universal, and more true.

Love Is the Most Important

Many speak of priesthood for women, and they ask me what my opinion is about this issue. Everyone knows that it is still a hotly debated topic, in particular for its ecumenical implications, for instance in the relationships with the Anglican communion. First of all I would like to say that women, within the ecclesial structure, carry fundamentally unique values, and that, in God's plan, they are placed in the Church to defend those values that are inherent to their specific vocation.

It is a fact that Jesus did not speak on this matter, yet he has given the feminine world a unique model from whom all great Christian women have drawn inspiration through the ages: He has given his mother, Mary. In her, every woman who really wishes to serve the Church can discover a model.

Aside from all the false and exploited views of women, by looking at Mary, Christian women will be able to understand that they should not aspire to the priesthood, because, just like the Mother of God, they have a different role in the Church, also very important and indispensable. They must assert, in a way that only they can do, the *value and the primacy of love* over all other gifts, over all other components that make up our religion, including the most exalted dignity that is shared by those called to the priesthood.

Indeed, love is more important than any gift! Everyone knows that one does not go to heaven for being a priest or a bishop. One goes to heaven because one has love. Priests and bishops, who still are the pillars upon whom Christ has built his Church, can be found in hell. Yet neither men nor women who have love can be found in that place.

Love is the most important thing of all. This is attested to also by the fact that the hierarchy and the sacraments are meant for this world, while, on the other hand, love remains even in the world to come. It is therefore necessary that part of God's people should give witness to this truth without possibility of error.

It is in loving with a supernatural love, and it is for love and with love that women, already entirely permeated with natural love, which brings them to endure any sacrifice, can find their proper place in the Church. Hence they are ministers of love; through the centuries, they have kept Mary's presence alive in the Church, just as they do today. In fact, as ministers of love, they make fully productive what priests and bishops do, and they remind them that, as Paul has stated, to give one's body to the flames without love is vanity; indeed, even being God's minister without love is not in accordance with God's will. When there is no love, everything is pure formality and mere ritual.

Therefore, although "they are not called to the priesthood," as the pope has said, and though "the teaching of the Church on this point is very clear, this does not change in any manner the fact that women are truly an essential part of the Gospel plan of proclaiming the Good News of the Kingdom."[11]

Women can carry out this task mainly on account of the greatest of all the charismas, charity.

"Just as it is true," the Holy Father said on another occasion, "that, through her hierarchy, the Church is ruled by the successors of the apostles, hence by men, it is even more true that in the charismatic sense women guide her just as men do and perhaps even more so!"[12] These words come from the pope!

He himself readily confirmed a statement by theologian Hans Urs von Balthasar, according to whom "Mary is Queen of the apostles without ever claiming for herself the power of the apostles. She possesses something else which is a better gift."[13]

Thus women, by living fully their vocation, with Mary's faith, nobility, and love, can be for the Church the revelation of the "Marian dimension of the life of the disciples of Christ"; they can help to keep alive in and to reveal to the Church her essential Marian profile.

A Living Presence of Mary

In conclusion, I would like to add something concerning the presence of women in the Church.

More than mere enunciation of principles, what counts is the present day practice of the Church. In my estimation, it shows some signs of a change of direction.

I would like to recall just one fact, but of great relevance, which touches me directly. Pope John Paul II knows our movement, made up of lay people consecrated at various levels, religious men as well as sisters; as I have already mentioned, he has emphasized its Marian nature on various occasions. Since it is our intention that the movement should maintain its Marian characteristics in the future, not simply in its inner spiritual nature, but also in its external appearance, namely by preserving God's design upon it, which is evidenced in the fact that he entrusted its beginning and growth to a woman, one day I dared to ask the Holy Father in total confidence whether he thought it possible to set down in our rules that the president of the movement should always be a woman. His spontaneous reply was, "And why not? Indeed!"

Now our updated rules, officially approved by the Holy See, contain this norm, which perhaps constitutes a novelty, at least in the field of ecclesial movements. The rules state that a woman, though not endowed with sacred orders, may preside over an ecclesial organism, whose membership includes, alongside lay members, also many priests, religious men, and sisters, as well as a good number of bishops who share in the spirituality of the movement.

In my opinion, all of this gives an indication of new horizons for the role of women in the Church.

In our rules we read that our movement "wishes to be—in as far as possible—a presence (of Mary) in the world and as it were a continuation (of her)" (Article 2).

However, a small but significant episode of the early days of our movement can perhaps help us understand the special place that Mary has in this movement.

War was still brutally going on. One day, we, the first Focolare members, had taken refuge in a shelter dug out of the rock, not too safe, however. All of a sudden, an airplane dropped several bombs directly over the shelter, almost at its entrance. A tremendous pressure wave sent us all sprawling to the ground while filling the narrow passage with dust. Personally I had never felt so close to dying as in that moment. In such a predicament, my face glued to the floor, at the thought of having to die, I felt only the acute pain that I would never be able to say the Hail Mary again here on earth.

In that very instant, I did not understand the meaning of such a singular perception. Later, however, much later, when I witnessed the movement's growth as a work linked to Mary, as a spiritual edifice dedicated to her glory, and as a work of praise to the Mother of God, I understood the reason. Indeed, this work belongs to Mary; not just because it is named after her but because it is animated, sustained, and guided by her.

Later on, five or six years after the beginning of the movement, in a time of intense spiritual life and special blessings, there were ever newer insights about her; she was better perceived as what she really was, the Mother of God. She appeared so noble and so elevated that we felt as if our previous notion of her divine mystery had been nothing in comparison. Moreover, she who treasured all God's things, pondering them in her heart, was envisioned by us as completely God's Word, namely all-encompassed in God's Word, as it were. If Jesus was the Word, the incarnate Word, then she appeared to us as living Word on account of her fidelity to the Word.

We contemplated in Mary the image of the perfect Christian woman, to whom all the followers of Christ would be able to look. On our part, furthermore, as members of this new movement, we understood, with an intense and distinct perception that will never fade, that in Mary we should contemplate our *"model to be,"* as each of us had a *"possibility of becoming like her."*

Living for love and for mutual love, living in order to "generate" the spiritual presence of Christ among people, makes women feel particularly close to Mary, who physically gave Jesus to the world. They try to imitate Mary in everything, because she is the model of the virgin, fiance, wife, mother, and widow. At the same time, she is open to and interested in the vast problems of humanity, as we can see in the Magnificat. Better still, perhaps it is Mary herself who models these women, feeling that she, too, has been engaged by God to give back to women their dignity, a demand of our times. Above all, she teaches them the primary secret of true Christian love: the cross, sacrifice. It was especially through the cross that Jesus showed his love to the world. Through the cross, Mary, sharing in her Son's passion, became the mother of all mankind.

In following Mary, women must take the same way, so that, to some extent, they, too, can become mothers of many others. And they are. A very strong characteristic of women is their spiritual maternity, and it is one of the greatest gifts that God can give to a woman. This maternity makes them fruitful not only in human society, but also in the Church.

Women contribute to bringing about the living presence of Christ among people, and the effect of his presence is immense. Through them, he conquers hearts, converts, and removes divisions between generations, among people of different races, among different nations, between the rich and the poor. He forms new people. He calls people to follow him in many different ways. He renews whole portions of the Church.

With a love that leads to believing, "May they all be one so that the world may believe" (Jn 17:21), women are able to open fruitful dialogues with Christians of other churches, with the faithful of other religions, and with all people of good will.

Yes, today there are women who are a real hope and example for many others, because the Holy Spirit is at work in their favor. Who knows what surprises he is still preparing in the laboratories of the Church and elsewhere?.[14]

Chapter 2

The Joy of Being a Woman of God

RONDA CHERVIN, PH.D.

A Profound Conversion

*A*re there any who have more joy in being women of God in the Catholic Church than those of us who come to this treasure chest from the bankruptcy of atheism?

When giving talks about Christian womanhood, I often start with this provocative opener: my militant atheistic parents never taught me that men were better than women. We were equal. Equally nothing, that is—a collection of atoms and cells of no more intrinsic worth than a pail of sand on the beach. Yet, just the same, God help anyone who trod on our toes!

My mother was proud to be a woman. A woman, she thought, could do anything a man could do if she tried hard enough, and also have babies if she cared to. My mother was brought up by atheistic, leftist, Russian immigrants, who had fled the old country to come to the United States, not because of their Jewish ancestry but because they were part of an underground Communist network. My grandmother, a doctor's wife, considered herself to be above the level of the Polish Jewish settlers in Brooklyn, New York, because they were from the ignorant peasant class. They were just housewives, whereas she was a sort of lady, with a Polish servant.

Regina Rosenson was an intellectual, but she had no scope for her abilities, since English was only a second language and she also had to manage the household and help her husband in his practice. She bequeathed to her daughters a dislike of all domestic chores. They were to be interesting individuals in their own right, not merely wives of men who were doing something in the world.

My mother expressed her horror of conventional roles for women by eloping with a journalist and spending her early womanhood in the cafes of Paris, in this way becoming part of the legendary literary and artistic left-bank group that included ex-patriates such as Hemingway. In my autobiography, *En Route to Eternity,* I give many details about my mother's lifestyle, which I will not repeat here.[1] What is important for the topic of the joys of being a woman of God is the contrast between the idea of the feminine my mother conveyed to us, my twin sister and myself, and the one I would find within my circle of mentors and friends in the Catholic Church.

The word "feminine" in my childhood was never used in a positive sense. Feminine was a synonym for silly, weak, luxury-loving, vain, slavish, mushy, sentimental, unadventuresome, stupid, and cowlike. It was not bad for a woman to have feelings, but these had to be glimpsed only through a certain coat of armor consisting of a masculine type of strength, daring, and grit. My mother's favorite actress was Katherine Hepburn.

What is remarkable is that, in spite of these views, my mother herself was actually a warm, affectionate person, and even nurturing to any girl or woman she loved. She especially excelled in empathy for our problems, being willing to spend any amount of time untangling these. Her large bed, with lots of room in it after my father left when we were eight years old, was always available for middle-of-the-night comfort.

These positive feminine qualities, however, were combined with lots of independence and survival-strength as a single parent. A brilliant intellectual who worked in the field of publishing as an editor, my mother taught me to be objective, analytical, and articulate, as well as to be aggressive and argumentative. Men, we were taught, as long as they were intelligent or creative, were fascinating but slippery creatures, to be seduced, talked about endlessly, but always held in suspicious distrust. Above all, men should never be allowed to exploit women by forcing them into "traditional" roles.

I do not remember my father ever suggesting that he would have preferred to have sons instead of the twin daughters that emerged from his union with my mother. Nonetheless, in many ways, I would realize later on in life, he treated us more like sons than like daughters. The entire emphasis was on learning. My father, whose occupations in life ranged from seaman, zoologist, musicologist, editor, and sales manager to technical writing college teacher, had an encyclopedic mind. He simply assumed that loving children translated into ramming as many facts as possible into their heads. Unfortunately, neither my sister nor I have ever had the slightest interest in facts, being much more intuitional and conceptual.

Not only did my father treat my mother as an equal, intellectually, he also took over many of the household duties that she detested. He would cook and clean when he came home from work. My mother liked reading to us, talking to us, and taking walks, but otherwise devoted every spare moment to her own reading or conversation with my father.

Imagine my surprise and amazement after eight years of living within this pattern to find that my father was leaving us to marry a totally conventional woman whose favorite occupation was cooking. She was a long-haired beauty and not an intellectual!

As any psychologist could predict, a background like this would produce much conflict in a little girl. Raised to be an exact replica of my mother, I was suddenly forced to see that my father actually preferred the exact type of woman my mother despised. The choice that seemed open to me was to be adored by a feminist mother and deprived of masculine love, or to achieve love from males only by becoming a servile female.

This was the dilemma I was trying to resolve at the age of twenty, as a graduate student of philosophy. My mind was masculinized. I had been trained to destroy every theory that came along through analytic logical techniques. I dressed in a traditionally feminine manner, with long hair and longish flowing skirts. In my conversation with men I would go back and forth between silly flirtatiousness and aggressive debate.

I was astonished when I met philosophical Catholic women for the first time. Women such as Madeleine Stebbins of Catholics United for the Faith, and Alice von Hildebrand, were intelligent, charming, interesting, objective, and at the same time warm, sweet, nurturing, delicate, and dependent on strong men!

Here is how this encounter began. It was the year 1958. I was in despair from studying nonreligious philosophies of life. My mother turned on a television program by chance. It was called the "Catholic Hour," and featured Dietrich von Hildebrand and Alice Jourdain (later to become von Hildebrand). I had been brought up to think all Catholics were stupid superstitious throwbacks to medieval times. When I saw that these two philosophers on television actually believed in truth, beauty, goodness, and love, I was so moved that I wrote them a long letter. I told them how I had been looking for truth in philosophy for years as a student and could find nothing.

The story of the graces that brought me into the Catholic Church is profound.[2] Briefly, it involved an intellectual conversion from skepticism to the understanding of objective truth and morality by means of taking graduate courses with Dietrich von Hildebrand, as well as a conversion of soul through miraculous mystical events: the face of Christ in a picture came alive, and the same expression could be seen on the face of the pope (Pius XII), seen in Saint Peter's. I was baptized in 1959. Five years later my twin sister became a Catholic, and ten years later my mother entered the Church.

It was only years later, when women's issues became red-hot in the Church, that I came to see that my conversion also involved a new way of being a woman. Being something of an extremist and also very proud, as soon as I realized that a baby had greater value than a book, I wanted to leave academe and become a mother of thirteen children.

My role model was Zelie Martin, mother of Saint Thérèse of Lisieux.

Of course, I would first have to find an ideal Catholic husband. This turned out to be harder than I thought.

Instead, I wound up marrying a more familiar type of man: a divorced atheistic Jewish playboy who loved Jesus! After three years of waiting to get his previous marriage dispensed, I found myself wed to an almost-Catholic man who adored me and the pre–Vatican II Church. We had twin girls. This woman who had never taken care of a baby for more than an hour as a sitter once by chance was plunged into twenty-four-hour-a-day service of the most unphilosophical variety!

Guess what? I couldn't do it. Even though I loved the little souls of my baby daughters with passionate intensity, I disliked spending all day doing material things rather than intellectual things. Too proud to admit that I needed help, I persisted in full-time mothering, weeping with frustration when I couldn't figure out how to teach tots how to tie their shoelaces.

God found a painful solution. My husband became deathly ill with late-onset asthma. I was "forced" to finish my degree and teach phi-losophy full time to support the family. In those days (the late 1960s) no one thought of home-schooling or going on welfare. If the husband couldn't work, the wife did. Period. I had three miscarriages during this time, then gave birth to a son, and then had three more miscarriages.

So what was I doing that was feminine while I was a professor? First of all, there was the joy of breastfeeding my son. When my twins were conceived, I was too frightened of pregnancy to experience delight in carrying a new human being in the womb. I just endured it. The year 1962 was just before nursing became popular, so they were bottle-fed. The nurturing, feminine part of being a woman of God was expressed the most with my daughters in teaching them how to pray.

Eight years later, nursing was all the "fad" among Catholic moth-ers. Nothing gave me more of a sense of the utter privilege of being a woman of God than having a body created to give perfect food (an analogy to the Eucharist) to a tiny little baby.

In my marriage, the feminine side of my nature was always in conflict with the masculine side. On the one hand, I loved the surrendering aspect of falling in love, and of delighting in my husband's physical and creative strength. After he became ill, he left book sales and started writing Catholic plays and novels. I loved sitting at his feet after the children went to bed and listening to what he had written during the day. On the other hand, I was always in a state of resentment at having to do the cooking and cleaning as well as working full time as a teacher. My husband was brought up by an orthodox Jewish mother of the type of Golda in *Fiddler on the Roof.* He refused to help in the kitchen or with laundry and cleaning, even though he was home a lot of the day because of his illness—that was "woman's work."

Because I had come from a broken home, I was afraid to be more assertive with my husband's faults, fearing he would leave me if I weren't submissive. Instead, I thought that if I just added more prayer to my schedule I would become more holy and then I would love to do the chores and to obey!

Looking back, I wish that instead of dreaming about being a saint I had gone to a Christian marriage counselor. In fact, the way toward renewal of my marriage was by means of a combination of the healing graces of forgiveness and general counseling, leading to the adoption of more practical solutions to daily conflicts.

During my thirty-three years of marriage and family life, what sustained me most was daily Mass, Holy Communion, and fidelity to the Magisterial teaching against divorce. For an overachiever and workaholic like myself, having an hour a day where I didn't have to produce anything, but could be surrendered to the Lord, loved and nurtured by him, has always been most wonderful. Sitting at the feet of Jesus in quiet prayer, magnifying him in prophetic charismatic utterance, letting the strength of his grace pour into me—what a feminine role!

I also found my relationships to my students to be intrinsically mothering. It was a joy for me to find ways of making the truth "palatable" to disaffected Catholic youth. To bring them back from skepticism or rebellion into the path of Christ in the Church so that they could be nurtured with the sacraments was my mission. I also loved to feed older people in the Church with the wholesome nutrients of truth by means of speaking and writing. As is the case with many women lecturers and writers, we have a feminine way to convey our ideas—more personal and existential than in the writings of many male counterparts. What a feeling it is to bring a healing truth to a Catholic woman or man who has become frozen in pain and despair! A special privilege was to teach for seven years at a Catholic seminary in California. When I would allow myself to be wide open to the inspirations of the Holy Spirit, I truly felt like a mother to these men, future priests, in the image of Mary: Queen of Apostles.

Feminine, Free, and Faithful

Around the year 1975 Catholic feminism began to take off. This challenge would help me to formulate into theory what I had been experiencing myself personally as a wife, mother, and professor. Asked to teach the philosophy segment of our women's studies program at Loyola Marymount University, I realized that I would need to do a great deal of research and engage in much thought to formulate an overarching theory that would not only be teachable to women and men taking the course but also be inspirational for my own life.

I spent a year assiduously reading Scripture, von Hildebrand's *Man and Woman,* Edith Stein's *Essays on Woman,* Steve Clark's *Man and Woman in Christ,* and, on the most negative side, Simone de Beauvoir's *Second Sex.* I also became interested in rereading classical novels to find out what combinations of negative and positive feminine and masculine traits played themselves out as comedy or tragedy—*Anna Karenina* of Tolstoy is a gold mine on this.

After teaching the course for a few years, I came up with a formulation with which I was happy. It became the title of the book

Feminine, Free, and Faithful.[3] The basic thesis of this book is that no woman should have to choose between being feminine and being free. The key to being warm, sweet, nurturing, and intuitive and also being strong, daring, and objective is to be faithful not to human tradition or human innovation, but instead to the Holy Spirit as expressed in the teaching of the Church and in personal leading day by day.

I adhere to what I call a modified complementary theory such as can be found in von Hildebrand, Edith Stein, and John Paul II, where the emphasis is on complementary qualities rather than fixed roles (except for priesthood and motherhood). On the other hand, I do believe that pro-life feminism has a lot to offer in the way of promoting assertiveness in areas of real injustice, including seeing abortion as a covert form of negative masculine irresponsibility.

My theory includes analysis of positive feminine and masculine traits and negative feminine and masculine traits so that one can see the roots of some of these virtues and vices in culture and one's own character. The teaching of the Church and the model and intercession of Mary and the women saints is likewise essential in forming Catholic women to be feminine, free, and faithful.

Practical Applications

I would like to summarize some of the insights about these teachings that the Holy Spirit gave me as I wrote *Feminine, Free, and Faithful* and also as I spoke and gave retreats in this area.

On the issue of birth control I came to see how thinking of the fertile time of the cycle as "my bad time," as contracepting women come to do, was a form of self-hatred. The fertile time is a miraculous time when God can use the elements he has created in man and woman to bring into being the place for the coming of a new human person into the world. A truly liberated woman should think of her fertile time as her "glow" time. If, as a married woman, she cannot use that fertile time for openness to creation because of grave reasons, she can post-pone its use for sexual union, but never should she be thinking of it as a negative or as a space and time to desecrate by means of gadgets and pills.

Well, after the original publication of *Feminine, Free, and Faithful* by Ignatius Press a miracle took place. John Paul II wrote the Apostolic Letter *Mulieris Dignitatem* (On the dignity and vocation of women). Tears filled my eyes as I realized that God had lifted off my shoulders the impossible duty of persuading those without and within the Church that the teachings of the Catholic faith were actually liberat-ing for women and not repressive. Here was a document that achieved the synthesis for which many Catholic thinkers such as myself had been aiming.

Essentially, the Apostolic Letter roots the dignity of women not in changing male attitudes in society and the Church but simply in our unity with God. The document of the pope does not whitewash male responsibility for female wounds. It rightly condemns such attitudes. On the other hand, John Paul II does not give into the false way some feminists make it seem that only men have original sin. Bad treatment of women he considers to demean the man as much as the woman. Yet women need to rush to God's mercy when they express their own resulting frustration, for example, by hurting the babies in their own wombs.

Opening up the passage in the Apostolic Letter about women find-ing their inherent dignity in their union with God, I was able to understand in a special way why daily Holy Communion has always been essential for me. Even when I was taking care of little twins, I would stroll them over to the Church, ride them around during the readings and sermons so they wouldn't disrupt the service, and then rush in for the period from Consecration until Communion. Whereas the problems of raising children would leave me breathless and some-times crazed, in the Church I could feel how Christ wanted to unite him-self to me in the Eucharist, no matter how harried I was. At times of sorrow in marriage where I felt rejected, there was the celestial Bridegroom leaping from heaven, as it were, to plunge into the depth of my heart with his real presence. Yes, I had infinite worth in the eyes of my God, no matter what!

In *Mulieris Dignitatem,* John Paul II reviews the personal ways that Jesus came to individual women as depicted in the New Testament. Some of these passages mirrored for me times when I could come to Christ only as a sinner in the sacrament of Reconciliation. Often through the mercy in the face of the priest, I could see that even when I was most unworthy, I was still loved. This realization brought great peace.

Going back to an earlier time, in the late 1980s the U.S. bishops decided to write a Pastoral on the Concerns of Women. I was chosen to be one of the women consultants to the bishops in this endeavor. The experience of sitting face to face with women consultants of mostly different perspectives, as well as reading some ten thousand pages of input from women all over the country, was quite illuminating. Some of the areas of pain for women I came to understand much better than I had before, include battering (psychological as well as physical), the unwillingness of some clergymen and laymen to take the feelings of women seriously, and the marginalization of single and divorced women. From the other side, I was thrilled to see the birth of the organization "Women for Faith and Family," which gathers signatures of thousands of women throughout the world who love the teachings of the Church on women and whose grievance is the failure of some clergy and bishops to stand up against illegitimate feminist incursions into Church life.

The pastoral was voted down, yet many of us on the committee came out with our own books as a compensation for our frustration. In my case, I became interested in trying to cut through the debate on rancorous issues, to get to the core of the pain. I devised healing seminars for women under the title of *Freed to Love: Healing for Catholic Women.*[4]

With the help of local teams, I travel the world, conducting week-end workshops for women. Through the sessions we touch on areas of wounding of heart, mind, and spirit. Each segment involves witness talks, teachings, sharings, and personal prayer. Women who have been sexually abused and feel healed enough to speak of it pray over women who have never given such pain to the Lord. Women who have spent years as radical feminists and slowly come to see the truth of Catholic teaching are able to reach out to women who still have doubts and frustrations. During the second part of the retreat we have witness, teaching, sharing, and prayer concerning Mary, women saints, and mystics, and how the Holy Spirit is leading each woman in her role in the Church.

My newest experience of joy in being a woman of God has come about, again, through suffering. My husband died in 1994. Our marriage had become much renewed over the years. His death was a crisis for me. I had always wanted to be a full-time apostle, free of burdens of family. Once able to try that cherished dream, however, I found that I was miserable! I hated being a single woman. I missed marriage and family terribly. I chose to leave a perfectly wonderful job and ministry situation at Franciscan University of Steubenville to move in with one of my daughters and her husband and children, and to be closer to my other daughter and her husband and family.

Once feeling more secure and enriched by family life, I was able to open myself to a possibility I had considered and rejected earlier on in my widowhood: the life of a consecrated woman.

When I first heard about this potential consecration, I was not interested for myself, because I was so eager to find a second husband. After some months, however, I received an interior vision and locution. Jesus appeared as a Bridegroom. I was dressed as a bride. I asked him if he wanted me to make this consecration. He said yes. I was overwhelmed with peace and joy.

After trying many different possibilities, on Saint Joseph's feast day of 1996 I felt gently moved to try it for six months. Immediately I felt a peace I had despaired of feeling ever again in my life as a widow. Researching the widow-saints for another book I was working on, I was more and more impressed by how many such women found intimate joy in accepting Jesus as their Second Bridegroom.[5] Of course, the widow-saints were not without sufferings. Who is? Nonetheless, their consecration lifted them off the cross of the *unredeemed* suffering that comes from simply feeling unlovable, old, ugly, and rejected—a state of mind that can lead many widows into addictions and depression.

So, as I enter into my sixties, I am experiencing a new springtime in my femininity. I sometimes feel as if Mary, the true Handmaid of Nazareth, has entered into my heart and is expanding it to include everyone she loves, to magnify and sanctify me from within.

"My spirit rejoices in God my Savior." May you rejoice also for me and with me as I conclude this witness to the joy of being a woman of God.[6]

Chapter 3

To Serve God Is to Reign

ALICE VON HILDEBRAND, PH.D.

Everything Is Grace

*E*verything is grace"—these are the last words that Bernanos puts in the mouth of a dying priest, the hero in *The Journal of a Country Priest*. May God grant us all the grace of dying with words of gratitude on our lips for all the gifts he has given us throughout our lives, laced with words of deep contrition for not having better responded to them.

Whether one's life has been easy or difficult, happy or unhappy, smooth or rough (and in most lives these contradictory traits are interwoven), gratitude is the proper response, for, supernaturally speaking, "everything is grace." Whatever happens in the course of our existence always contains a message coming from God, a message that can be properly deciphered *only* in an attitude of faith and humble receptivity.

Looking back upon my early life, certain events stand out in my consciousness that have left an indelible imprint on my soul and now trigger in me a flow of gratitude. I still see my father taking me to church every Sunday from the time I was four years old, and upon entering the sacred building, reverently taking off his hat, genuflecting in front of the Blessed Sacrament, and being so recollected throughout Holy Mass that I knew I was assisting at something *sacred*. Just in back of us, there often was a little boy of about my age who had a curly pageboy hairdo. He reminded me of the picture depicting Little Lord Fauntleroy on a book cover my mother was reading to us children. This boy looked lovely and I yielded to the temptation of turning back to have a look at him. Yet I read on my father's face such a sad and severe expression of disapproval that I immediately felt how improper my behavior was. He was a shy and reserved man; he said little, and he was mostly in the background. Yet, at age four, I already knew one thing: He was a deeply religious man for whom God was at the very center of life. Every single day, rain or shine, he went to 6:00 A.M. Mass (regretting that there was not an earlier one, for he was a very early riser), but never mentioned it to us; he was back home when the rest of the family was slowly climbing out of bed. Another thing that struck me was that every morning, his rosary was to be found in his bed. I knew that he went to sleep speaking to the Holy Virgin.

I do not recall that he ever mentioned her to us; but we knew that he had a special devotion to the sweet Mother of God. This love was mirrored in his attitude toward my mother. My father was so secretive, so shy at showing his feelings that the message and lesson he gave his children was not formulated in words, but was living in his reverent attitude toward her. Thanks to him, I sensed at a very young age that to be a woman was a mysterious privilege. Obviously, at that young age, this consciousness was not clearly articulated in my mind, but my father's reverence planted this seed in my soul.

When I was five years old, I got double pneumonia. At that time there were neither myacins nor penicillin, and soon I was at death's door. I recall vividly lying in my little white wooden bed, so weak that I became totally passive. It is easy to die when one's roots in the soil of life are still very tenuous.

Yet then something happened that, once again, left deep marks in my soul: My mother bent over my bed and said, "Darling, how I wish I could suffer this for you." I was too weak to open my eyes, I was incapable of responding, but I said to myself, "Lily, don't ever forget this; this is true love." At the age of five, I understood that an infallible test of true love is to wish to suffer *for* another. Through my mother's remark, I made the acquaintance of the very essence of Christianity, "for there is no greater love than to offer one's life for one's friend" (Jn 15:12-13).

When I started going to school, my father never questioned me about my grades; I was a girl, and at that time studies were not considered to be important for them. Much as he worried about my brother's performance in school, he did not pay much attention to mine. He was certainly pleased that I was doing well and loved books, but had my grades been poor, it would not have concerned him much. There was, however, one branch of knowledge to which he attached an enormous importance: the catechism and biblical studies. Every single semester, he would ask me, "When is your catechism test?" He would then invite me to come to him, sitting at his big oak desk, and he would question me carefully; I knew the questions and answers by heart. I realized that my grades in religion were all-important to him, and I studied hard to please him. I always received excellent marks, and it made him happy. Even though he did not play the role that my mother played in our lives (for she was always with us and we saw relatively little of him, except at meal times, when the whole family was always gathered together), I felt a deep love for him.

As I turned twelve, my love for my father deepened considerably. My only brother, aged fourteen, was going through a typical puberty crisis. Some of his school comrades had given him coarse information about the sexual sphere and this had upset him deeply. He shared his newly acquired knowledge with my sister (aged thirteen) and myself. It was very troubling for both of us, and we felt helpless. Even though my father probably suspected that my brother was going through a severe crisis, I do not think he fully realized how much my brother needed help. There was, unfortunately, little contact between father and son: both were reluctant to speak about personal matters. At that time, parents recoiled from speaking openly to their children about the genesis of life. My parents were no exception, but I did know that my father was very severe when it came to the sixth commandment, and I felt instinctively that his very severity would harm my brother if I spoke to my father about my brother's difficulties. I decided to say nothing. Yet through God's grace, every time my brother would repeat the same depressing refrain, I would strongly antagonize the views he was defending. Deep down, I knew they were lies. To my joy, I could feel that my challenging him was a comfort to him: He needed to hear "another music" than the discordant sounds his comrades were shouting in his ears. With female intuition, I felt that, deep down, he was sickened by the vulgar views propagated by his peers.

Providentially, that very year, my mother became pregnant for the fifth and last time. It was quite a revolution in our family; the fourth child was going to be seven, and somehow, no one had thought of the possibility that the family would still grow larger. The coming of a new baby was bound to shake the framework that had been ours for several years.

Clearly inspired by the Holy Spirit, my shy father decided to come to our bedroom (that of my older sister and myself) every single night for a brief chat, and in simple, moving words, he spoke to us about the greatness of pregnancy, and the drama and joy of childbirth. I shall never forget the words that he uttered, his lovely blue eyes moist with tears: "I was with your mother at each one of your births and never have I experienced so closely God's presence and greatness. My awe and reverence for her, suffering agonizing pains to bring you into the world, moved me to the very depth of my being." That my reserved father should become so eloquent made a tremendous impression on me. How was it that, all of a sudden, someone who by nature was so secretive burst out in what sounded like an exultant song of praise?

That was the only "sex education" I ever received, and it was the best. Thanks to the noble person God gave me as father, I intuited so deeply the sacrality, depth, and mystery of the sexual sphere that I was thereby shielded against the onslaught to which so many young people are exposed. I then understood his devotion to his own mother, whom he treated with a respect that edged on veneration. It was very much as if, every time he saw her, he recalled vividly that she had suffered to give him birth.

He had planted in my soul the seeds of reverence for the mystery of sex, and an awareness of the mysterious connection existing between love and suffering; it was clear to me that to give birth is to accept suffering so that another person may live.

Of course, like most girls in their teens, there were moments when I resented the fact that I was a girl and that there were many things my brother could do (for example, at that time, horseback riding) and that my sister and I were not allowed to do. Yet, thanks to my father, I had been made aware that to be a woman was a costly privilege (privileges have to be paid for) that I would learn to appreciate more and more as I grew older.

How grateful must I be! What an unmerited gift I have received! May God give me the grace of gratitude. May I realize more and more how, in his love, he has protected me from so many dangers to which young people are exposed!

My parents sent their children to the best Catholic schools. Historically, then, they were truly taught their faith. Young people today would be amazed if they saw the textbook we used in high school: 439 pages long, in small print. And we studied it carefully from cover to cover. Today, alas, children are given sex education textbooks in so-called religion classes. They are taught the various methods of birth control, are informed about various sexual perversions, but usually do not know the Ten Commandments. A teenager today is likely to be an "expert" in a domain in which we were and remain ignorant, and to be totally illiterate concerning his or her faith. I recall a word of my grandfather (whom I never knew) that my father liked to quote: "There are things which I do not know, and do not want to know." I am sure that there are children who would welcome remaining ignorant of certain things that, according to Saint Paul, "Should not even be mentioned among you" (Eph 5:3) and are actually forced down their throats in so-called religion classes, with predictable catastrophic results. Those responsible for this scandal should meditate on the words of Christ: "But whoever causes one of these little ones who believe in me to sin, it would be better for him to have a great millstone fastened round his neck and to be drowned in the depth of the sea" (Mt 18:6). Alas, "Something is rotten in the state of Denmark."[1]

Another grace that God has granted me was the discovery of Pascal at a young age. When I was twelve, we studied seventeenth-century French literature in school, and I made the discovery of Pascal's *Pensées*. One of them, written in the purest, most beautiful French, made an indelible impression upon me. I memorized it, and loved to repeat it to myself:

> Man is but a reed, the weakest in nature, but he is a thinking reed. The universe need not arm itself against him in order to crush him; a vapor, a drop of water suffices to kill him. But if the universe were to kill him, man remains greater than that which is killing him, because *he knows that he will die* and the advantage the universe has over him, the universe knows nothing of this.[2]

After school, my best friend and I often met to read Pascal together. I recall vividly that we hid ourselves behind huge armchairs in her parents' living room, to create the atmosphere of intimacy and mystery necessary to penetrate into such sublime domains! One day, Nicole's grandfather unexpectedly came into the room and, discovering us hiding, said, "What are you doing there, girls?" My friend answered, "Grandpa, we are reading Pascal," clearly enjoying the surprise written on her grandfather's face! Amusingly enough, some forty-six years later Nicole's path and mine crossed once again. I reminded her of our love for Pascal, and she told me that when her grandfather died, she had inherited his diary, in which he relates that, to his joyful surprise, his granddaughter, aged thirteen, was reading Pascal!

Rites of Passage

A profound experience, which has marked me very deeply, is related to my first crossing of the Atlantic, with my older sister in 1940, to escape the Nazi invasion of Western Europe. We had an uncle and an aunt (my father's sister) who had left Belgium in September 1939, rightly foreseeing that Hitler's appetite was not going to be satisfied with the eating up of Austria, Czechoslovakia, and Poland. Early in May 1940 (May 5, to be exact), they sent us a telegram inviting my sister and me to pay them a visit. For two teenagers, to see the United States for a few weeks was a most tempting prospect. Yet things changed radically when exactly five days later—on Friday, May 10, 1940—the Germans invaded Holland and Belgium, and we realized that crossing the ocean would imply a long separation from our parents. To make a long story short, the whole family left Belgium, just hours ahead of the invading army, and after a real odyssey, arrived in Bordeaux in southern France. My father had constantly kept his relatives in New York informed about our itinerary. Even though my sister and I were no longer eager to take the trip that would cut us off from our parents, it was decided that it was safer for two teenaged girls to be on the other side of the Atlantic. It is a well-known fact that invading armies usually behave coarsely and brutally.

In spite of great difficulties (only American citizens were admitted at the consulate in Bordeaux), my uncle, who had powerful friends in the financial world, managed to have the State Department "request" that my sister and I be given American visas. An employee at the consulate was dispatched to our miserable living quarters (Bordeaux was filled with refugees), informing us that we had to rush to the consulate: The last American ship was leaving from Le Verdon (not far from Bordeaux on the Gironde) the next day, on Saturday, June 8. Within hours, we received our visas, Belgian passports, and our tickets, and the next morning, deeply moved, we said goodbye to our father and mother and to our two younger sisters (our brother was in a Belgian training camp and we could not say goodbye to him) and arrived in Le Verdon, where the S.S. *Washington* had docked. We did not see our immediate family again for six full years! The whole thing went so fast that both my sister and I had the feeling of having been hit over the head. I shall never forget the sadness I felt when the ship started moving and the coast of France receded into the background. On that fateful day, my sister and I embarked on a great adventure that would give to our lives an unforeseen and radically different direction.

The S.S. *Washington* first headed for Lisbon, where it was scheduled to pick up American citizens coming from Spain and Portugal. It crossed the Gascogne Gulf, well known for its stormy sea, and both my sister and I got hopelessly seasick—quite an experience. Monday, June 10, we arrived in sunny Lisbon. For the first time in my life, I contemplated with delight a southern landscape. The sky was different, the intensity of colors was ravishing, and the sun was brighter. I, who had always longed to travel, felt that I was discovering the world, and in spite of a deep sadness at having left my family, I tasted a bit of the enchantment of wanderlust. We were not allowed to land on Portuguese soil, but watched throughout the day the lively activity of the ships crisscrossing the harbor.

The S.S. *Washington* was a fine vessel that usually carried nine hundred passengers, but because of the emergency, the living rooms had been transformed into dormitories and the crew was ready to host two thousand passengers. From Lisbon, we were scheduled to go to the West Coast of Ireland (Galway) and pick up the American citizens fleeing from the British Isles. On Tuesday, June 11, at about 5:00 A.M., I heard a series of ominous gongs. Being a light sleeper, I immediately woke up and opened the door of our cabin.

To my utter amazement, I saw people running with their life jackets on! I realized that there was an emergency, but my anemic school English did not allow me to understand what was going on. All cabins had double occupancy, and my sister and I shared one with two women. They, too, were now awakened, and inquired into the cause of the hullabaloo and came back with the fateful information that the S.S. *Washington* had been stopped by a German submarine that had given the captain one hour to put passengers in life boats; then the ship was going to be sunk. (The Germans had sunk the American ship *Lusitania* in 1915; was history repeating itself?)

My sister and I quickly put on light summer dresses (I recall that mine was a navy blue cotton dress with polka dots), took our life jackets (which were actually our pillows), and rushed to the corridor. We then experienced what the word "panic" conveys: people were pushing and pressing to reach the upper deck more rapidly. I was terrified at the thought of being separated from my sister, who was everything to me in this moment, and locked my arm in hers from fear that the flow of panicky passengers would push us in different directions. I had noticed in our cabin that in case of emergency, we were supposed to report to lifeboat number ten. When we got there, however, the lifeboat was full. The captain had announced that (in view of the unusual number of passengers) only women and children were to enter the lifeboats, but husbands did not want to be separated from their wives and were jumping in all the same. There was not room left for us. My sister and I found ourselves standing on deck, convinced that our last hour had come. The weather was foggy and grayish; from time to time, we could see the submarine flashing messages. The captain of our ship was talking on the loud speaker, giving directions and trying to keep the passengers calm. We could not understand most of what he said, but a kind gentleman next to us translated his message for us. Humanly speaking, my sister was all that was left to me. We desperately clung to each other.

The clock was ticking, and soon the one hour granted us would be over. We were doomed to die. It was clear to me that I was facing death, and I was convinced that my last hour had come; there was no escape. Then, something amazing happened to me, so amazing that I can only hint at it; it is impossible to put it into words. Suddenly, in what seemed a split second, I saw my whole life in front of me: what

I had done, failed to do, thought, felt, imagined, willed, and so on. The experience was overwhelming; it was as if I was "above time," contemplating my life from eternity. As I said, it lasted only for a flash, but it was an instant that to me had the value of eternity. A few moments before, I had been a child; then, quite suddenly, I was a woman. The consciousness that one may be facing God face to face in a matter of seconds is an awesome experience. It is a grace, because, inevitably, in such moments one perceives with pitiless clarity the hierarchy of values, the things that matter, those that matter less, and those that do not matter at all. One perceives that much of one's life has been dedicated to the pursuit of things that have no "weight." "How long will you love vain words, and seek after lies?" (*"ut quid diligitis vanitatem ad quaeritis mendacium?"* [Ps 4:2]). In a moment, one discovers one's poverty and misery, and one's need of redemption. It is an overwhelming experience, and simultaneously a deeply humbling one. One sees that the precious years God has granted us have been, to a large extent, given to things that will soon "be gone with the wind." One sees how many graces one has received, and how badly, how ungratefully one has used them, or possibly misused them. Once again, Pascal comes to mind when he wrote:

> It is a monstrous thing to see in the same heart and at the same time this sensibility to trifles and this strange insensibility to the greatest objects.[3]

After a couple of hours of suspense, the German submarine, which had telegraphed to Berlin to receive its orders, was informed that the S.S. *Washington* should be allowed to proceed. The captain informed us of this fact. The ship, which had come to a full stop during the emergency, was put back into action, and headed north to Galway, where more American passengers awaited evacuation to the United States.

I cannot say that the portentous experience of facing death has always remained in the forefront of my consciousness, but somehow it lived in me "superactually," and resurfaced as soon as I "found myself in my depth." It was a great grace, to which, alas, I responded poorly.

Man is a mystery. He can know with perfect clarity that his relationship to God is the "one thing necessary." He can be fully aware of how superficially he spends the short period of time allotted to him on this earth—these precious drops of time that will decide his eternal fate—and yet live from day to day totally absorbed by the small, petty concerns of everyday life, cut off from the tapestry of eternity. How deeply humbling it is for me to realize that the "call" I heard on the S.S. *Washington* did not have the effect that it was meant to have: Namely, to give me a full awareness of the relativity of purely earthly concerns, which, whether fortunate or unfortunate, have, when seen against the background of eternity, the seal of nothingness.

One Thing Necessary

After some time, another milestone in my life occurred. It was my first meeting with Dietrich von Hildebrand, and taking his graduate courses at Fordham University. I first met him while studying at the Manhattanville College of the Sacred Heart, where, after being locked up at the Waldorf Astoria, New York, for two years, my aunt finally allowed me to pursue my studies. My philosophy professor was Dr. Balduin Schwarz, a German refugee, and one day he asked me whether I would like to attend a lecture that his great friend and mentor, Dietrich von Hildebrand, was giving in his apartment at 448 Central Park West. This talk would revolutionize my life. As noted previously, I had received a very sound Catholic education, but surprisingly and sadly enough, these dear nuns had not opened to their students the beauty, sublimity, and depth of the Liturgy. Strangely, I owe this momentous spiritual discovery to a layman for whom the Liturgy had been his main spiritual food since his conversion. I read with passionate interest his book *Liturgy and Personality*—a book that is so rich in insights that I keep re-reading it. Dietrich von Hildebrand made me aware that praying the Liturgy not only unites one in a unique way with the whole Church, but that, moreover, it is the very prayer of Christ himself, the Priest par excellence, who leads man to God.

"Lex orandi; lex credendi." A reverent and contemplative perusal of the Liturgy puts the thirsting soul in contact with the whole splendor of Revelation. The magnitude of its message is such that I must limit myself to a few hints that have a direct bearing on my topic: the mystery of femininity and the privilege of being a woman. Christ, the God-man, the Second Person of the Holy Trinity, is at the very heart of the song of praise that is the Liturgy. Yet the role assigned to his Holy Mother (*tota pulchra est, Maria*) carries, for those who have ears to hear, a magnificent message to women, revealing to them the unique beauty of their mission in the Church.

Even though Mary is, after Christ, the most important character in the gospel, she is very little mentioned. Neither Saint Matthew nor Saint Mark quote any word coming from her blessed mouth; yet, in Saint Matthew's Gospel, we hear the voice of the mother of James and John, sons of Zebedee, begging Christ to give her children the first places in his kingdom—and no doubt this devoted mother was a very secondary character. It is Saint Luke who gives us precious information about the Annunciation, the Visitation, and Christ being lost and found in the Temple. It is to Saint John that we owe the story of Christ's first miracle at Cana, where, twice, we hear Mary's sweet voice. And yet, the few words that have come down to us teach women all they need to know about their extraordinary vocation, and the unique role they are called upon to play in the economy of redemption.

Her Loving Presence

Great Christian thinkers have, throughout the ages, given us sublime meditations on the very few words uttered by the Blessed One among women. When the angel Gabriel informs Mary that she has been chosen to become the mother of the Savior, there is no trace of prudishness in her response. She knows the role that the husband plays in the conception of the child, and chastely mentions her virginity. When the angel Gabriel makes it clear it is the Holy Spirit that will fecundate her, she utters only a few words, but these words contain the secret of Christian perfection: "I am the handmaid of the Lord, be it done to me according to thy word." It is impossible to say more in fewer words. The whole program of sanctification is contained in them. Human beings are creatures; they owe everything, absolutely everything, to their Creator. It is their glory to serve him and to do his will. The whole of Mary's holiness is contained therein. In the gospel, she is assigned a background role. She does not teach. She does not correct. She does not perform miracles. Yet her loving presence is felt through her holiness, her love, her humility, her purity.

It is only in the Magnificat that all the wealth of her spiritual life is revealed in a flash. It is like a torrent of loving gratitude for the miracle of grace that has taken place in her, she who at that very moment carried within her womb the infinite being that "the whole universe cannot contain." *"Virgo Dei Genitrix, quem totus non capit orbis, in tua se clausit viscera factus homo."* That the womb of the Holy Virgin should encompass what the whole world cannot embrace calls for reverent amazement! That a woman should have been granted such a privilege shows how pathetic is the feminist claim that women have been treated by the Church as second-class citizens.

When, after three days spent in anxiety, Mary finds Christ in the Temple, speaking to the doctors of the Law, she gives expression to her motherly anguish. Yet when her Son tells her that he has to attend to his Father's business, she silently accepts her secondary role and must have repeated in her heart the words that are the motto of her life: "I am the handmaid of the Lord." She knew that her Son belonged to God, and that the immense privilege granted to her must be subordinate to God's claim over him.

Saint John is the only Evangelist who reports on the first miracle that Christ performed at Cana. Once again, the very few words uttered by the Blessed One among women contain a whole spiritual program. It is so very feminine that she notices that the hosts are running out of wine and will thereby be humiliated. Is it not a special charism of femininity to cater to the needs of others, to feel oneself into them, to gently relieve their anxieties? It is Mary's mission as co-redemptrix to draw her Son's attention to their hosts' predicament. Furthermore, when he seems to turn down her request ("My hour is not yet come"), she, who knows his infinite goodness and his infinite power, does not allow her faith to be shaken; she simply tells the servants, "Do whatever he tells you." Once again, a whole program of sanctification is contained in these few words. Man should *do what Christ tells him to do.* That is all that is required and that is what Mary has done. She has obeyed her divine Son. How incredibly simple is the way to holiness when one's heart is pure!

One cannot imagine a more splendid intellectual and scholarly basis than the one offered in the gospel about the Holy Virgin. All the words we have referred to amount to half a page of a printed text, but their riches are inexhaustible. We know that Mary, leading the pious women, followed Christ to Golgotha. We know that she witnessed the atrocity of his crucifixion, standing at the foot of the cross. We know that she was spiritually crucified with him. She therefore fully deserves the title of "co-redemptrix." Her inexpressible grief and pain have found sublime expression in Thomas de Celano's poem, "Fifteenth of September," in which she is called "Mater Dolorosa," the "Sorrowful Mother."

In the stations of the cross, Catholic tradition and piety commemorate Mary's martyrdom (let us not forget that she is the Queen of Martyrs), when Jesus meets his Holy Mother. Not a word is spoken between mother and son, because there are situations in which silence is infinitely more eloquent than words. Throughout the stations of the cross, women are in the foreground. Veronica wipes Christ's holy face with her veil; the women of Jerusalem cry over him. Where are the apostles? They all fled, even though Saint John came back later and was present at Calvary. In the fifth Station, one man is mentioned, Simon of Cyrene. However, Saint Luke informs us that Simon was *forced* to help Jesus carry his cross (see Lk 23:26). He did not volunteer; he was clearly anxious to go home and rest after a day's work. How willingly the holy women would have taken his place!

How eloquent are these devotions! How much do they tell us about the beauty of the female vocation! To love, to share, to comfort, to suffer with. The liturgy extracts for the faithful the plenitude of spiritual food contained in them. It is like a sublime nectar offered for our sanctification.

Once again, the texts offered us are few, but they are so pregnant with meaning that the soul opened to the supernatural can feed on them forever.

We are told explicitly that "salvation" has been put in the hands of the Blessed One among women. (*Adonai Domine, Deus magne et mirabilis, qui dedisti salutem in manu feminae, exaudi preces servorum tuorum* [*Sabbato ante Dom. IV Sept.*].) It is an amazing statement in the Liturgy, and sheds light on the fact that, supernaturally speaking, to be in the background is to be in God's foreground. All that the Holy Virgin said was "fiat," and through this "fiat" she has opened the door to redemption. Christ alone is the Savior of the world, but because of her closeness to her Son, she partakes in a unique way in his redemptive action.

Mary, the gentle one, "O clement, o loving, o sweet Virgin Mary," is, at the same time, the one Satan dreads. In his momentous work on the Liturgy, Dom Prosper Gueranger writes, "Satan fears Mary not only more than all angels and men, but in some sense more than God himself. It is not that the anger and the power of God are not infinitely greater than those of the blessed Virgin, for the perfections of Mary are limited, but it is because Satan, being proud, suffers infinitely more from being beaten and punished by a little and humble maid of God, and her humility humbles him more than the divine power."[4] The same thought is expressed in the Liturgy, the gentle maid of Nazareth is compared to an army arrayed in battle (Canticle of Canticles, 6:4).

Humility and Receptivity

We live in a world dominated by "activism." Everyone seems to be running from morning to night, "creating," "producing," "inventing," "planning." The most successful people in our society are usually "workaholics," slaving without stop until they drop dead. This activism, condemned under the name of "Americanism," is bound to blind people to the overwhelming superiority of "being" over "doing." How often do we hear feminists lament over the fact that the male "imperialism," "autocratism," and "sexism" have prevented them from developing their talents and from becoming leaders in the Church? The Church judges differently, for example, having proclaimed both Saint Catherine of Siena and Saint Teresa of Avila to be doctors of the Church. These two women are set up for us as great examples and yet they had no education to speak of. Due to their receptivity and humility, they received a knowledge and understanding of divine truth that puts to shame many a contemporary scholarly theologian. They had no diploma, did not spend hours in libraries, toiling over books, but while on their knees they were taught by God himself. They were completely receptive to his divine message.

In her autobiography, Saint Teresa of Avila tells us that more women than men receive mystical graces, and this claim is echoed by Saint Peter Alcantara, for women are *more receptive*. Those who open their soul to grace, and are transformed in Christ, never fall into the danger of "activism." Yet, they are those whose accomplishments have a lasting effect. Their "deed" will flower because they do not have their roots in flamboyant and noisy activities, but in prayer, recollection, and love of God and neighbor. No workaholic can compete with the amazing accomplishments of Saint Teresa of Avila, who reformed the Carmel and founded innumerable convents. Never was this superhuman work accomplished in feverish tension; it was always performed in quiet recollection.

In his admirable book, *The Soul of the Apostolate,* author Dom Chautard writes the following: "One of our great Bishops, overburdened with his duties, explained this to a statesman, who also had too much to do. The latter asked the Bishop the secret of his constant calm and the admirable results of his work, 'My dear friend, add to your other occupations (half an hour's) meditation every morning. Not only will you get through your business, but you will find time for still more.'"5

Let us not forget, once again, that the Liturgy is the official prayer of the Church; this is why its content is to be received with special reverence, on one's knees. How contemporary scholars would benefit from meditating on the following text: "Rejoice, Virgin Mary, for you have single-handedly annihilated all heresies. For you have believed the words of the Archangel Gabriel" (Mass of the Common of the Holy Virgin, Tractus).

Because Christ is the Truth, and because Satan is the father of lies, it is inevitable that, as long as the world exists, there will be constant attacks on the sacred teaching of the Church. Heresies are like the heads of a hydra; when one is cut off, another immediately appears. Oftentimes, a heresy that has been refuted resurfaces after centuries but under a different form. This cheats people into believing that another flaw has been discovered in the teaching of the Church. Again and again, the Holy Spirit has sent out knights for truth who defend the sacred deposit of faith confided to the Holy Bride of Christ. Let us recall how Saint Athanasius refuted Arianism, which was spreading like wildfire. Let us remember that Saint Augustine spent much of his time as a bishop attacking and refuting the heresies that were fashionable at the time: Donatism and Pelagianism. Yet no Father of the Church, no doctor of the Church, great as he was, has managed to refute *all* heresies. This amazing mission has been given to the humble maiden of Nazareth, the Blessed One among women; Mary, the Theotókos. That the Church should officially proclaim her to be the conqueror of all heresies testifies to the unique place that she grants to *femininity*. She annihilates heresies not through scholarship, not through eloquence, not through teaching, but through *her holiness*. What a program of sanctification she offers her daughters! How honored should they be to share the sex of the blessed one who has carried the Savior in her womb.

No doubt, contemporary feminism has seriously harmed the Church; many are those who, like Eve, have listened to the lies of the serpent. For God has put "enmity between him and the woman," and the duel that started in the Garden of Eden will continue until the end of time as depicted in the Apocalypse. Either the woman, in putting all her trust in God, will triumph, or she will, once again, be conquered, and thus jeopardize her unique role in the economy of redemption. It is noteworthy that feminism has originated in Protestant countries where devotion to the Holy Virgin has been eradicated since the so-called Reformation. Feminism can be conquered only by turning to her, she who declared herself to be God's servant.

A Special Note of Sacredness

God always has the last word. At the very moment when, for the first time in Christian history, many women have rebelled en masse against "male chauvinism" in the Roman Catholic Church, God has placed in the Chair of Peter a Holy Father who has shed new and admirable light on the greatness of femininity. He has truly understood the "Kairos"—the call of the hour. The teaching of the Holy Father on women is a divine response to the spirit of the times, for the wave of feminism offered a challenge to the Church to deepen her teaching on women. Our Holy Father has responded to this challenge with his admirable Apostolic Letter, *On the Dignity and Vocation of Women, Mulieris Dignitatem*. Had feminists not shot their poisonous arrows at Christianity for its "mistreatment and denigration" of women, the Holy Father would probably have turned his attention to other themes. He understands how crucial it is to highlight today the greatness of femininity in a way that has never been done before. Thanks to the feminists, Christian literature has been considerably enriched, and will remain a precious patrimony for future generations. Unwittingly, their revolt has been instrumental in deepening the Christian understanding of women's roles and mission in the Church. Indeed, God always wins in the end.

While proclaiming the complete ontological equality of men and women, our Holy Father shows the admirable complementarity of the two sexes; each one is to play the instrument that God has confided to him or to her, and thereby create a symphony of true beauty. The woman is marked by a special note of sacredness, for it is in the secret of her body that God creates the human soul. This is why her body, like all sacred objects, calls for veiling, and why any note of immodesty in her way of dressing or in her "body language" actually sullies her.

The consciousness that she carries a mystery within herself, far from giving the woman a feeling of smugness, should, on the contrary, give her a feeling of humbling reverence, laced with gratitude for the privilege granted to her. This is why the sexual sphere is especially confided to her. By this we do not mean to say that sins of impurity in a woman are worse than those in a man; any sexual abuse is equally detestable in both men and women, and equally offends God. Yet, humanly speaking, a woman who falls into the sin of impurity is more deeply sullied than a man, for in sinning she has betrayed a mystery especially confided to her.

It is noteworthy that in both the breviary and the missal, saints whose feast is celebrated are listed under the categories of apostle, martyr, pope, bishops, and so on. For women, the list is much shorter: martyr, virgin, nonvirgin. Priests who have taken the vow of celibacy and have led pure lives are also "virgins," but the Church, in her wisdom, reserves this title to women, and this is deeply meaningful.

What Shakespeare calls "the precious jewel of her virginity" should remain a closed garden (*hortus conclusus*), until, with the divine blessing in the sacrament of matrimony, the woman gives its keys to her spouse. It is to him and to him alone that she can unveil herself in the privacy of their love. Even though it is the husband who fecundates his wife, in giving her a living seed, it is she who gives herself to him. For this reason, it is easy for a woman to understand the evangelical teaching that it is in "giving oneself that one finds oneself."

The richest in the kingdom of God are those who have given everything to God, or rather, returned to him what he had given them—for all gifts come from him—including one's virginity.

The Charism of Femininity

It is the woman who carries the child in her womb, in a closeness that nothing else can match. She is the one privileged to feel life growing within her. She is the one who endures the humbling position of giving birth, unveiling herself so that the fruit of her womb may make its entrance into the world. Since original sin, giving birth is linked to deep anguish and suffering; every time the sacred writers make allusion to something immensely painful, they compare it to a woman in labor. Yet the woman understands intuitively that love and suffering are intimately linked in this vale of tears, and this is why a mother embraces her pains so that her child may live. This is why any woman worthy of this name has an intuitive understanding for the sacrifice of Christ, redeeming the world through his agony and death.

The devil therefore achieved his most horrendous victory the very day that he succeeded in convincing some women that giving birth, in fact, placed them in a position of inferiority with regard to men. He succeeded in convincing some that it was purely a "biological affair," in which rats and rabbits excel (as Simone de Beauvoir claims), and that women had an innate right to "liberate" themselves from this unfair shackle.

The feminist attack is taking place at the very moment that the charism of femininity is more needed than ever before. Let us face it; we are living in a world that is masculinized to excess and that is heading for a dehumanization if it is not counterbalanced by feminine virtues. The mind-boggling advances of technology in the course of the last fifty years (the atomic and hydrogen bomb, computers, the Internet, television, fax, e-mail, genetic engineering, and so on) are conquering the world. If this technological conquest is not curbed and tempered by divine *wisdom*, it will inevitably lead to the downfall of humanity. It is not by accident that the Greek word for wisdom is *Sophia*—a feminine word. The feminine element tends to be totally ousted by technological advances. Let us think only of the field of medicine, in which machines now replace more and more the personal contact between doctors and patients. Let us realize that, for centuries, loving and holy nuns have taken care of suffering and dying patients and given them not only medical services but patient and understanding love. Today (there are of course exceptions), every sane person must dread the thought of falling into the hands of the indifferent and soulless personnel who see the care of the sick as another type of "job," when it is in fact a mission. How beautifully our Holy Father has understood the need for the feminine element in this and in all fields of social involvement.

In a lecture that Saint Edith Stein gave in Salzburg in 1930, she sketched admirably the main feminine characteristics: The precedence that she gives to persons over things, to the concrete over the abstract, to the living over the nonliving, to the whole over its parts. In the world in which we now live, the scale is tipped in favor of things, abstractions, inanimate beings. Animals are often placed on a level with human beings, and even above them. What costly efforts are made to save a stranded whale, while millions of babies are being butchered. A dehumanized world is necessarily a de-feminized one. The great mission of educators is to reawaken in women a sense of the glories of femininity, to assist women in becoming aware of the fact that to be a woman is a *privilege,* although a costly one, for it was in a female womb that the King of the universe found a place of rest and a loving nest.

May Mary, our beloved mother, through her power of intercession, grant us the grace of understanding the beauty and fruitfulness of our mission. May she teach us that it is by repeating her words, "I am the handmaid of the Lord," that women shall, with God's grace, reconquer the world for Christ. May she also remind them that the women who followed him to Calvary were also the first witnesses of his Resurrection. Indeed, *"Servire Deo, regnare est."* To serve God is to reign!

PART TWO

Prayer and Contemplation: Temple of Welcome

*"From this day all generations will call me blessed:
the Almighty has done great things for me,
and Holy is his Name."*

*A*s one responds to the divine initiative of love, the initial conversion process begins. This is a process of maturing in prayer based also upon the grace of baptism. In this manner, a person then enters into a *living* relationship with God. The community of Divine Persons come and make "their dwelling place within" the Christian. This living relationship is nourished through continual prayer, communion with God, and the sacramental life. In the Blessed Virgin, the indwelling presence of God was manifest from the moment of her conception through the gift of being "pre-redeemed" by her Son. She is a constant reminder of how crucial this living relationship with God is:

> Always know how to gather and preserve the first roots of your being, which are the will of the Father, the grace of Christ, the power of the Spirit—the three most holy Persons, welcomed and working in the most pure heart of the Mother of God from the very first moment of her conception. May you also be, like the Child Mary, the blessed place, the temple of welcome of this infinite Mystery, so that shattered and disheartened humanity might find consolation, light, and rest in this "place."[1]

In her relationship with God, Mary becomes for us the pattern of the Church's holiness, and her heart is the "resting place" for all God's children. Women are, given their nature, predisposed to place high priority on the "values of the heart," as John Paul II likes to point out. With this capacity in mind, women are capable, then, of seeing persons *with their hearts*. It is not unusual to find the feminine, empathetic soul fostering a whole movement or work that benefits the many poor and less privileged around her. Just as Mary's "fruit was blessed," these works, too, the fruit of a deep and loving relationship with God, are blessed.

When the Virgin was proclaimed blessed together with "the fruit of your womb" and proclaimed blessed for having believed, she replied, "yes," but then *changed the person whom she addressed,* for she began to speak to the Lord, and raised a marvelous song of praise to him in her lowliness of a servant. The *Magnificat* is the real Song of Songs of the New Testament, resounding on our lips daily, brethren. Let us try to intone it with particular fervor … so that, in spiritual union with Mary, we may repeat it … almost syllable by syllable, and so learn from her how and why we, too, ought to bless the Lord.[2]

Nourished by prayer, we come to realize the precious gift of a living relationship with God; the natural response is one of reverential awe. God is awesome! God is holy! It is only normal to want to proclaim this in thought, word, and deed!

She (Mary) teaches us that God alone is great and therefore ought to be called magnificent by us. He alone saves us; therefore, our spirits should exult in him. He bows toward us with his mercy and raises us to him through his power. Grand, indeed, and lofty is the lesson of the *Magnificat.* Each of us can and should make it his or her own, in all conditions of life to attain comfort and serenity—beyond the gifts of grace and light—even in trials brought by tribulations and in sufferings of the body itself.[3]

Like Mary, for example, whether as virgin, bride, or mother, women are capable of achieving great works of God though their "yes" today. The next three chapters explore the various vocational callings and responses to God's grace. With "burning enthusiasm to be handmaids of infinite and merciful Love,"[4] these authors demonstrate the powerfully evocative symbolism of the feminine presence in the Church today. In each is "expressed the very essence of the Church, as a community consecrated with the integrity of a 'virgin heart' to become the 'bride of Christ' and 'mother of believers.'"[5]

In their public proclamation of their faith, these women witness the awareness that while they are indeed his servants, God *first* loved and served them!

Mary is the first to share in this new revelation of God and, within the same, in this new "self-giving of God." Therefore, she proclaims, "For he who is mighty has done great things for me, and holy is his name." Her words reflect a joy of spirit which is difficult to express: "My spirit rejoices in God my Savior."[6]

Let us read now of these lives, formed through prayer and contemplation. Let us, with these women, recognize the great things God has done for them and in awe respond together, "Holy is his name!"

Chapter 4

Closer My God to Thee:

A Personal Testimony to the Gift of Faith and Femininity

SUSAN MUTO, PH.D.

Pure Faith

Dear sisters, together let us reflect anew on the magnificent passage in Scripture [Genesis 1:27] which describes the creation of the human race and which has so much to say about your dignity and mission in the world.[1]

I received the gift of my faith years before I was born in Pittsburgh, Pennsylvania, on December 11, 1942. I did nothing to merit or deserve this gift. It came to me through the bloodline of bedrock belief, from the nobles and peasants, landowners and farmers, religious and laity to whom I trace my maternal and paternal heritage in southern Italy. During Holy Week, 1998, when I made a pilgrimage to Malta, it was as if I were also witnessing the faith my ancestors cultivated in Calabria. Interspersed with Maltese and English were the melodious tones and prayers I had heard in childhood, mostly from my maternal grandmother, Elizabeth, to whom I attribute in great measure my initial faith formation. When she died of stomach cancer in 1954, I had only had the privilege of knowing her for twelve years, but it was enough to sense myself in the presence of an extraordinary woman of faith who greeted suffering with heroic surrender, hatred of immigrants with infectious humor, and family feuds with effective

93

peacemaking. Her illiteracy revealed no lack of intelligence. Her wisdom was proverbial, her prayer life epiphanic, her wit accurate and spontaneous in any language. When I try to imagine the hardship of her life, I have no other explanation for her joy in the face of it than pure faith.

Though there was no real future for my grandmother in her home country, it must have caused her great pain to be wrenched from her roots, from the fresh-mown fields and flowers she so loved, and sent onboard an immigrant ship to America to consummate an arranged marriage with my grandfather, Vincent, a man she hardly knew. Though she bore eleven children, between infant deaths and various influenzas she lost five of them. Of her remaining children, two sons and four daughters, my mother was the fourth-oldest. It does not surprise me that of all of her siblings my mother remained the most loyal Roman Catholic, for she stayed the longest at home with my grandmother, marrying only at the age of thirty-three. She loved her dearly and nursed her to her dying hour. She also made sure in the ensuing years that I, myself the oldest child, and my two brothers, lived nearby our "Nunny."

So dear is my grandmother's memory to me, so formative of my faith has this unnamed "saint" been, that I write of her in *Womanspirit*, the book of mine most dedicated to the gift of femininity.[2] Were it not for Elizabeth, were it not for the witness of her faith, I sometimes wonder, would I have kept mine? Would I have remained through the turmoil of the 1960s—when so many of my friends and acquaintances left the Church—not only a loyal Catholic but a single laywoman who found her vocation in its service?

When we say that the woman is the one who receives love in order to love in return, this refers not only or above all to the specific spousal relationship of marriage. It means something more universal, based on the very fact of her being a woman within all the interpersonal relationships which, in the most varied ways, shape society and structure the interaction between all persons—men and women. In this broad and diversified context, a woman represents a particular value by the fact that she is a human person, and, at the same time, this particular person, by the fact of her femininity. This concerns each and every woman, independently of the cultural context in which she lives, and independently of her spiritual, psychological and physical characteristics, as, for example, age, education, health, work, and whether she is married or single.[3]

In some way, to vow fidelity to God, to proclaim one's undying faith, is to seal one's future. If I were to be worthy of Elizabeth's witness, it meant not being afraid to be different or to sacrifice popularity for the sake of setting my priorities in order. That meant, among other things, going from eight years of elementary school at Saint Catherine of Siena to four more years of Catholic education at Saint Mary of the Mount. Then it would be on to college at Duquesne University, where, two years after my graduation in 1964, a special encounter would change my life and channel it in the direction Divine Providence had decreed. Yet let me retrace a few more steps.

"Statu Conversionis"

Here I was, a "cradle" Catholic blessed with an early "love affair" with God, a woman clearly not called to the religious life who surprised herself by finding her vocation to the single life in the world. When I finished college, I felt convinced that I was destined to pursue a career in journalism, though that fall I enrolled in the master of arts program in English literature at the University of Pittsburgh. By the mid-1960s the Charismatic Movement was in its first flowering. We were on the verge of a technological revolution in the West. Young people were torn between the amoral atmosphere of Woodstock and the responsibility thrust upon them for the Civil Rights Movement. Believers were only beginning to grasp the impact of Vatican Council II and the changes afoot in the Church. All of these developments made the question of life's meaning impossible to ignore.

By that time I knew enough about myself and my own reflective needs to know I simply could not graduate and go to work. I had to have space to be present, leisure to think and pray, an excuse, so to say, to return to my roots. The chance came when I signed on in the summer of 1964 for a three-month youth hostel trip to Europe. Our group would tour cities like Copenhagen, London, Paris, and Munich. I would set foot for the first time in the land of my origins, visiting Florence and Assisi, Rome, Naples, and Venice, and coming close enough to Calabria to catch precious glimpses of my grandmother's face in the many faces of Italy. Many times during that trip—in Winchester Cathedral in England, at Chartres in France, at Saint Peter's Basilica in the Vatican City—God touched my life and reminded me in no uncertain terms that there was another aim intended for it: not to be a journalist in the ordinary sense of that term, but to become a spiritual writer, editor, and teacher. God would be a jealous Lover, but One whose gifts to me far outweighed the gift of my heart to him.

Authentic knowledge of the God of mercy, the God of tender love, is a constant and inexhaustible source of conversion, not only as a momentary interior act but also as a permanent attitude, as a state of mind. Those who come to know God in this way, who "see" him in this way, can live only in a state of being continually converted to him. They live, therefore, in *statu conversionis;* and it is this state of conversion which marks out the most profound element of the pilgrimage of every man and woman on earth in *statu viatoris.*[4]

The design of Holy Providence began to reveal itself in earnest when I returned home. I received the dose of humility I probably needed when I found myself jobless until the first of the year. After a brief stint in retail advertising (for which I am grateful because it gave me a sure indicator that I might be in the wrong field), I was hired by a friend of mine to serve as the assistant director of public relations for the United Jewish Federation of Pittsburgh. My main task would be to help with its annual fund-raising endeavors.

This experience, as I would later come to understand, was also part of God's plan for my life. It offered me an unprecedented opportunity to learn more about my Judeo-Christian faith tradition, and it opened the door to the job I would next hold as one of the editors of the *Jewish Chronicle*. While I loved the social and historical side of my work, I became increasingly despondent, spiritually. Something was not right, but what could it be? Young as I was, I had tasted journalistic success, but it left me feeling strangely empty. Doors were opening for career advancement. So why wasn't I happy? The joy I knew did not come from bylines and recognitions but from reading the Hebrew Scriptures and going to night classes in English literature at the University of Pittsburgh. I felt a hole inside my heart no one and nothing but God could fill. I was not content with routine Catholicism, but joining a prayer group or an awakening movement did not appeal to me, either.

Without quite realizing the implications of what I was doing, I began to beg God, with what can only be called peasant faith, to lift the depression from my soul and to show me the way not I but he had decreed for my life. My daily prayer became, "Grant that my whole being, no matter how tiny, may be an embodiment of your eternal, infinite love for souls." It was around that time that I discovered the Jesus Prayer ("Lord Jesus Christ, Son of God, have mercy on me a sinner"), and it, too, became a great comfort.

In the fall of 1966 the unhappiness and confusion I had managed thus far to hide under the cover of careerism came to a head. I was at a banquet honoring dignitaries of the Jewish community. I think I was the only non-Jew at the head table. I sensed our publisher's admiration for my work editorially as well as for the technical skills I brought to the operation. The food was splendid but halfway through the meal I experienced for the first time in my life a distinct psychosomatic symptom: I could not swallow anything, neither food nor water. My throat closed up. Embarrassed and distraught, I excused myself from the table and ran out of the building to get some air, lest I faint. It was a crisp night. The stars were extraordinarily bright. I felt a little crazy, or maybe like a "fool for Christ," for the next thing I knew I was kneeling on the cold pavement with my arms raised to heaven, saying aloud, though no one was on the street to hear me, "Unless you show me what you want me to do with my life, I will be lost." No sooner had I uttered this plea then a great calm came over me. I gave everything over to God. Then I returned to the banquet as if nothing had happened, as if I had only excused myself to go to the restroom.

Three weeks later the answer came. What I did not know was that at the very time I was praying for direction of my life, a priest at Duquesne University was praying to find a person to serve as the assistant director of a new institute of spiritual formation it was his life's task to establish. I received a call "out of the blue" from the then chairman of my old journalism department. He said that Father Adrian van Kaam wanted to see me. He was a Holy Ghost priest and professor I already admired from a few elective courses of his I had taken in the Department of Psychology as an undergraduate. I assumed that Father needed some freelance publicity for his new institute. I thought that was the least I could do to help him. We met for the first time in October 1966. I came to his office armed with notebook and pen in eager anticipation of the story he had to tell.

Formative Spirituality

It started in the Netherlands in 1935. Together with his soul-friend and fellow seminarian Marinus Scholtes, he started a group called the "pioneers of Mary." It consisted of religious and laity who wanted to share their faith, read Holy Scripture and the writings of the spiritual masters in a formative fashion, and seek ways to offset the danger of an arrogant expression of Catholicism that was perilously close to forgetting its humble roots in the teachings of Jesus. The "pioneers" foresaw in some way the agony of war, occupation, and utter dehumanization that would soon overtake Europe with the rise of Nazism.

By 1944 their direst forecasts had come true. During this terrible year before the liberation and prior to his ordination in 1946, he credited God with planting the seeds of his life's work. Catapulted out of the seminary into the hiding places that became his home, he discovered the distinction between denominational faith traditions (what people believe) and the vast variety of formation traditions (how people live these beliefs in everyday life). He came to see, as did his peer in Poland Karol Wojtyla, later Pope John Paul II, the absolute necessity of respect between all people, however different their religious or ideological backgrounds may be.

History has shown that the passage from nationalism to totalitarianism is swift and that, when states are no longer equal, people themselves end up no longer being equal. Thus the natural solidarity between peoples is destroyed and the principle of the unity of mankind is held in contempt.

The Catholic Church cannot accept such a vision of things. Universal by nature, she is conscious of being at the service of all and never identifies with any one national community. She welcomes into her bosom all nations, races, and cultures. She is mindful of—indeed she knows that she is the depository of—

God's design for humanity: to gather all people into one family. And this is because he is the Creator and Father of all. That is the reason why every time that Christianity—whether according to its Western or Eastern Tradition—becomes the instrument of a form of nationalism, it is as it were wounded in its very heart and made sterile.[5]

The more Father van Kaam spoke, the more furiously I took notes. His story was truly fascinating. Here I was in the presence of a person who had founded a new science, anthropology, and theology of human and Christian formation, a new field of study he had come to call "formative spirituality." Father's call was to unfold these disciplines in a systematic way in service of the Church as a whole with special attention to the needs for in-depth spirituality expressed by many in the wake of Vatican Council II. His was a vision of Church and world I would henceforth follow with great interest.

After Father's ordination, his work aroused the attention of the then secretary of state of the Vatican, Monsignor Giovanni Baptista Montini, later Pope Paul VI, who recommended that he pursue this formative approach to faith-filled living on a full-time basis and per-haps eventually develop his ideas for a comprehensive formation theology on the university level. Father thus arrived at Duquesne University in Pittsburgh in 1954.

He confirmed my own intuition that in our time people were inclined to be more psychological than philosophical, more pragmatic and empirical than speculative and analytical. The clarion cry was "show me" or "prove it." The Church could not ignore this state of affairs. In addition to starting the program at Duquesne on psychology as a human science, he continued to develop his pre-theological formation science and anthropology. Interestingly enough, Professor Karol Wojtyla, later Pope John Paul II, was crafting at the same time his remarkable, and in some ways similar, existential-phenomenological thinking on the acting person.

After nine faithful years the opportunity came in 1963 for Father van Kaam to begin a new institute devoted exclusively to the question of "formation." Here he could pursue his conviction that the well-being of the Church in the twentieth century would depend in great measure on one's addressing the empirical-experiential sciences in the same way as Thomas Aquinas had to address in the thirteenth century the philosophical-speculative insights of Plato and Aristotle. He was right in his assumption that my generation was not falling over itself to resolve the great questions of philosophy. On the contrary, we were fascinated by contemporary psychology, and especially by the self-actualizing teaching it promoted. I could see from my experience in the working world how easy it was becoming for young people to separate their faith tradition from the influences of psychologism, careerism, materialism, and consumerism permeating their formation traditions. It was an easy step to displace Christ as the center of our lives and to replace him with the self. Many of the old values I had seen lived to the full by my grandmother were literally "up for grabs." People my age were interested in a "spirituality" not grounded in a classical faith tradition but bent on human experience alone—be it psychedelic or Far Eastern—without sufficient critical discrimination. After all, this was the "Age of Aquarius!" Mood rings were sources of serious guidance. Gestalt psychology, marathon therapy, encounter groups, every kind of counseling were gravitated toward like new religions.

I could see why Father Adrian needed a separate graduate institute to pursue his goals, and I hoped whatever I would write would be of some help to him.

"Life Call"

I looked up from what I had noted and began to apologize in advance for the possibility that I would not do justice to his story. He looked puzzled, as if for a moment we were on different wavelengths. Then he sensed my confusion and smiled. In a few short words that changed my life he explained that this interview was not about writing a story but about asking me if I wanted to serve as the assistant director of the institute. In a flash that sealed my vocation and answered my prayer, the word "Yes!" popped out of my mouth. Christ called, and I heard his voice through the invitation of his priest.

> Both in her earliest days and in her successive development, the Church, albeit in different ways and with diverse emphases, has always known women who have exercised an oftentimes decisive role in the Church herself and accomplished tasks of considerable value on her behalf. History is marked by grand works, quite often lowly and hidden, but not for this reason any less decisive to the growth and the holiness of the Church. It is necessary that this history continue, indeed that it be expanded and intensified in the face of the growing and widespread awareness of the personal dignity of women and her vocation, particularly in light of the urgency of a "re-evangelization" and a major effort toward "humanizing" social relations.[6]

With the blessing of my publisher, I left the *Chronicle* and came to Duquesne. Father insisted that I not only get my master's degree in English literature but also pursue a Ph.D. in this field, so as to be qualified to teach graduate courses.

We had a trained faculty, a research methodology, an excellent library, and, most of all, a keen sense of service to the Church. By that time our students, laity, clergy, and religious came from twenty-six different countries around the world. We felt called to steer a steady course through churning waters. By this time I had also published a trilogy of books on the art and discipline of formative reading (*Approaching the Sacred, Steps Along the Way,* and *The Journey Homeward*) along with a standard text in the field entitled *A Practical Guide to Spiritual Reading*. Once the doctoral program was in process, new books were authored and co-authored by us along with the editing of several journals, including *Envoy* and *Studies in Formative Spirituality*. Then, in 1980, Father Adrian suffered a heart attack and subsequent bypass surgery. After what he called, in characteristic fashion, the "blessing of a coronary," I became the first laywoman to direct the Institute of Formative Spirituality at Duquesne University.

Epiphany—Praying Pioneers

It was at that time (1979), at the height of our academic careers, when both of us were tenured professors, that another disclosure of our call unexpectedly announced itself. It was to resurrect the prototypical association of "praying pioneers" Father Adrian and friends had started in 1935 in Holland, now under the title "Epiphany." Now, as then, people outside university circles, living their Christian lives in the world, needed special preparation for the work they were being called to do in the Church. There was an outcry among laity, clergy, and religious for in-depth spiritual formation. Circumstances made it impossible for all but a few to pursue formal graduate courses. With the help of like-minded friends in Pittsburgh, we co-founded the Epiphany Association to fill this need. Little could we know then that it would be the place where the field of formative spirituality would come to its full flowering.

The work of the Epiphany Association understandably became more demanding. It was not, as we had thought originally, destined to be a weekend activity. The hunger of "people in the pew" for a deeper walk with Christ, for a life of holiness, was not sporadic but epidemic.

The vocation to holiness must be recognized and lived by the lay faithful, first of all as an undeniable and demanding obligation and as a shining example of the infinite love of the Father that has regenerated them in his own life of holiness. Such a vocation, then, ought to be called an essential and inseparable element of the new life of Baptism, and therefore an element which determines their dignity. At the same time the vocation to holiness is intimately connected to mission and to the responsibility entrusted to the lay faithful in the Church and in the world. In fact, that same holiness which is derived simply from their participation in the Church's holiness, represents their first and fundamental contribution to the building of the Church herself, who is the "Communion of Saints."[7]

Another event of ministry aided the ongoing appraisal of my "life call." In 1984 I accepted an invitation from Bishop Joseph Imesch of the Diocese of Joliet to became the principal writer of a planned pastoral letter of the National Conference of Catholic Bishops on the concerns of women for the Church and society. Busy as I was with university teaching and the directorship of the institute, a number of outside speaking engagements, and, of course, the work entailed in being, along with Father Adrian, Epiphany's co-founder, I said another life-changing "yes" to the bishop. Little did I know then that this work of service to the Church would occupy the next nine years of my life, along with the writing of four complete drafts of the pastoral for the committee of bishops and scholars involved in this project. While the pastoral as such was not destined for final publication, its twenty-five action items were unanimously approved by the National Catholic Conference of Bishops in 1992 and subsequently influenced many other American documents favorable to the dignity of women—a theme dear to our Holy Father's heart. His groundbreaking Apostolic Letter, *Mulieris Dignitatem* (1988), had a major influence on the work of the pastoral committee and on my personal life.

If we look at today's world, we are struck by many negative factors that can lead to pessimism. Yet this feeling is unjustified: We have faith in God our Father and Lord, in his goodness and mercy. As we enter now into the third millennium of the redemption, God is preparing a great springtime for Christianity, and we can already see its first signs. In fact, both in the non-Christian world and in the traditionally Christian world, people are gradually drawing closer to gospel ideals and values, a development that the church seeks to encourage. Today there is a new consensus among peoples about these values: the rejection of violence and war; respect for the human person and for human rights; the desire for freedom, justice, and brotherhood; the surmounting of different forms of racism and nationalism; the affirmation of the dignity and role of women.

> Christian hope sustains us in committing ourselves fully to the new evangelization and to the worldwide mission, and leads us to pray as Jesus taught us: "Your kingdom come, your will be done on earth as it is in heaven" (Matthew 6:10).[8]

In 1989, I was immersed in full-time service to the Epiphany Association. Father Adrian was assigned, following his retirement from Duquesne, to be our full-time researcher and chaplain-in-residence. The university made the decision to phase out this graduate-level program of the institute, in order to focus its resources more on undergraduate and professional education. Holy Providence had ordained that Epiphany would be in place, so that, as the university phase of our work ended, its apostolic, formative, educational, and resource development phase would begin.

Today we maintain the advanced, postgraduate Epiphany Certification Program, known as ECP, one in Pittsburgh and the other in Indianapolis, as well as the twice-yearly, five-day Epiphany Lay

Formation Academy, known as ELFA. Epiphany foundations are also active in Moscow, Russia, and in the city of Seoul, Korea, where students and graduates of ours are stationed.

A Vision for the Church of the Twenty-First Century

In May 1991, I had the privilege of traveling to Rome with the bishops and secretary of the pastoral writing committee to present our work to a worldwide assembly of bishops and also to the Holy Father. Never will I forget the morning I attended Mass in his private chapel and stood face to face with him in his library. In my hand I had a copy of my companion text to Saint John of the Cross's *Ascent of Mount Carmel.*[9] This was the year the Church celebrated the saint's four-hundredth anniversary. The Holy Father had written his own dissertation on faith according to John of the Cross, so it was a singular privilege for me to give him my book in person.

This meeting was quite providential. I was deeply moved by the person of the Holy Father and realized that we needed a way to integrate the contemplative and active sides of our life as Pope John Paul II does so beautifully. I see these two components in splendid unison in the figure of our Holy Father. The feminine side of his personhood explains his veneration for our Blessed Mother, his salute in many letters and documents to the "feminine genius," and his defense of human dignity. The masculine side of his wholeness manifests itself in his world travels, his self-sacrificial nature, and his determination to combat the forces of materialistic atheism and individualistic consumerism.

I have had the privilege during my nine years of service on the pastoral committee to study his writings on the gift of femininity and found in them the help I needed to remain faithful to my vocation as well as to the mission and ministry of our association.

I saw the saintly courage of John Paul displayed once more in person when Father Adrian and I were among the pilgrims meeting him in the privacy of his library in July 1996. We were in Rome representing the association on the Golden Jubilee pilgrimage we were making to celebrate Father's fiftieth anniversary in the priesthood. We had many occasions to identify with the Holy Father's teachings on ecumenism, on the culture of life, and on the need for wise and balanced efforts at evangelization. In fact, his vision for the Church of the twenty-first century goes to the heart of our own concerns.

> Among the most fervent petitions which the Church makes to the Lord during this important time, as the eve of the new millennium approaches, is that unity among all Christians of the various confessions will increase until they reach full communion. I pray that the Jubilee will be a promising opportunity for fruitful cooperation in the many areas which unite us; these are unquestionably more numerous than those which divide us. It would thus be quite helpful if, with due respect for the program of the individual churches and communities, ecumenical agreements could be reached with regard to the preparation and celebration of the Jubilee. In this way the Jubilee will bear witness even more forcefully before the world that the disciples of Christ are fully resolved to reach full unity as soon as possible in the certainty that "nothing is impossible with God."[10]

Indeed, as I look back on my life as a celebration of the gifts of faith and femininity, I can truly say, "Nothing is impossible with God." I often begin my lectures on formative spirituality by reminding my listeners that "formation is narration." It is the telling of our story of the journey of faith that makes us sense our oneness in Christ Jesus and the fact that we would not have come this far without the guiding hand of the Father and the inspiration of the Holy Spirit. I have chosen the narrative format in this testimonial to show why I am not only content to be Catholic, as one would be content to behold a reasonable, convincing tapestry of truth, but why it excites me to be a member of the Church. I want to walk in the footsteps of faithful women over the ages, women like Catherine of Siena, Teresa of Avila, and Thérèse of Lisieux, saints named doctors of the Church, whose belief was no less intense than that of unknown holy women like my grandmother. If Christ chooses to use my witness as he used theirs to draw other souls to himself, I could imagine no better outcome of my vocation.

I am happy to say that many hearts are being touched through the work of the Epiphany Association and its endeavors to enhance the life of the spirit in foundational formative ways. I believe in the old catechetical saying that faith is less taught than caught. It is a gift that appeals eternally to that part of us that does not doubt but believes, even if we do not see, that hopes in the impossible, and that dares to proclaim, in the face of every destructive force on the face of the earth, that love is stronger than death. Who better than our Holy Father, himself the victim of an assassination attempt, deserves to have the last word? This word appropriately is an ode to womanhood and to that woman, Mary, whom he addresses in prayer as the Mother of Life and who to us is Our Lady of Epiphany:

O Mary,
bright dawn of the new world,
Mother of the living,
to you do we entrust the *cause of life*:
Look down, O Mother,
upon the vast numbers of babies not allowed to be born,
of the poor whose lives are made difficult,
of men and women
who are victims of brutal violence,
of the elderly and the sick killed
by indifference or out of misguided mercy.
Grant that all who believe in your Son
may *proclaim the Gospel of life*
with honesty and love
to the people of our time.
Obtain for them the grace
to *accept that Gospel*
as a gift ever new,
the joy *of celebrating* it with gratitude
throughout their lives
and the courage to *bear witness to* it
resolutely, in order to build,
together with all people of good will,
the civilization of truth and love,
to the praise and glory of God,
the Creator and lover of life.[11]

Chapter 5

The Catholic Woman Finds Her Vocation in Imitation of the Church

GENEVIEVE S. KINEKE

To Whom Should We Go, Lord?

*A*s a convert, I would love to say that I came to the Church through careful study, intellectual discussions, or sorting through complex theological minutiae. The pride in me would like to take credit for recognizing the truth and having the courage to pursue it at all cost. Yet I am in the arms of Holy Mother Church by the grace of God, through the spiritual wealth of an infant baptism he magnificently arranged, and because of the prayers of persevering souls in the Mystical Body of Christ that I will probably never recognize this side of the veil.

Now that I have had the privilege of studying the teachings of the Church and meditating on the person of Our Lord who deigned to visit us, I praise God for his mercy, his order, and his tremendous charity. The invitation not only to participate in his work of redemption but to be lifted up and embraced within the unity of the Trinity is beyond all comprehension and adequate appreciation.

The invitation to live within the Blessed Trinity, extraordinary as it is, is meant to be carried out in the ordinary, so that the mundane is linked to the miraculous in a coherent, rational way. This is what we mean by the Incarnation, which, although it refers to a particular event in history, the event indeed through which all history is interpreted, also indicates the transforming potential of our everyday thoughts and actions. Thankfully the Church provides the coherence and unfolds the rationale in season and out.

With the contemporary challenges in the realm of the person and his sexuality, the lessons of the Church are particularly applicable to understanding the gift inherent in our feminine nature. Thus if we look at mercy, order, and charity in light of the person of Jesus Christ, his Blessed Mother, and his bride the Church, we can find a deeper awareness of what it means to be in the image and likeness of God as a woman.

First, I must explain how God drew me into his Church. Truly, the infant baptism given under extraordinary circumstances had the power to lay the necessary foundation. I lay dying in a strange land, a few months old, after the sudden death of my mother. Yet family—in the sense of the Mystical Body of which we are all a part—took precautions for my soul as the doctors cared for my physical needs, and the script God had in mind took flesh. I learned of these events only after I had taken actual steps to enter the Church and, although it surprised me, now knowing a little about how God works, it shouldn't have.

I was raised in a nominally Protestant home that carried all the residuals of a once conservative, God-fearing culture. This meant that all of the behaviors once linked to the practice of the faith were instilled in us, granted in sometimes Jansenistic fashion, yet Christ and a personal devotion to him were absent. The framework remained but there was no core. Particular actions, then, were promoted out of a combination of duty, guilt, and the desire for human respect. This can protect one to the extent that one submits to the ground rules—which can mirror a rather righteous life—but it runs the risk of alienating anyone who questions the rationale for the framework.

One of the particular aspects of Catholicism that drew me as a child (admittedly it is difficult from such a distance to peg) was the fact that Catholics knelt. American children kneel in play or while play-acting other cultures or eras, and adults kneel to pull weeds or perform other menial tasks. Yet the active choice to kneel, not in humble service but in humble adoration—in the latter twentieth century—was jarring to my sensibilities. My thoughts certainly weren't this deep at the time; I just thought it was overwhelmingly different from everything I knew about people and what they did and didn't do.

The thought of grown men in this generation—American men!—kneeling led me to another indistinct but clear conclusion: There must have been something really important inside that Church that caused this submission. Catholics are equally guilty of the same trap into which any other faith community can fall. The gestures and actions can lose their connection to God and become merely cultural. Yet God can take these gestures and use them with or without our recognition of their transcendence (who of us is always *present?*) for his glory. And so it was.

I was intrigued enough to commit myself to participating as soon as would be feasible, which would have to wait for when I left home.

Needless to say, finding the Catholic Church was a challenge that took nearly a decade. From the fuzzy faith of a campus ministry where Father was "Bob" and sin was nonexistent my pendulum took me to the reactionary traditionalism of the anti–Vatican II crowd. After all, I thought, if the tremendous faith of the early portion of this century had crumbled after the council, perhaps we should rewind the tape and live as those earlier generations had.

That road eventually led down a frightening path that snapped me out of this nostalgic dream world.

So what was left? Christ, of course! As Saint Peter beautifully stated, "To whom should we go, Lord? For you have the words of eternal life" (Jn 6:68). I was fully committed to the Holy Father as our true shepherd, so perhaps it was time to stop listening to people telling me what the pope *meant* and listen to the man himself. *Ubi Petra, ibi ecclesia!*

True Anthropology Reveals True Femininity

In school I had studied anthropology and even considered specializing in that field, but as much as it intrigued me, the secular courses didn't keep my interest or satisfy the desire to understand man. Societies were paraded across the chalkboard, identified, quantified, and categorized—with no transcendent criteria. It seemed useless, or at best, intellectual curiosity for its own sake.

Instead, I chose history, where we turned our secular eyes to events near and far, from the distant past to recent years. The standards by which we analyzed these events were off the mark, to be sure, but the years were by no means wasted. The knowledge is now useful as I look with the Church at the current dilemma over the relationship between the sexes. We never want to look backward in the sense of nostalgia for a past era, but to look backward to learn lessons from our errors is very helpful to making the future more pleasing to God.

Unless we know what questions to ask, though, we do not know where to go in our quest for authenticity. In searching for the answers, John Paul II goes back to the beginning to probe our unfallen state in order to find the ideal man, the ideal woman. There, in the garden, in harmony with our Creator, he shows us that the "nuptial meaning of the body" is the key to unlocking the truth about our femininity.

> When man—"the male," awakening from the sleep of Genesis, sees man—"the female," drawn from him, he says: "This at last is the bone of my bones and flesh of my flesh" (Genesis 2:23). These words express, in a way, the subjectively beatifying beginning of man's existence in the world.[1]

Here, Adam's solitude, which is noticeably a drawback, ends and the complementary relationship between man and woman begins. The pope continues:

Precisely by traversing the depth of that original solitude, man now emerges in the dimension of the mutual gift, the expression of which—and for that very reason the expression of his existence as a person—is the human body in all the original truth of its masculinity and femininity.[2]

What this beautiful philosopher has to offer women is the Church's teaching on the essence of their being:

The body, which expresses femininity, manifests the reciprocity and communion of persons. It expresses it by means of the "gift" as the fundamental characteristic of personal existence. This is the body: a witness to creation as a fundamental gift, and so a witness to Love as the source from which this same giving springs.[3]

So where do we find women and their understanding of themselves today? Always in the past, the Church has reacted to heresies that threatened its deposit of faith. Similarly, the Church is reacting to the assault on the notion of a two-sexed universe and the rejection of the protections provided by the family. Today there is a united attack on the basic premises of society, such as marriage, chastity, fidelity, and purity. Many have worked hard to blur the distinctions between men and women by promoting androgyny, promiscuity, and the rejection of fertility.

Their focus is the self, indulging the baser instincts, and the rejection of consequences or responsibility. The family hangs precariously in the balance, and the children are left without love or guidance. We must remember that a woman is the critical link from generation to generation. Her body binds them physically, forming the bridge between the old and the young, and bringing traditions into the present. If the women let this task go and fail to make the traditions alive and practical to another age, how can society but suffocate and founder?

While only a few years ago I rejected feminism out of hand as completely unjustified power-mongering by bitter women, maturity has come with age and I can see where the seeds lie. Exposure in various ways to bygone generations has brought revulsion and frustration—at the way women and their talents were dismissed out of hand and left untapped, at the way women were considered chattel and sexual toys by men, and at the way work was distributed so unfairly that women were little better than slaves. Some societies still reflect a real bias that never gives a little girl proper dignity or a chance to achieve her legitimate dreams. Chauvinism is reprehensible—anywhere, at any time. Opportunities for education, health, and autonomy are only fair and should be available for women as well as men.

Curiously, though, women, who head most of the cadres of rebellion, end up harming themselves in the ways they insist on fighting chauvinism. Since they have suffered from being sexual objects, they, in return, insist on making sexual objects of men. After being hurt by unfaithful men and promiscuity, they insist on having available the same means, which requires contraceptives and no-fault divorce. Instead of learning from the men who put power and wealth before relationships, women insist on access to the same avenues, and, in turn, reject their own fertility and offspring for the same reasons.

Another factor that affects the discussion is the course the English language has taken in recent generations. It is sad that our culture has charged the word "sex" with erotic and indelicate baggage. This phenomenon has made the discussion of the vocation of men and women that much more difficult and imprecise. This is exacerbated by the sexually charged atmosphere of our era so that even to consider the nuptial meaning of the body often assumes that that potential must be fulfilled in order for the essence to be realized. Thus it is important to restore a sense of purity to the discussion so that chastity can be understood and appreciated as the dignified state of man.

What is interesting is that the war of the sexes that has permeated recent decades has metamorphosed into a heavily fortified, uneasy "truce" called androgyny, or the blurring of the distinctions between the sexes. Sadly, this battle has consumed our study of literature and Western culture, has used language as a tool of manipulation and identification of loyalties, and has so charged the atmosphere of everyday living with sexuality, innuendo, and perversion that it is nearly impossible to live chastely or purely. It is a truism that nature abhors a vacuum, and the attempted deconstruction of God's two-sexed universe has led to curious behaviors that fall far short of the dignity that is ours by design. Androgyny, which pervades the media, the school hallways, the towers of academia, the marketplace, and the streets, is at best confusing and at worst injects an insidious element into society that destroys families and corrupts individuals.

"Theology of the Body" Is the Church's Response

This heresy is strangling the world, yet forcing the Church to define the person in terms heretofore unseen. As children grow up hungering for truth, a truth is being hammered out and voiced that will surpass all understanding until now about men and women. In her well-guided mission to staunch the flow of casualties from this onslaught, the Church, and our present pontiff, John Paul II, especially, are revealing to the world a vision of the human person unencumbered by stereotypes and false dichotomies.

This pope recognizes the pain of our fallen condition and has written to his sons and daughters from the heart. He has woven together a body of work that explains our creation, our original unity, and what God revealed about himself in our human bodies. John Paul II has expressed to every nation God's love and plan of redemption. He exhorts all peoples to partake of the gifts of the sacraments, Our Lady, and the ability to cooperate with God's plan. He could not be more fatherly; he could not be more passionate. His writings could not be more eloquent. *He himself is a gift,* and we would do well to take him and his words to heart.

The search for the true person and his Creator has particular consequences for a woman because in the different communities, a woman has a varying significance. Men, up to the present, have had their vocations pretty well under control because of the simplicity of their working life. They forge a living in a manner based on resources, talents, technology, and the ever-present "market." They contribute to the family they naturally create as their working life allows, and their level of dedication reflects their understanding of morality and responsibility.

For women, the world is now far more complex. The new and growing numbers of completely secular women have no definition of womanhood save that which each carves out for herself, based on her culture, her temperament, and her opportunities. Her conclusion naturally impacts on the men in her life and the children she produces. For many, their choices have left men bewildered and their children neglected.

For a Christian, there is simply the Bible and its prescriptions for salvation, which channel a lot of her choices morally yet leave a lot of material details up to interpretations by her faith community. Unfortunately, as important as Scripture is to these communities, many of the conclusions are based on man-made traditions and later become indefensible territory.

The Catholic woman finds her vocation in imitation of the Church, which is the spotless bride of Christ. The Church is virgin, bride, and mother, embracing the essence of the various paths all women take and expressing the nuptial truth at the heart of the universe. It reminds us of true love, everlasting commitment, and the fathomless communion in which man and woman are invited to share in marriage as they become one flesh. This supernatural reality, which transcends all of human history, must be made manifest in tangible ways by women in all times and places, in all states of life, and in purity and truth. Our glory as women is to study the bride, embrace the bride, and be the bride for all of mankind to see.

As the eyes of the maid are on her master, so the Church looks to Christ for inspiration and direction in the way to live the virtues. In a particular way, women must study the Church's method of expressing the divine will of her Founder in order to guide their own actions and responses in everyday life.

Mercy

Our God is a merciful God, and this was clearly manifest in the God-Man, the Savior. Christ lived mercy, and our imitation of him must reflect that. In the tangibles of society, of the legal system, of the economic system, of the social strata we've woven for ourselves, mercy is jarring and out of sync. These attempts at justice are critical to the smooth operation of our culture, and yet they provide a framework where mercy can, while being misunderstood, be countercultural and even a little piece of heaven. Mercy speaks to the person at his core, and when he finally recognizes it, at the hands of a neighbor, for what it is, he grows enormously in his recognition of the infinite capacity for mercy he will find in God.

God's love is unconditional and so must ours be. Thus, though a woman's heart is often more vulnerable to pain, hers must also be capable of constant and thorough forgiveness of the foibles and daggers of others. As women we often hold on to resentments. The feminine nature "ponders these things in the heart," taking the time to turn events or words over and over, analyzing and even brooding until they can be understood. Too often, though, we allow them to define us. We react to injustices in a particularly personal way—perhaps because of our inherent physical bond with the "other."

Forgiveness is critical, for our growth, for the spread of the truth, and for the peace so desperately needed in this fallen world. This is only possible through union with Christ and our recognition of the nature of his Mystical Body. The cross is inherent in every wound we suffer, every indignity we undergo. To embrace our particular, temporal suffering as having been suffered by Our Blessed Lord in his passion and having been more painful to him than even to us is the first step of letting go. Our union with him transforms our pain into cooperation with the Divine Plan and allows us to offer it truly for the good of those who hurt us. We can all allow ourselves to be nailed to Christ's cross, as comfort to him, balm for ourselves, and a channel of grace for mankind.

Mercy cannot be based on emotions, but based on will, which a woman must hone and strengthen. It is incumbent on her to make divine mercy manifest to those in her sphere. Mary is a creature who is distinctly immaculate from sin yet fully human. She is also fully dedicated to her particularly maternal task of providing a channel of mercy, a sense of order, and a beautiful, tangible example of imitating the charity of her Son. Our Lady is such a model for this, especially as she stood beneath the Cross, accepting not only his death in agony but the charge to mother those who betrayed him, scourged him, and rejected him—then and through all ages to come. She became then, and remains forever, Our Mother of Mercy. That is the degree of forgiveness we must show. That is the challenge to all of us.

Order

Women must imitate Our Lady and Holy Mother Church in another dimension, which is in the realm of order. Mary is constant. The imagery of the Church helps us. How many pieces of art have we seen over the years? She is always holding the Child, always at the foot of the cross, always gazing at the lifeless Christ draped across her lap, and perpetually coronated in submissive, radiant humility. Is this boring? Perhaps to some, but the subtlety of this consistency lays its seeds in the human mind. Are they just more "religious pictures"? No, this is, among other things, the lesson of *her constancy*.

Children who are raised on these images carry them for life, whether they want to or not. One of our children, at age two, recognized Our Lady in every picture of a mother holding a baby, regardless of the circumstances, the retinue, or the wardrobe. She lisped, "Oh, Blessed Mudder, Baby Jesus." And so it is—another dimension of the Incarnation we know as the Mystical Body.

Order is a part of the Church year. There is the endless cycle—Advent, leading to Christmastide, giving way to Lent and Easter. There is ordinary time, which is part of our everyday lives as well and surrounds the parade of feasts. The Church carries us through the seasons and before we know it we're back to another Advent. Mothers also set the order in the home, establishing customs according to the personality of the family and setting the tone that underlies each. She, being the heart of the home, can imitate the Church and make its life resonate within the life of the family.

There is an interplay here as the Church revitalizes her so that she, in turn, can build up the Church. A woman may become distracted or overly tired, she may balk at the demands the Church makes on her. Yet the Spotless Bride of Christ will encourage her to more constancy and fidelity. It may be that faithful priest who is waiting in the confessional that leads her to bring souls to him. It may be the excitement of the children over last year's successful Lent that will bolster her energy to bring the season alive in the home once more. Even yet it may be her insistence on the availability of the sacraments or a fervent round of devotions that revitalizes the waffling priest.

Order is critical to the well-being of souls, from infancy to old age. It is in our nature to want to know what is expected of us, what parameters exist, and what will happen in the near future. It is common knowledge that children thrive in an orderly setting and perform better when limits are set and consequences understood. Order frees the mind and safeguards the body. The Church provides such, and a woman can manifest that in her sphere in a very personal and loving way. This order leads very logically to unity when minds are focusing on the same ideal, and ultimately to peace. Her sphere may be small or large, but joined with Christ, her example and efforts toward this end can build miracles.

Charity

Charity, of course, is the pillar of our faith, the everlasting virtue that defines Christianity. Women, due to their intimacy with the formation of the young and their personal attention to those around them, can carry the love of Christ to so many who would otherwise never experience it. This love can manifest itself through acts of hospitality, through generosity of the body, and through the attentive love for the person that she can show in a concrete and effective way.

The means provided to integrate our Christian ideals into life are really an ongoing reflection of the Incarnation. In condescending to visit us he thereby allows us to lift our whole being to God. Christ used real flesh, real water, real dust, real stones, real hunger, real pain, and real bread. He also gave us the tremendous gift to do likewise—to take the realities of our tangible universe and allow them to be laden with grace and sacramental power in spiritual order.

Thus, charity can bring God into the home in a particular way when it is hospitable to the guest, to the wayfarer, and to the neighbor. The warmth of a home is often hard to quantify but is easily recognized. Women have a critical role here in establishing hospitality—because openness to the person leads to openness to the gospel. The Church's foundation was hospitality to the Word, first by the Woman, then by many women, and this must continue in order to make Christ present and loved.

A woman's generosity toward new life is her crowning glory and her special distinction in the created order. She has been asked to cooperate in this unique way with the generation of souls, and here femininity boasts its likeness to the Creator and revels in his gift to her. This is an extraordinary regeneration of the Incarnation as we recall the words of Genesis, that she will be saved through child-bearing. Motherhood is painful—indeed, labor is only the start. Yet it is one of our treasured means of sharing in the paschal mystery of Christ.

The physical demands that co-creating and sustaining life entail draw the woman to the cross and nail her to it. As living waters flowed from the side of the Christ, giving birth to the Church, so she suffers and gives of her flesh to people that Church, to carry the seed to fruition and give glory to the Father. And when our lives are not undergoing this particular life-giving trial, women assist in their particular way the growth and maturity of nearby souls—through nurturing, teaching, nourishing, and performing whatever tasks their talents will allow. When no immediate corporal works are needed, they take their place at the side of Our Lady, in imitation of her faithful prayers for her Son's intentions. They pray for those in need, in pain, in distress, or in doubt. They imitate Mary's faith in a two-fold manner; first in the fact that this suffering, when united with Christ, will bring good to the world, and secondly, in that their faithful presence will thus console the Church Suffering.

Charity bids us be open to new life, to welcome its arrival, to nurture and protect it, and to provide it with an understanding of its existence. This will be the source of pain, misunderstandings, fear, resentment, complications, and exhaustion. All of these must be smoothed by charity and overcome by grace.

How like the Church are all of these everyday actions, for what are the sacraments but acts of welcome, cleansing, growth, and healing? Who is the bride but *"mater et magister"*—our mother and our teacher? What does she do but pour herself out from age to age for the benefit of the souls in her care?

We, like the Blessed Virgin, are invited into the Trinity, into its mysteries and its eternal joy. This generous God of ours lifts up our nothingness and links it to his awesomeness so that the ripples of grace can touch more creatures. Our cooperation is free, and souls depend on it. Women can never be considered less in the scheme of life—without them, God's world as he ordered it would be barren.

Most certainly, women can never be considered less in life—indeed, in the plan of God, we hold an exalted place.

Pope John Paul II writes in *Mulieris Dignitatem* these stunning words that should shake us to the core of our being: "In God's eternal plan, woman is the one in whom the order of love in the created world first takes place."[4] We are fundamental to the transmission of the most precious commodity in the universe, and he continues, "The Bridegroom is the one who loves, the Bride is loved: it is she who receives love in order to love in return."[5] We are his ambassadors of love and the bridges of his union with mankind. It is our privilege and our crowning glory.

God's Call in My Life

With this in mind, I have responded to my particular call, which is to help women to understand their femininity. I have benefited from extraordinary examples of women all around me as mothers, friends, professionals, and mentors. Years ago I saw an article written by Dr. Ronda Chervin in the *National Catholic Register* suggesting that a forum for women be established to discuss authentic womanhood. This caught my attention and spoke to me in a profound way, so I applied my abundant enthusiasm and yet limited skills to the establishment of a journal for women. I'm not sure that what developed was what she had in mind, but God has blessed this project abundantly. *Canticle* magazine continues, growing in stature, quality, and confidence through the contributions of its writers and the providential, inspirational mentors given to me at critical times.

Our articles deal specifically with women and the Catholic faith, including topics from their vocations to their family relationships, the virtues, life's challenges, and the devotions that bring them to God and define the way they live in society. *Canticle's* goal is to help women provide light, salt, and leaven to the communities in which they live. The tasks to which women are called in this generation are broad and diverse, so we hope to combine the eternal dimension of their vocations with the practical details of modern life.

Of course the writings of Pope John Paul II are the heart and soul of *Canticle* magazine. He has a personal and very human love for women. This is clear in his travels, his addresses, and his everyday life. His affection for babies has been evident to all who have watched him in a crowd thoroughly enjoying the presence of women and children. His life's story is such that he appreciates what a mother can provide and he recognizes how she affirms the maternal provisions the Blessed Mother will make for all her children.

It is important that *Canticle's* forum not be limited to any particular age group, vocation, charism, or culture. It is meant to be broad, international, and inclusive in the sense that single, married, or consecrated, old or young, all women will be enriched. Granted, our vocations are lived out with particular and differentiating details, yet discerning the core of womanhood and God's plans for his beloved daughters is our ultimate aim. This will help in the struggle to break through the peripherals and discover the essence of femininity, truly, the gifts of femininity!

It is an intriguing time to be a woman and a particularly blessed time to be alive. As the words of *Mulieris Dignitatem* make clear, it is incumbent on women to restore God's rightful place to society. Women can transform themselves, but only if they see the need—men cannot do it for them or push them in any way. The dynamics of the sexes, for better or worse, are such that men may have the authority but women must have the autonomy within the relationship to initiate change for the right reasons. The Church fathers wrote eloquently in the closing documents of the Second Vatican Council:

> The hour is coming, in fact has come, when the vocation of women is being acknowledged in its fullness, the hour in which women acquire in the world an influence never hitherto achieved. That is why, at this moment when the human race is undergoing so deep a transformation, women imbued with the spirit of the Gospel can do so much to aid mankind in not falling.[6]

God's generosity will bring about enough grace to turn the tide and glorify his self-giving love. We must cooperate in his plan at this particular juncture and witness to his faithfulness. This requires accepting the enormous crosses of our generation with a cheerful and steadfast spirit and turning to our brothers and sisters who are in need. By spreading the word about the true meaning of the human person and injecting our culture with the mercy, order, and charity of our loving Father, we will win back the confused and discover the fullness of joy inherent in being women in the image and likeness of God.

Chapter 6

Opening Your Heart to Him

JOANNA BOGLE

Unchanging Truth

*E*ach generation in the Church has to stand for particular truths and teachings that may be challenged. In Britain at the time of the Reformation many died for affirming Catholic teachings. Often, they were dying for something that, within the memory of many, had been affirmed by the whole community and regarded as a basic part of a common faith that formed the basis of the nation's life. Today, Catholic men and women have to affirm beliefs about some of the most important and beautiful things of all—the right to life itself, and the naturalness of a union between the two different sexes. We can often unite with Christians from other denominations, and with people of goodwill from all backgrounds, to make a stand in defense of these common values. However, we have to know that in the end, if necessary in defense of truth, we may have to follow the example of martyrs in the past. We may have to stand alone while recognizing that any hardships we face are tiny in comparison to the torture and death endured by those gone before us.

It is a joy to affirm unchanging truths and to find new meaning in them: the Church of the future will be enriched by the struggles that are taking place today to defend truth from error, orthodoxy from heresy. To affirm these truths takes courage, however, and realism.

The Catholic teaching on male priesthood is centered on Christ's actions. He could easily have picked women to be his first priests, as all the pagan religions in that part of the world had. He knew exactly what he was doing, and he was not conditioned by his time and culture, since he is *omnipotent and chose the exact moment in history to be born and dwell among us.* Christ himself was male, and born of a woman. There is a meaning and significance in all of this, and we need to ponder it. I myself have been greatly blessed and edified by the teachings of Christ through his Church.

To be a Catholic woman is to be part of a long tradition going back to the women who, while several of the men ran away in fear, stood faithfully at the foot of the cross. I'm not brave enough to do that, and am perfectly convinced that I would have run away too. At one time I might have deluded myself that I would not have, but recently I heard a graphic description of just exactly what happened at a Roman crucifixion, in all its horror. I know that I would have run away retching, terrified, trying to get the thing out of my mind.

It is a huge privilege to have been baptized as a child and taught the Catholic faith in a cheerful, loving, and united family. This was my experience. I am grateful every day of my life that this is what happened to me. I have no dramatic conversion story to tell and nothing of heroism in the faith. Yet I do have the experience of a life in the Church, which I think is a common enough one among my contemporaries and not adequately described or explained. I'm very happy to set it down in writing.

As a child, I found that the Catholic aspects of my life were, on the whole, extremely attractive ones. I was raised in a secure home in the London suburbs, with parents who had married shortly after the end of the Second World War and thought themselves extraordinarily fortunate to be raising a family in happiness in a house with all the modest trimmings of middle-class Englishness.

I mention this because it seems to be fashionable today to emphasize how lonely, or miserable, or misunderstood one was in a Catholic childhood, and I have to say that this was simply not the case with me. We were and are an affectionate family, with lots of laughter and jokes and idiosyncratic ways of doing things.

We were taught about God and we certainly prayed to him with a sense of confidence. Sunday Mass and nighttime prayers were year-round features of our lives. When my parents had married (in 1949), there were strict rules in the Catholic Church about the way a non-Catholic spouse should raise a child. My mother was the Catholic in this case, and my father the non-Catholic. I owe *each* of them a huge debt for the happy home they gave us, and something about the background of each is relevant to this story.

My father came from a straightforwardly Christian home, in which Catholicism was unknown and probably, if mentioned at all, was regarded as weird and slightly sinister. His mother, a devout Methodist lady whom I remember with great affection, taught him to pray, and he retained throughout his life a strong faith and a firm adherence to Christian teachings. When he died and we went through his papers, we found a wartime diary of life on a troopship and then in the desert battles in Africa. In a description of an evening in Cairo he noted that some of his companions went to a brothel and he commented forcibly, "None of that for me. I intend to keep myself for the girl I will marry. I intend to stick to this." And he did. He communicated to us, without ever getting involved in much religious talk, a steadfast message about the right way to live. I think this is one of the best things a parent can do.

His family and my mother's had been neighbors and knew each other well. After my mother came back from Staffordshire, where she had been an evacuee during the Second World War, and my father returned from war service, they met and married. Their courtship was at Army dances and the local tennis club, and the religious division was not a major problem. My father once told me that it was a case of, "Well, the priest said I had to sign on the dotted line to say that all the children would be brought up as Catholics, and that seemed all right to me ... so ... I agreed." Having once committed himself, he never went back on this and was insistent about our going to Mass and living as Catholics!

When we were in our early teens, we started saying Grace at meals, but "family" prayers were not a major feature of our home and we certainly had few of the "Catholic trimmings" that we sometimes noted at the homes of some of our friends. We tended to regard such things as prominent rosary beads or statues of Mary as rather extreme! Catholicism, for my siblings and me, was something true, important, and intellectually coherent. Catholicism was essentially the explanation for why we were all created. "Who made you?" the old Catechism asked, and then gave the answer: "God made me." "Why did God make you?" "God made me to know him, love him, and serve him in this life and to be happy with him for ever in the next." This seemed to make sense, and formed my understanding of things quite well.

My mother's father had converted to Catholicism in the years after the First World War. He and Granny had been enthusiastic Fabians and socialists in their youth. They had eloped and married in the face of family disapproval and then had been caught up in the universal patriotic enthusiasm and idealism of the Great War. In the trenches as a young officer, Grandpa, wounded and gassed, experienced the questioning and disillusionment of so many of his generation. Later he was one of those who found his way into the Catholic Church. By that time he and Granny had four children, and it was more or less automatic that they would enter the Church too. My mother was about twelve at the time.

This, then, was the religious background at home: I remember being told that "Catholicism is the one religion where the more you ask questions, the more you'll get answers." Quite early on, I was told about writers like Ronald Knox and G.K. Chesterton, and in my late teens I delighted in reading them—although by that time both were very unfashionable (this was the late 1960s/early 1970s—they are back in favor again now!).

Being Catholic meant belonging to a tradition of strong women. My patron saint is Joan of Arc—a soldier, a patriot, and a martyr. She was a woman whom God had called to be a visionary; someone utterly certain of her role. Once I discovered the details of the story, I was, for a time, worried by the fact that she had fought the English. (Surely we were always on the right side, so how could she be against us?) Once it was established, however, that she had been perfectly correct to do so, I thrilled to her story. She was a source of immense inspiration, a role model, and a defining image in my childhood and throughout my formative years. She still is. I had been named for her because my parents watched George Bernard Shaw's "Saint Joan" while expecting me. They decided then and there that if the baby were a girl she would be named Joanna and have this saint as her patron. My older sister, Barbara, is named for the patron saint of the Royal Artillery.

This notion of the strong Christian woman was reinforced at school. My Catholic education included daily formation by large numbers of confident nuns, bustling around, organizing everything, and generally inspiring awe in students' parents.

Priests seemed very much in awe of them, too. I never saw priests as figures of power: On the contrary, they were clearly at the service of people and tended to be quieter and more anonymous than the nuns. I remember old Father Ward, saintly, friendly, venerable, who gave me my First Holy Communion. There was a young jolly curate and then at school occasional priests came to say Mass, but as personalities they never impinged on us. My relationship as a Catholic was primarily with God.

I knew about the pope—I remember being shocked when I discovered he wasn't English! I understood about the structure of the Church, but it was God, and specifically Jesus Christ, that mattered. I minded terribly about his suffering on the cross—I think most children feel this way when they are told the story—and knew that it was sin (yes, including mine) that had caused this. I also knew Jesus as a source of comfort, inspiration, and courage. I could talk to him very privately about things like being scared, or wanting ballet shoes for my birthday. I knew Jesus in a very childlike and personal way.

We didn't go to Mass in a church when I was very small—it was said in the tea-hut in the local park. I knew that England had once been Catholic but that four hundred years earlier the churches had been turned into Anglican ones. We walked past the beautiful old local parish church on our way to Mass each Sunday. The nearest Catholic church was some distance away. Later we moved house so as to be nearer to it. Mass was important: this was where God came to dwell on earth in a moment of drama, and I knew about this with a certainty and confidence.

I was not a particularly devout child; Catholicism just seemed logical, interesting, and important. God was certainly real enough. I wanted to cooperate with him, too, in tackling issues like suffering and hunger and people unjustly imprisoned. This last area was a particular feature of my prayers. These were the years of the "Cold War," and in some book I discovered an account of the dreadful labor-camp system in the Soviet Union. I decided, with the confidence of childhood, that when I became an adult I was going to do something about it all.

Sunday Mass was simply a part of life. At school, however, religion had more exciting moments, such as processions in honor of Mary in May and of the Blessed Sacrament on the Feast of Corpus Christi.

Testing and Challenge

Life's pattern changed when I became a teenager. The dominating influence was the social revolution of the late 1960s. In the summers of 1968 and 1969, students were rioting in the streets, the pop music industry was creating a whole new culture, and the message to the youth was that "pop, pot, and the pill" had radically changed everything previous generations might have known. This message filtered down to every ordinary suburban family. I remember the horror with which my parents viewed the youth fashions that were designed, expensively, to look as scruffy as possible. Their own youth had been so utterly different. They had spent it dressed in uniform, serving their country and undergoing hardships. They gratefully cherished modest pleasures and accepted concepts such as sacrifice, loyalty, and duty. No one had rebelled; there was a war on! People of my parents' generation simply couldn't imagine a culture in which students burned down a university building in order to enforce their demands for co-ed dorms. Neither could they have imagined students storming the streets of London in support of some foreign political cause.

We were all torn in our loyalties: I didn't care for people who raged the streets, burning American or British flags, and I strongly suspected many of them did not understand the real issues involved any better than I did. However, I was disinterested with adults who appeared to criticize those students merely for their hairstyles or for being young.

On the other hand, some issues presented themselves differently. I was a schoolgirl when Parliament passed the 1967 Abortion Act, which legalized abortion in my country. I was sickened and angry when I found out about it. No one had asked my friends, or me, how we felt about the issue. We all thought abortion was vile. We were the young women on whose behalf the adults who enacted this law claimed to be speaking, but they did not truly speak for us. We thought that if you slept with someone and became pregnant, it was cruel and merciless to kill the baby.

We talked endlessly on this topic: "Should you sleep with your boyfriend, or not?" Sexual moral issues were the very subject of discussion. Our ideas, unfortunately, were confused. We were strongly influenced by the fashionable clichés of our time and lacking effective guidance from a Church that *seemed* to be confused too!

Surely it was okay to do it if you simply loved someone very much?

I didn't really think so. I wanted to wait until marriage. I was emphatic about this, and it had a lot to do with self-respect. I had rather too much of what is today called "personal self-esteem." Of course, I relied as well upon the teachings of Christ and the love and respect I felt for my parents. Already several girls quite clearly felt differently. The wider subculture regarded my opinion as weird and even unhealthy. It was difficult to find much to support or encourage coherent thinking. It was at this time that I discovered the writing of C.S. Lewis. His work *Mere Christianity* made good sense, as did Chesterton and Knox.

It was a time of testing and challenge. The message from school was that the old rules were changing. There was confusion and conflict within society and within the Church as well. The religious sisters were discarding their habits, the Liturgy was being turned into a silly mess, and the hymnals were being thrown away and replaced with popular songs with rewritten words. This last upheaval was something of a disaster; the songs were out of date by the time they were used for Mass. Their words sounded trite. The message we intuited, unfortunately, was that the nuns couldn't think of anything better to sing about than our own subculture regurgitated!

People kept implying that the Christian teaching on many matters had changed. Had it? Once you *really studied* the matter, one discovered that the Church had not changed her stance at all! I found I wanted to know more about the eternal truths present in my faith. I liked what I discovered. Christianity had a coherent explanation for things. Sadly, few people charged with the responsibility to do so seemed prepared to give these explanations. The media was saturated with an anti-Christian doctrine on life. On television, the dominating means of communication, champions of Christian orthodoxy rarely seemed to be given a voice.

School was over and I was flourishing as a junior reporter on staff with a local newspaper, getting active in politics.

The Church in those years seemed to me rather wounded—feeble in affirming what I knew to be its teachings. The Liturgy, as experienced in suburban parish life, was quite ghastly. Our local church had been remodeled and now was demoted to the equivalent of a hideous, modern concrete tent, the inside of which was lined with pale green blocks. I knew Catholicism was true, but what was happening around me on the local level was not "truth" expressed at all. I joined campaigning groups within the Catholic Church that explored the faith and urged bishops to speak more clearly. Before this time, I hadn't really thought about the position or office of the local bishop. I learned the importance of the laity, and that meant being "involved."

What made a difference was something named the Faith Movement. The Faith Movement was a group for young people that had been started at my brother's school by a dynamic young priest who taught science there. The essential focus of the movement was and is to bring together in a new synthesis the teachings of the Catholic faith and the insights of modern science. What a combination for young people to embrace! What I found in the movement was simply a coherent and consistent presentation of the truths of the Catholic faith, given in an atmosphere of humor, wide-ranging discussion, informality, and friendship. I stopped thinking that I had to lobby bishops and found a new approach. The Liturgies that were celebrated with the movement were reverent, the talks were dynamic, and the possibilities for questioning and debate were excellent. The movement also automatically assumed a lively and committed approach to social, community, and political life. It was with friends from this group that I campaigned to oppose abortion and speak up for better values in the mass media. I became very active with the Society for the Protection of Unborn Children and the National Viewers and Listeners Association. I began to understand that the Church had a positive and very specific social teaching. This teaching was dynamic.

I had always been interested in the nineteenth century, and now learned more about the "Second Spring" of that era and the revival of the Catholic Church in my country through such leading figures as Dominic Barberi and John Henry Newman. The latter is someone whose life and writing have helped so many English people and have been an influence on our family, with its tradition of conversion.

Life was opening up in numerous ways. I stood for election to the local borough council, won election, and put my whole heart into this position. Underlying all of my endeavors was my faith: Faith in action, a faith that had taught me much about my role in society and my influence upon cultural issues.

I was offered a job at the House of Commons and started to become a serious debater at universities and women's groups. Major issues, such as abortion and the defense of human life, opposition to the growing menace of pornography, and the escalating crudity on television and in films presented themselves for debate. I didn't see myself as a "moral crusader," nor did I wish to become one. However, it seemed absurd to ignore the fact that these concerns were a dominant influence in our culture and no one involved in politics, especially someone with a Catholic education, could afford to ignore them.

Christ and His Church

Well, all that was a long time ago now. I'm looking at it all from the perspective of a quarter of a century later. I'm now more passionately committed than I could have imagined on issues that are the same yet different for our era. Back in the 1970s, we were caught up in the bleak aftermath of a massive social revolution and an embattled Church. Now we have to deal with the results of the devastation of those years. Our culture at first tolerated and now strongly promotes homosexual and lesbian activity. Pornography is part of mainstream magazine and newspaper publishing, not to mention prime-time television. Contraceptives are routinely given to schoolchildren, and abortion on demand even until the last months is sanctioned. I am glad I became a "campaigner" when I was young, because it trained and formed me, enabling me to tackle the issues.

In today's Britain, nearly half of all marriages end in divorce and many people never marry. Children born out of wedlock are not rare, almost 30 percent of births being illegitimate. Our suicide rate is high and climbing, as is our crime rate, especially among the young. We desperately need a return to sane human values. There is a climate of tension surrounding any discussion of these issues—people are worried that they might be quoted as having politically inappropriate views, and this can be a serious matter if you have a career in the public service or in the media. Politicians in particular will preface their remarks with careful phrases so as not to antagonize specific lobby groups such as homosexual campaigners or men and women cohabiting outside of marriage.

The Catholic Church has a different understanding of these things. She teaches that marriage between a man and a woman is a *sacrament,* that it is lifelong, that it is profoundly linked to the bond between Christ and his Church, that sexual union outside of marriage is wrong. She is unafraid to teach the truth about human biology, and rejoices in the glory of what God has made. She sees dignity in motherhood and fatherhood. She recognizes that there is a "nuptial" pattern in God's plan that began with the great idea of Christ and his Church— that he is the original Bridegroom, she the bride, and that this gives a thrilling meaning to manhood and womanhood and matrimony.

I was working in Parliament as a researcher when the news about Pope John Paul II's election was announced. I recall the thrill and excitement of having a Polish pope. There was much talk about the implications. At that juncture, I was with people who mostly saw and discussed the political side of things, but of course, it is the spiritual things that matter. The two interconnect all the time because God is active in our world, a world that he created. In the long run, a Polish pope meant the downfall of Communism, no matter the assassination attempt. How exciting it was to watch the rapid movement toward freedom in Poland, to see firsthand the thronging crowds that pressed to greet "their" pope on his triumphant progress around his country.

Yet the reality of this pontificate has been much, much more than that single event. The same preaching of human and sacred values that brought the end of Communism also spells a challenge to the decadent and bleak lifestyle of the West.

To be a Catholic woman today is to belong to a Church that takes a radical and refreshing approach to so much in modern Western life. Pope John Paul II has provided tremendous leadership in speaking out against what he refers to as this present "culture of death." He has affirmed the God-given and radiantly important differences between males and females and spoken of the "theology of the body," giving light to a new understanding of the importance of matrimony. He has drawn attention to the nuptial meaning of the Eucharist and the nuptial imagery that runs throughout salvation history—giving deeper insight into the male priesthood that is the unchanging teaching of our Church.

I find the Church today, more than I ever did as a child or adolescent, a source of endlessly fascinating and thrilling teachings. There is always something new to learn.

New Insights

I met my future husband at the House of Commons. We were both attending a committee meeting of a Catholic group, which just happened to meet there, as the chairman was a Member of Parliament. A small crowd of us had supper together afterward. There was much talk and laughter about Catholic things. Jamie is a convert to the Church and was still radiating a terrific joy in this, coupled with an infectious enthusiasm. We had everything in common, plus the joy of sharing in new things, too.

Amazingly, with engagement, then wedding plans underway, and happy days of courtship in London, came new insights into many aspects of the faith. Jamie, too, had been profoundly inspired by John Henry Newman and was a convert in that tradition, which was familiar to me. He had also been helped immensely by the writing of the English journalist Malcolm Muggeridge, who at that time (1979–80) was still alive and living in Sussex. It was a joy to be able to introduce Jamie to him. I, too, owe Malcolm a great deal, not only for his wit and for the brilliant way he denounced the absurdities of the pop culture that had so affected my generation, but for his knowledge of history, for his splendid use of English at a time when jargon proliferated.

I had a faint perception of the graces of the Sacrament of Matrimony when we married in 1980. In the years since then, I've discovered more and more of what it all really means and why Christ gave us his first miracle at a wedding. In many various and mystical ways, there is a bond between man and wife that is like that of Christ and the Church.

The Rosary, which when younger I rarely used or thought about much, has become an important prayer that Jamie and I often say together and is associated with the "domestic church" that is our home. We like its simplicity, the fact that it gets you thinking about major events in Christ's life. Through the meditations of the Rosary, these events can be linked with particular petitions we offer up: work we are doing, friends in trouble, family needs.

I find new meaning, as I grow older, in the lives of saints—especially the women martyrs of England at the time of the Reformation, such as Margaret Clitheroe, Anne Line, and Margaret of Scotland. As my work still keeps me very much in the public eye, I find it helpful to know about these women who played major roles in political life and upheld Christian truth there.

Before the fall of Communism, Jamie's job took us to live in West Berlin. I met at firsthand the reality of a divided Europe. How grim and out-of-date the great Berlin Wall seemed, almost as if it really belonged in an old black-and-white film of the early 1960s. We were on the side that was "free," with beautiful shops, prosperity, and a most enjoyable way of life. The East, on the other hand, had outdated slogans ("With Marxism-Leninism, We March Toward a Better Future," and the like) and an almost tangible sense of despair and discomfort. Yet, on our side of the Wall, we had problems that were of a different nature: Lines of prostitutes jingling their keys in the Tiergarten at night, and punk-rockers lounging listlessly in the seedy areas, sniffing glue, as well as additional evidence of a not-so-underground drug culture.

Learning a foreign language widened my outlook. Living in Berlin gave me a taste for travel that has never left me. I studied history and relished discovering libraries and museums and reading everything I could reach to fill in the gaps in my knowledge. I loved finding my way across Europe on trains and buses and improving my atrocious German and French, and thoroughly enjoyed reading foreign newspapers and magazines.

Being formed in the Catholic faith alerts you to the intriguing aspects of things. Why is the Cathedral in Berlin named after Saint Hedwig? Who was she? Where is Stauffen-bergstrasse? What happened there in World War II? Would I have been brave enough to oppose Hitler if I had been a German officer in 1944? And so on and so on … I have never taken it for granted that hundreds of thousands of seemingly "average" people have gone before me, struggled in their faith, and lived silently heroic lives. The few thousand that we know of are canonized: saintly, shining examples of holiness.

Most of our married life has been spent in London, where my husband and I are tremendously involved in the Catholic apostolate, regarded as eccentric and certainly very happy! Teachings of the

Church that I rarely thought about as a teenager—such as the ban on the use of contraception—hold a great deal of meaning for me today. As virtually a lone voice, Mother Church speaks with wisdom, affirming human dignity and the rights of ordinary people, especially the poor. Attendance at the United Nations conferences has confirmed my abhorrence at the gross way my country and others are attempting to enforce population control on other nations. Meanwhile, we are dying; our birthrate is low, and our family culture is collapsing. Basic ideas, such as parents and children sharing a common surname and marriage as a lifelong bond that brings together people as in-laws and cousins with mutual responsibilities are fading. Not surprisingly, the collapse of marriage has meant the collapse of much else, so that even institutions such as our Monarchy are now under threat and seem meaningless.

If I have learned one thing that remains true, the faith of those gone before me brings hope, no matter how dark the present moment. I'm grateful for our family tradition of humor that is closely connected with our Catholicism, and for the laughter that is shared with my teenage nephews (whose views on Liturgy and music are like mine, but stronger). I'm grateful for places of pilgrimage that have drawn me to God and to a better understanding of my country's history: Walsingham; Stonor, and its links with Saint Edmund Campion; Saint Thomas More's cell in the Tower of London; and Feryhalgh, where Our Lady has been honored for more than a thousand years. I'm grateful for the opportunities I've had to visit centers of Catholicism throughout Europe, for the gift of praying the Rosary with Austrian friends at a mountain shrine, for midnight candlelight processions at Paray le Monial in France on a warm summer evening, and for the unbelievable experience of celebrating the Feast of the Assumption at Poland's national shrine when Solidarity was beginning its great freedom crusade.

A Divine Purpose

The Catholic Church in my lifetime has been the beacon of hope to which millions have looked, and not in vain, for an end to Communism and the cold war. It's now a voice of clarity and sanity in an era of sexual anarchy and vicious denigration of all that is beautiful. It is a sign of exciting contradiction, making politicians' cliches sound trite and affirming embarrassing truths with serenity and joy.

The Catholic Church is a perpetual challenge at the personal level as well. The straightforward faith of my childhood was nourished and informed by the debates of my teens and twenties (though I still regard those as having been bleak years in the Church, from which in so many ways we are still suffering). I continue to meet people who tell me, quite erroneously, that "since Vatican II we don't need to go to Mass every Sunday," or, "Confession was abolished in the 1960s," and still, "In the modern Church divorce and remarriage is okay." These are mostly older people, in their sixties or seventies, who seem trapped in the culture of twenty-five or thirty years ago. Yet the Church of tomorrow will be different, enriched and strengthened by the New Catechism (published during the pontificate of John Paul II), a useful, modern summary of Catholic doctrine and an excellent resource, and by new trends in the Liturgy that emphasize the sacrificial nature of the Mass.

I belong to the Association of Catholic Women, founded by women who want to voice their glad assent to the teachings of the Church. It is one of a growing number of such movements in different countries. The work to promote family life is also exciting. My husband organized a massive International Congress for the Family in Britain in 1990, and we've been involved with similar events in other countries since then.

In my work as a writer, I've loved exploring history and discovering heroes and heroines of the faith. Through Jamie, I learned about the nineteenth-century Englishwoman Caroline Chisholm, whose hard work and selfless crusading helped to transform Australia from a brutal penal colony to the "lucky country" where millions could find prosperity and raise families. My book about her inspires people throughout Australia and Britain where it is available. Her life, like that of so many Catholic saints, continues to remain a source of encouragement to all who learn about her.

Like all Christians, I've had to learn about prayer. I am still learning. You need to give time to God. This means real time; time allocated during the day when you kneel and talk to him, opening your heart to him. I have met men and women of real devout prayer who also pour themselves out in generous and courageous service. I've revised my opinion of priests, too, as I have met those brothers in Christ who are truly holy. I have received help more than once from a wise confessor, benefited from real scholarship via books and lectures and conversations, and begun to recognize that the Sacrament of Holy Orders is a treasure from God that my generation was not taught to honor properly. This treasure is a real link with the apostles and with heroes and martyrs down through the centuries.

I am not sure that the women of my generation will match up very well to those of previous centuries in the Church. We were encouraged by popular culture to value our own opinions very highly, to reject the values of our parents and grandparents, and to make excuses when we did anything wrong. We are not very tough on ourselves, but tend to complain of others a lot. We were encouraged when young to see the Church in political terms. We were not taught much about the lives of saints or about the meaning of the sacraments. In the end, we tend to see any restraints on our personal behavior as merely arbitrary and unfair. Those of my age and younger have found it hard to pass on the faith to their children. We are now seeing some new books, tapes, and videos that will improve matters for the future, part of a revival in the Church that is tentative, but real.

How do we support this renewal? We need heroes and heroines for the immediate future. It will be difficult to be a Catholic in a culture that accepts and promotes not only abortion but now euthanasia, that celebrates sexual vice and honors dishonesty and infidelity, and that denies the existence of a Creator God, let alone One who came to dwell among us. We are going to have to use our intelligence, humor, courage, and loyalty—and if we feel we need help in fostering these we must seek and find resources for this within our Church.

It will be challenging, exciting, dangerous, and heartwarming, and in the end we will see that there was a point to it all. Despite popular beliefs, through faith we learn that we were not created for nothing, that God loves each of us tenderly, and that the sacrifice on the cross would have been done for each of us alone. As Catholics, it is our task in these next years to show joyfully that life is ordained by a divine purpose. The old Catechism of our childhood is the foundation for the New, and as such, it remains true today and will be true tomorrow. "God made us to know him, love him and to serve him in this life and to be happy with him forever in the next." History will demonstrate whether the response of women in this generation proved worthy or not. To begin, we must first be willing to open our hearts to him.

PART THREE

Life-Giving Love:
God's Self-Revelation

*"He has mercy on those who fear him in every generation.
He has shown the strength of his arm, he has scattered the proud
in their conceit. He has cast down the mighty from their thrones,
and has lifted up the lowly. He has filled the hungry with good
things, and the rich he has sent away empty."*

*G*od's mercy, which is the mercy of the Trinity, is extended to every generation, from generation to generation. Fear of God is the beginning of wisdom. It is particularly important to note here that the early church fathers, as well as theologians today, understood the Book of Wisdom to be a symbolic reference to Our Lady herself. Scripture is rich with the example of women who are filled with divine wisdom and whose wise actions caused God's mercy to flow to their respective generation. Mary's spirit recognized this mercy in her life and she rejoiced at the eternal implications of it:

> *It is a joy that springs from amazement at the almighty power of God, who can permit himself to carry out "great things," in spite of the inadequacy of human instruments* (cf. Lk 1:47-49). It is a joy at the superior justice of God, who "has put down the mighty from their thrones, and exalted those of low degree; he has filled the hungry with good things, and the rich he has sent away" (Lk 1:52f.). It is, finally, joy at the mercy of God who, faithful to his promises, gathers under the wing of his love the children of Abraham, "from generation to generation," assisting them in all their necessities (cf. Lk 1:50, 54-55).
>
> This is Mary's song. It must become the song of every day of our life; there is no human situation, in fact, that cannot find in it adequate interpretation. The Virgin utters it while over her spirit there mount questions about the reactions of her betrothed, who still knows nothing about the future of this Son, over whom there hang disquieting prophetic words (cf. Isaiah 53).[1]

Once a commitment to charity is established in the heart and the mystery of God's self-revelation is experienced personally, one is able to move from *prayer and contemplation* into *ministry and outreach*. Here we see again the examplar of Mary, Mother of Mercy. She actively participates in the works of mercy, which she recognizes as the movement of divine strength. The power of God, working through her faith, encourages her to forever align herself with the "little ones" of God, while she realizes that it is *his* life and work in which she is privileged to participate.

> [F]aith is contact with the mystery of God. Every day Mary is in constant contact with the ineffable mystery of God made man, a mystery that surpasses everything revealed in the Old Covenant. From the moment of the Annunciation, the mind of the Virgin-Mother has been initiated into the radical "newness" of God's self-revelation and has been made aware of the mystery. She is the first of those "little ones" of whom Jesus will say one day: "Father ... you have hidden these things from the wise and understanding and revealed them to babes" (Matthew 11:25).[2]

Mary recognized that the spiritual food that her people (all people) are starving for is found in God alone. The Trinity offered her everything. As the new Ark of the Covenant that contains the heavenly manna, God wished to give this Divine Bread to the world through her. Mary agreed.

This third section of testimonies details the commitment to active works of mercy. Indicative of a firm faith, each author shares her experience of God's mercy and strength acting in and through her life. Their holy fear of God has matured into a deep wisdom. This wisdom is expressed above all in an attitude of trust in the Lord. Through personal experience these women have been lifted up, and their "hunger has been filled with good things." Now, like Mary, they joyfully participate in the works of mercy and bring the good things of God to others

Chapter 7

Authentic Femininity

MERCEDES ARZÚ WILSON

The Fabric of Our Lives

I was born into a deeply religious Roman Catholic family in my country of origin—Guatemala. Typical of many in Latin America, we had an extended family of several dozen cousins, united not only in faith but also with strong family ties and respect for our values and traditions. My grandmother and great-uncle were highly respected for their courage in fighting dictatorships and denouncing the communist regimes that had ruled in the past. My family's patriotic example made a deep impression on all of us and, I am sure, influenced my brother, as I write this testimony currently the president of Guatemala. My parents' example, their love and generosity toward us and others, has been the greatest influence in my life, and it is beautiful to see my brothers and sister following the same example of generosity toward their children and the less fortunate. Our faith was woven into the fabric of our lives; such gifts from God became an integral part of our being. It was not something to practice weekly, but to be lived daily.

From the time I was young, my two special interests were music and social services. I attended daily Mass in my teen years, and continued this practice throughout my life before I would go to work, though less frequently while my children were small infants. So, overall, the sacraments always nourished my spiritual hunger. It is hard to explain the inner desires of the soul, but when you faithfully attend Mass and Communion daily, and then, for reasons beyond your control, are unable to attend, there is a kind of vacuum in one's heart, a feeling of having missed something of great importance in your day, an emptiness, that secretly confirmed to me the importance not only of feeding one's body but also of nourishing one's soul.

My then-future husband, Hugh, a Protestant, belonged to the Anglican Church, but seemed to be drawn to my family because of the strength we received from our faith. We met on a golf course during a tournament in Guatemala. Hugh, a geologist, worked for Shell Oil, and shortly after our meeting I started to work for the same company. I was twenty-one years old and we had dated for about six months when he received instructions to transfer to the Middle East. We wanted to get married before he left Guatemala, but my parents' advice was that we should wait and write to each other and, if, after a year, our feelings were still as strong, then we could marry. At the end of the year, our love and commitment for each other had continued to grow and we were married in Rome in May 1962. My sister had married in Rome a few years earlier at Santa Andrea del Quirinale, a beautiful chapel designed by Bernini, so we decided that we would begin a tradition and be married in the same church. Rome was also the halfway point for our respective families, who were coming from Guatemala and the United Kingdom. This tradition continued when our daughter was married in Rome some years ago and prior to the wedding received a special blessing from Pope John Paul II. At the young age of twenty-two, I was uprooted from my native land to accompany my husband to faraway lands that included Arabia first, and then England, Australia, and finally the United States.

I did a lot of observing and analyzing as I raised my young family, comparing lifestyles, values, and traditions of the Middle East, Europe, Australia, North America, and Latin America. After living three and a half years in the Middle East from 1962 to 1965, we arrived in England at the end of 1965 with our baby daughter, Dominique. It was a culture shock to go from living in Arabia, an environment that had changed little from the time of Christ, to the environment of the mid-1960s, with its rebellion against all established forms of authority. It was not long after we had settled in England that my first surprise was to read in the national papers that the archbishop of Canterbury and his fellow Anglican bishops, shepherds of one of the so-called advanced nations of Europe, had agreed to support the legalization of abortion in the United Kingdom. The Christian churches teach obedience to the Ten Commandments, and this decision was in clear violation of the fifth commandment, "Thou shalt not kill," since it is the killing of an innocent baby, the most vulnerable of all. It was then, in 1966, that I wrote my first letter of dismay and indignation to the archbishop. These early scandals within Christian countries were very shocking to me, having lived only in developing nations. I was still growing in my faith, but I did have the advantage of a very solid faith formation and foundation developed within me by an order of Belgian nuns in Guatemala during my adolescent years. I stated to the archbishop that if this was what happened to countries that became affluent and regarded themselves as "civilized," it would be better for my little country, Guatemala, to remain poor and backward. We might not have too much to feed our bodies, but we would save our souls. I expressed my disbelief that religious leaders would accept such barbaric practices as abortion. His reply was that he agreed with me, but that the majority of his fellow bishops had outvoted him.

As Pope John Paul II later stated in *Evangelium Vitae*:

[O]ver and above the specific missions of parents, the task of accepting and serving life involves everyone and this task must be fulfilled above all toward life when it is at its weakest.[1]

Although there are no direct and explicit calls to protect human life at its very beginning, specifically life not yet born and life nearing its end, this can be easily explained by the fact that the mere possibility of harming, attacking or actually denying life in these circumstances is completely foreign to the religious and cultural way of thinking of the People of God.[2]

Our Holy Mother the Church teaches that the sanctity and sacredness of each and every human life is to be protected according to the will of God, since we are created in his image and likeness. What has happened to Great Britain and the rest of Europe is history now. This incident, as I look back, was the beginning for me of a public ministry. At the time I would not have seen it as extraordinary. Today, however, I realize that perhaps God was preparing and strengthening my faith for a more difficult task.

After two years in the United Kingdom, we were transferred to Melbourne, Australia, in 1968. Our family consisted of my husband, Hugh; our daughter, Dominique, then two; our baby boy, Philip, who was about two months old; and myself. Having had both children by Caesarean section, severely affecting future pregnancies, we were strongly advised by my physician that I should not get pregnant again. Imagine my quandary, as a young Catholic wife and mother, being told that my life would be in jeopardy should we attempt to have additional children. It was "coincidentally" the famous year of *Humanae Vitae*, the encyclical of Pope Paul VI that specifically addresses the issue of sexuality and birth control. A few months prior to Pope Paul VI's historic encyclical, I was fortunate to read in the inside pages of the major Melbourne paper of a new, natural method of family planning. As any woman in the world would react, I was delighted and intrigued to know more about this advanced natural method that would be harmless to my body and, best of all, was approved by the Catholic Church, who asks us to always respect the natural laws.

It was also during this time in Melbourne that we developed a strong friendship with Msgr. Hannan. The Monsignor and Hugh would spend hours at our home discussing the different aspects of faith and especially the teachings of the Catholic Church. It was through this friendship and discussion that Hugh made the decision to become a Catholic. He entered the Church in 1968. Needless to say, my prayers were answered that our whole family would be united in one faith. This unity added even more importance and meaning to our sharing the sacraments together and helped me understand the Church's position on mixed marriages. The mere thought of not sharing the same beliefs to jointly pass on to one's children can be divisive and the source of conflict in a marriage. It is my observation that the mother of the family is one of the greatest influences in her children's lives. Should their father not practice his faith, unlike their mother, the children usually keep the faith. However, if their father has a strong faith but their mother does not, the children often lose their faith.

As an average young couple in dire need of Church-approved family planning information, we discovered that it was compulsory for couples to attend the classes together on the Ovulation Method of Natural Family Planning. Although it was the 1960s, most husbands continued to leave the responsibility for family planning and the accompanying fertility issues to their wives, accepting as little involvement as possible. Nevertheless, Hugh and I went to learn this natural method together, never realizing how such knowledge was going to change our lives forever! Even before his conversion to Catholicism, there was never any conflict between us regarding respect for the natural laws and rejection of the use of artificial birth control. Therefore, there was only positive response in our marriage to the Church's latest teaching, and joy resulting from respecting the natural laws. I experienced a sense of peace, knowing that God, in his wisdom and kindness, had given me the opportunity not only to learn this knowledge but to share it with a passion and eagerness so the world could be taught the good news of achieving or postponing conception naturally.

Humanae Vitae and N.F.P.

Our first introduction to the "Ovulation Method" took place at the Catholic Family Centre in Melbourne. We had the privilege of having Doctor Evelyn L. Billings, a pediatrician who was assisting her husband, Dr. John Billings, a neurologist and the originator of the Billings Method, as the teacher who instructed us in this "authentic alternative."

In learning about this "new" method, I discovered that the knowledge itself was not new at all, but really as old as Adam and Eve; only the implementation of it was new. Earlier references to this knowledge exist in scientific literature as far back as the middle of the nineteenth century.

Dr. Billings had developed a revolutionary method of Natural Family Planning that he called the Ovulation Method. I was amazed that such a simple method was not made known to the whole world. Though I was skeptical at first, as time went by and everything I was taught occurred within my cycles, I knew this method was the true family planning answer to many women's problems, including my own. Here was a method that perfectly corresponded to my Christian faith!

While we were learning the Ovulation Method, the Catholic Church was being attacked for the pending decision of Pope Paul VI to oppose the use of the birth control "Pill." Since I was already confident that this new natural method was the answer, I was intrigued by the criticisms of the pope emanating even from those who did not profess our faith. When they would criticize and ridicule the pope, I would ask them, "Why are you so upset? As a Catholic, I am obligated to obey the teachings of the pope, while you are under no such obligation. I feel certain that he will never approve the use of any artificial means of birth control and I am very happy about it." In contrast, people of other faiths, agnostics, and even atheists were very upset at Pope Paul VI's upcoming decision, even though they could use any method they wanted. Their reaction was a clear indication to me of how important the teachings of the Church are to everyone. Even though most people won't admit it, they do listen to the pope's rulings, because deep down they know that the Catholic Church is the only Church that won't compromise its beliefs for the sake of popularity. My inner feelings told me that the pope would never compromise the truth, even knowing what an explosive issue this would become worldwide.

Subsequently, under the leadership of John Paul II, the Church not only has held fast to its precepts but also has addressed the issue of natural conception regulation. Not only are couples required to be open to new life in their marital relations but also every human life must be the result of a conjugal act between a man and a woman. The goal of contraception is the prevention of the existence of human life rather than the killing of innocent human life. The most effective way evil can frustrate God's plan is by diminishing the number of people God chose to create with the possibility of spending eternity with him in heaven. Furthermore, the ruthless intrusion into the process of human reproduction to produce life separate from the marriage act is an even greater moral violation than abortion, because it distorts the very meaning of physical human love—made flesh—and therefore, humanity. As John Paul II explains about artificial reproductive techniques in *Evangelium Vitae,* "They are morally unacceptable, since they separate procreation from the fully human context of the conjugal act."[3]

Even if the Church would allow it, however, I would never use any artificial method, because, first of all, it is against the natural laws, in addition to being wrong and harmful. In the 1960s, I was only following my female intuition, which I equate with those same qualities that God, in his wisdom, has endowed upon the poor, who must guard themselves against the exploitation of the powerful. They are also suspicious of medications that interfere with the normal functions of the human body, which is what all artificial methods of birth control do. When on July 25, 1968, the big headlines in the world's papers came out saying, "Pope Says No to the Pill," I knew that the battle was just beginning. In *Humanae Vitae*, Pope Paul VI calls upright men to reflect upon the consequences of artificial birth control. Prophetically, he asks us to consider "how wide and easy a road would thus be opened up towards conjugal infidelity and the general lowering of morality," and how man might come to the point of considering the woman "as a mere instrument of selfish enjoyment, and no longer as his respected and beloved companion."[4]

I decided to act as a volunteer to the Billings Center, as I was convinced of the validity of increasing my knowledge of the Ovulation Method, which at that time was not taught as simply and succinctly as we do today. Having inherited an affinity for challenges, especially in defense of the poor, I truly believed that God had led me to this opportunity to help women and their families by sharing with them this natural, Church-approved method of Natural Family Planning.

As my interest in this method continued to grow, I asked to meet Dr. John Billings, himself, in order to become more knowledgeable in my understanding of the method for teaching others. Dr. Billings will go down in history not only as a remarkable Catholic leader, but also as an outspoken defender of the Catholic Church's teachings regarding natural family planning, and a pro-life, pro-family advocate. There is no question in my mind that Dr. Billings has had to defend his research in the midst of tremendous criticism from his own colleagues. God chose a truly great and obedient man to do his work. As Hugh's assignment to Melbourne was ending, Dr. John Billings and several other doctors and scientists showed their kindness and interest by preparing me to be more proficient in teaching the Ovulation Method.

The Faith of the Poor

When my husband was transferred to the United States at the end of 1969, I spent over six months waiting in Guatemala, with my children, for my resident's visa, the famous green card. This gave me the opportunity to begin teaching the Ovulation Method of Natural Family Planning to family and friends and subsequently the poor. By this time I realized that I had to simplify the concept so that everyone could understand it. I felt driven by a sense of obligation to my faith to provide leadership in this field and assistance to those that need it the most, the poor of our developing countries. The help and assistance I received from missionary priests and religious in the regions of Guatemala and El Salvador, who live and experience the pain of the poor and the great need to assist them in spacing their children, was invaluable. In contrast, the developed countries' taxpayers are financing, wittingly or unwittingly, programs that change traditions, morals, and values of the poor in developing countries through the dissemination of artificial birth control. Sterilization programs are now the most widely used means of birth control in the world, disguised as "women's reproductive rights," "sexual rights," "women's liberation," and so on. I am saddened to see how poor countries' governments put aside their peoples' beliefs and principles, for the sake of securing loans and other material benefits for their countries. My eyes were opened to the war between good and evil that you hear about but do not necessarily experience. I realized my mission was to provide the tools to enable people to follow and defend the natural laws. I began by developing materials that would enable even those who couldn't read or write to follow the teachings of the Church through the Ovulation Method of Natural Family Planning.

As I started teaching the poor in Guatemala during 1970, I noticed that they were able to follow this natural method with simplified materials I had developed just as easily as I had learned to follow it. I realized that we were on to something very important for the future of the Catholic Church. I was also astonished to realize how much stronger is the faith of the poor. After all, they possess little material wealth, yet their spiritual wealth is in many ways surprising. Most of our teachers are poor. Seldom do I see people from the upper classes volunteer their services in this field. Our impoverished teachers, be they from the People's Republic of China, the Philippines, Africa, or Latin America, are always willing to give up their weekends to teach others, sacrificing the little time they could have with their children or extended family, yet they give it willingly and happily. I realize that our apostolate is no easy task. The challenge in raising funds to clothe the poor or feed the hungry is easier than raising funds to fill the spiritual vacuum that permeates the world today. Obtaining assistance for nontangible items has been the greatest challenge of our mission. From my heart I am pleased and proud to say that the poor have taught me far more than what I have taught them. They are the true reason for the passion I feel that keeps me fighting what seems to be an impossible battle, but it is the battle for justice. As Pope John XXIII said, "If you want peace, you must work for justice."

This is a David and Goliath fight, as we are battling the gigantic pharmaceutical companies, anti-life organizations such as the International Planned Parenthood Federation, the United Nations, the World Bank, and the major Western governments presently committed to fulfilling a secularistic agenda. The powerful media, who are under instructions from those with a very specific agenda, have cleverly manipulated most public opinion. This agenda is being carried out not only through governments but also throughout most institutions of learning, which have fallen prey to the hypocritical and well-disguised policies. The majority of the good, law-abiding, God-fearing people fail to recognize the dangerous path to which we are letting them direct the world, and are also too busy in their own small worlds or too apathetic to act in their own defense. Many times I feel that we have gone so far down the road to destruction of the human race that nothing seems to be able to stop its course, yet I keep repeating to myself that "nothing is impossible with God." I am convinced that it will be the so-called poor and ignorant who will eventually save the world. After all, as we think back two thousand years, it wasn't the learned or the high priests who listened to Christ, it was the so-called poor and ignorant who helped and followed him. This is why he often said that we have to become like little children in order to enter the kingdom of heaven.

David and Goliath

In the Spring of 1970 I visited the Nuncio in Guatemala, asking him to forward a letter addressed to Pope Paul VI, in which I informed the Holy Father that this natural method was the answer to his prophetic encyclical, *Humanae Vitae*. I felt compelled to give the courageous Pope Paul VI the encouragement he needed. It was suggested to me that I visit the United States Agency for International Development (USAID) because they were funding artificial birth control programs and might decide to promote this natural alternative. It seemed like a very good idea. After making an appointment with the medical officer of USAID, I presented him with the successful results of our teaching of illiterate people in the Ovulation Method of Natural Family Planning. I told him that USAID must send back the Pill and intrauterine devices to the United States because the people of Guatemala were successfully following this simple, natural method. We were by now convinced that the poor were able to understand the simplicity of reading their own signs of fertility and were eager to help others learn about the couple's combined fertility. He was surprised at my candor and responded with arrogance and defiance. At this point my response was, "Look, this is my country, and furthermore it is a

Catholic country, and you must respect the culture and religion of our people. What you are promoting is against the teachings of the Catholic Church." By this time, he was exasperated with me and ushered me out of his office. Although the subsequent meeting was very uncomfortable for the director of USAID, the funding was grudgingly approved. This was to be the first of many such unpleasant incidents in my faith journey. Nevertheless, I feel compelled to speak out for those who have no voice or who have not been given the opportunity to speak. Those in discord with these teachings usually employ the tactics of verbal insults, shouting, or intimidation to sway opponents to their side. God, with his interesting sense of humor, seems to enjoy placing people like me, with such little knowledge and preparation but with a strong sense of right and wrong, to fight the good fight. It was a tremendous consolation when Pope John Paul affirmed in *Evangelium Vitae:*

> It is therefore morally unacceptable to encourage, let alone impose, the use of methods such as contraception, sterilization and abortion in order to regulate births. The ways of solving the population problem are quite different. Governments and the various international agencies must above all strive to create economic, social, public health and cultural conditions which will enable married couples to make their choices about procreation in full freedom and with genuine responsibility.[5]

The Holy Father's wisdom and insight in this encyclical give a powerful message of courage, as he stands very much alone in a world plagued with cowards, where a handful of legislators and outspoken pagan leaders in the fields of law, medicine, and the powerful media have managed to convert the world into accepting what is always wrong and reprehensible as acceptable behavior. The pope also offers positive and logical solutions for world leaders, international organizations, and institutions to adopt if they are really sincere in their desire to help the world. You cannot eradicate poverty by killing the poor or their offspring. You can help the poor only by providing each one of them the opportunity of a life with the dignity and honor that everyone deserves.

As God awakened me to the reality of the existing conflict between good and evil, I realized that the main victims are not only the poor in the developing countries, but also the middle and upper classes.

Guatemala was really the pioneer in the expansion of what is today called the Billings Ovulation Method of Natural Family Planning. I can only assume that all these happenings in my life were not pure "coincidences," but rather providential circumstances that God put in my life, with the freedom for me to accept the challenges or ignore them. Little did I know that he was guiding my life in a totally different direction from that of a typical wife of an oil company executive and mother of two small children!

There is no question that faith is a gift from God, and as you accept new challenges, you become more desirous of continuing to please him and resigned to accepting the challenges as they surface. And surface they do, because, as Mother Teresa used to say, "Sometimes he is very demanding," but through your acceptance your faith also becomes stronger.

The Family of the Americas and New Friends

Around Thanksgiving 1970, we moved to the United States. Once there, I delayed teaching about natural family planning for about six months. Looking back, I could say this was my time of personal, inner struggle. I knew that the moment I publicly shared my knowledge of the Ovulation Method of Natural Family Planning, my peaceful, comfortable, uncomplicated life was going to be over. How right I was! I struggled as to when I should begin, knowing that, once I started, I could not do it halfway.

As a Catholic wife and mother of two I had been successfully using the Ovulation Method for over twenty-four months. The Catholic Church teaches respect for the sanctity of life, and as our spiritual mother, the Church wants only what is good for us, not harmful. Hugh and I have always been in agreement about Natural Family Planning. We discovered the truthfulness of the Church's teachings in that a couple grows closer and more intimate with each other when there is no intrusion in the conjugal act. This intimacy is part of the divine plan and a blessing from God. Natural Family Planning draws a couple closer together in their marriage because by having to abstain for a few days each month, it becomes like a new honeymoon each month. Couples from various countries throughout the world have confirmed this.

Medical studies on the Pill were not complete, even though it was being distributed and used worldwide. Even to this day, no one is completely certain how artificial contraceptives negatively affect the human brain. I was only aware of the minor negative effects experienced by women who used the Pill, bloating, mood swings, depression, weight gain, and so on. On the other hand, the Ovulation Method of Natural Family Planning has no negative side effects, only positive ones: better communication between the couple, increased mutual love and respect, and a closer family unit. As Mother Teresa said:

God has created each one of us, every human being, for greater things—to love and to be loved. But why did God make some of us men and others women? Because a woman's love is one image of the love of God, and a man's love is another image of God's love. Both are created to love, but each in a different way. Woman and man complete each other, and together show forth God's love more fully than either can do alone. That special power of loving that belongs to a woman is seen most clearly when she becomes a mother.

Motherhood is the gift of God to women. How grateful we must be to God for this wonderful gift that brings such joy to the whole world, women and men alike! Yet we can destroy this gift of motherhood, especially by the evil of abortion, but also by thinking that other things like jobs or positions are more important than loving, than giving oneself to others. No job, no plans, no possessions, no idea of "freedom" can take the place of love. So anything that destroys God's gift of motherhood destroys his most precious gift to women—the ability to love as a woman.... I have often said, abortion is the greatest destroyer of peace in the world today.[6]

In our new home in the United States, I founded the organization known as the "Family of the Americas." Because of our rapid growth, we felt the need to incorporate, so Family of the Americas Foundation was officially started in 1977. As my children grew older and were in school all day, I opened a small office in Covington, Louisiana, the home of the famous American author Walker Percy. Walker Percy had a very strong influence in my work. He encouraged me to write my first book and very kindly edited my work. His influence and insight into our apostolate was magnified over the years as he came to realize the importance of influencing families to follow the natural laws. He experienced a conversion during this time as he witnessed the attacks that were directed at us by the enemies of the traditional family. My official working hours began as 9:00 A.M. to 3:00 P.M. Inevitably, as I continued teaching and training, through the 1970s, in Louisiana, word got out and invitations began arriving from Mexico, Puerto Rico, Dominican Republic, Europe, and other parts of the United States. No longer were my workdays only six hours long. There has been little rest since then.

Looking back on my days as a working mother, I have no regrets. As hard as it was traveling to far-away lands—I managed to stay just long enough to do my work and then promptly return to my family—there was never any doubt in my mind that I was doing what God wanted me to do. I'll never forget Mother Teresa's advice to become like a little pencil and follow God's instructions, to be a little instrument of his will. I felt driven by a force that is impossible to explain, but that is constantly reassuring me through the daily blessings of little gifts to gifts of great magnitude—blessings throughout my life. One of God's greatest such blessings came through a "chance" meeting.

It was in 1976 that I first met Mother Teresa at the New Orleans airport. She was returning from Guatemala, after visiting the country in the wake of the tragic events resulting from the 1976 earthquake. My family and I were on our way to visit relatives there. When I recognized her at the airport, I told my family, "Come meet a Saint." She was not renowned as yet, but I had read about her saintliness from Malcolm Muggeridge's *Something Beautiful for God.* After our introduction, I apologized to Mother for not being able to attend her lecture the previous night due to our family's departure for Guatemala. When she heard where we were going, she said, "I just came back from there. Can you please go and take care of my Sisters?" This was her first request of me. I immediately said, "Of course!" Once we arrived in Guatemala, it took us two weeks to locate the sisters. Their quest was to obtain a piece of land, where they would be able to do their charitable work in my country. My sister and I helped Mother Teresa acquire the land and begin her wonderful mission in Guatemala. My family also became very much involved in the development of the mission.

One treasure of the Catholic Church is found in her offspring themselves. The example given by the Missionaries of Charity throughout the world is challenging to emulate. They live as Mother Teresa intended, in similar conditions to the poor around them and whom they serve. Women who enter this kind of life are, in my opinion, great saints who give up literally everything to be at the service of the poorest of the poor. We became very much involved in teaching Natural Family Planning at her mission and have cooperated with her sisters in different countries of the world. This was the beginning of a great friendship with Mother Teresa; I felt free to call her at different times for advice and primarily to request her prayers.

In 1980, when we were overwhelmed by requests to go and teach everywhere, our foundation decided it was time to regroup. We resolved to organize a congress for the family in one of the countries of the Americas, where we could bring people from various countries to become trained teachers, providing them with materials and then sending them home to teach their own people. My faith and prayer life increased as the workload and pressures mounted. With more needs, and more demands on my time, I was always conscious of the importance of attending daily Mass and praying the rosary, for they renewed my strength and kept my focus on God's plan for me. As it says in Isaiah 40:31:

> They that hope in the Lord will renew their strength, they will soar as with eagles' wings; They will run and not grow weary, walk and not grow faint.

Also, at this time His Holiness John Paul II was becoming the most popular and influential figure in the world. As my faith increased, and remembering what my spiritual director, Fr. Pedro Richards, always told me—"Think big!"—I decided to extend an invitation to our Congress to the Holy Father through one of his close friends.

Pope John Paul II and the Congress for the Family

It was through yet another blessed "coincidence" that I met Wanda Poltawska, from Poland, in 1979. My friend Dr. Anna Cappela introduced me to Wanda in Saint Peter's Square. In February 1980, Wanda very kindly arranged an invitation to the Holy Father's private Mass.

When I left Guatemala for Rome, I decided to bring a letter from the president of the country, inviting His Holiness to visit Guatemala. One of the most exciting days of my life was when I entered the Vatican doors through a private entrance to attend John Paul's private Mass. I was very nervous but full of joy at the gift that had been given me, to be in the company of such a great Saint. The Mass was attended by only a handful of people—primarily the Sisters who serve the pope, his secretaries, Wanda, and myself. At the conclusion of Mass, I had the opportunity to present the president's invitation to attend the Congress and have a memorable conversation with His Holiness. It was the most interesting day of my life. He asked if I had experience in organizing Congresses, and I replied, "No, your Holiness. As a matter of fact, we don't even have the funding for the Congress that I'm here to invite you to." At this, he laughed and proceeded to encourage me in this ambitious endeavor. He requested that Mother Teresa be invited, to which I replied that she was second on my list, after him. I hold this conversation very dear to my heart, and as we said good-bye, he encouraged me to visit him whenever I came to Rome. As a result of this memorable experience, a profound friendship developed which continues to the present moment. The Holy Father is a spiritual father not only for the Family of the Americas, but for all of us.

Although John Paul II was unable to attend our first Congress in 1980, he sent an emissary, an assistant to the head of the propagation of the faith, who was a good friend and was instructed by His Holiness to help fund the Congress.

His Holiness John Paul II and Mother Teresa have been the greatest influence in my life. We have many canonized saints in the Church whom we can imitate. In these two great people, I have found sanctity worth emulating in our day. I feel I must work harder, not only for God and my Church, but also in order not to disappoint them. I almost feel the same way as when you don't want to disappoint your parents. At another meeting, years later, in early 1985, after we had organized seven very successful Congresses for the Family (in Guatemala, Mexico, and Venezuela) the Holy Father asked me to begin doing Congresses for the Family in Europe. He felt that the Europeans were in even greater need than the Third World. Thus, Congresses for Africa, Europe, and Asia followed. In total, we have done twenty Congresses for the Family. The last one was held in Moscow in September 1999.

These Congresses are designed to be working Congresses, because of the powerful speakers, who are masters of the various subjects that are covered. Topics are from a wide range of subjects: scientific research, psychology, social sciences, philosophy, spiritual growth, population, and economics. All presenters are supportive of the Church's teachings, whether or not they are Catholic. Mother Teresa, of course, had specific instructions from His Holiness, John Paul II, to cooperate with our Congresses, so as often as she could she attended them. The wife of the prime minister of France and the minister of health opened the Congress in Paris jointly. A Congress in Spain followed in 1987 and was opened by the Queen and Mother Teresa. In Belgium the Queen and the Princess, who is now the reigning Queen of Belgium, opened the 1988 Congress.

The 1988 Congress in Vienna, Austria, was also a tremendous success, as was the one in 1989 in Bonn, Germany. We have had other small congresses in Luxembourg, as well as Moscow, Russia. Past speakers include such masters as Jerome Lejeune, Viktor Frankl, Mother Teresa, Harvard professors in line with the teachings of the Catholic Church, and Jewish personalities such as Michael Medved or Melvin Anchell, who write so much against secular "sex education." Those who were lukewarm in their faith became fervent believers, while others who were deprived of the truth experienced a conversion to the truth. It was after the Paris Congress in 1986 that we heard of its impact from Mother Teresa. She informed us that the young people were inspired to hold their own first Congress for Youth in Versailles, followed by others in various parts of France. This is typical of the impact our Congresses have had in other countries.

There is no question in my mind that as our work expanded throughout the world, so did my commitment to God. I have become completely convinced that it is God who is directing our work, and it is his wish that it continue growing and expanding. The temptations that result from frustrations due to lack of funding or support, especially from those areas where you expect the most, are always present. So when people ask me, "When are you going to retire? How much longer are you going to be doing this?" I can think only of Mother Teresa, who in spite of great hardship and difficulties never retired, and when asked to rest would always answer, "I have all eternity to rest." The pope responded the same way when questioned about slowing down.

One of the Gospels that comes to my mind whenever I am tempted to slow down or to spend more time with my children and grandchildren, which I would love to do, is the Gospel of Matthew. Jesus said to his apostles in Matthew 10:37-42:

Anyone who prefers father or mother to me is not worthy of me. Anyone who prefers son or daughter to me is not worthy of me. Anyone who does not take his cross and follow in my footsteps is not worthy of me. Anyone who finds his life will lose it; anyone who loses his life for my sake will find it.

The Truth About Human Love

I have always felt that the work I do is not a gift I live, but rather an obligation to fulfill. Anyone who has been blessed with a comfortable standard of living and is given the opportunity to help others has an obligation to do so. There is a reason why God puts us in a specific situation and in a specific country to influence others.

I started my mission teaching only Natural Family Planning (NFP). After writing three books on the technique of Natural Family Planning, I realized that we needed to expand beyond just a technique, because it encompasses much more than just a method. Natural Family Planning encompasses sacrifice and communication between husband and wife. The fruit that we see coming from this work includes the moral and spiritual benefits that accompany respect for the teachings of God and his Church. It was in light of all the testimonies that I have heard from people in the United States, Latin America, Europe, Africa, Asia, Eastern Europe, and Russia, while traveling, that I realized all people are the same when presented with the truth. As Mother Teresa said, "People will always recognize the Truth; they may not always follow it, but they will recognize it."

Pope John Paul II gave the best illustration on the subject when he addressed the participants in a training course on Natural Family Planning on January 10, 1992:

Natural Family Planning, in fact, does not have a merely technical character, but always implies an essential moral dimension. Therefore, it is not simply a question of acquiring scientific knowledge about sexual physiology and the methods for diagnosing female fertility. Above all, it is a question of understanding the truth about human love in God's plan and of growing in sensitivity to the moral values involved in it. Thus, the increasingly accurate knowledge of the cycles of female fertility finds its appropriate horizon and the condition for its morally permissible use in the context of conjugal chastity, understood as a virtue of genuine marital love.

People may not always follow it, but they will always recognize the truth. It is our obligation, then, to present the truth of Natural Family Planning, and it is the decision of human beings endowed with God's gift of free will to either follow or not follow the truth. Many times the truth is denied, but later those who had first denied the truth come back to learn more about it. This often happens after they have been harmed through the use of artificial birth control, and may even have been left infertile. John Paul II best expressed how I feel when he said:

> Authentic love is not a vague sentiment or a blind passion. It is an inner attitude that involves the whole human being. It is looking at others, not to use them but to serve them. It is the ability to rejoice with those who are rejoicing and to suffer with those who are suffering. It is sharing what one possesses so that no one may continue to be deprived of what he needs. Love, in a word, is the gift of self.... The family, the great workshop of love is the first school, indeed, a lasting school where people are not taught to love with barren ideas, but with the incisive power of experience. May every family truly rediscover its own vocation to love! Love that absolutely respects God's plan, love that is the choice and reciprocal gift of self within the family unit.[7]

I thank God for the gift of life he has given me and praise him for the opportunity to teach others to be open to life and to live out fully their "vocation to love."

Chapter 8

Women's Roles in the Church

KIMBERLY HAHN

What I am about to share is not politically correct, but it is true. The Catholic Church has embraced a male-only priesthood. This follows Jesus' choice of men to be apostles and the early Church's example of selecting only men for the priesthood. Though some men and women portray the Church's stance as archaic, others understand it as tradition in the best sense. While some scorn the Church's teaching as anti-woman, others embrace it as a great blessing for women. Though the Lord calls all of his people, men and women, single and married, to serve his Church, he calls only some men to be ordained priests.

I did not always think so.

My Sense of Call to Ministry

From the time I was in the second grade until my junior year in college, I wanted to be a pastor, just like my dad. My father is a Presbyterian minister in a denomination that does ordain women as pastors.[1]

Each night at the dinner table my dad shared the most wonderful stories about being a pastor. Perhaps he had had the joy of leading someone to a saving knowledge of Jesus Christ. Or he had led a counseling session with a man and a woman who now had hope that their marriage could be restored. Or possibly he told us of the delight he and my mother had experienced as they led a Bible study with converts so fresh in their newfound faith.

Not only did my father relate the power and mercy of our heavenly Father through the work of the Holy Spirit in his life, but he included us in his sense of mission. We prayed for different people, welcomed some of them into our home to live with us, and met people who felt called to do the kind of ministry that my dad did. He encouraged men and women who loved Christ to commit their entire lives in service to him, either as pastors or on the mission field. Night after night, he would come home, incredulous that he was paid to do something he enjoyed so much.

In this environment, all five of us children were nurtured in our faith. Three of us—my two brothers and I—wanted to serve the Lord as pastors. I thought that there couldn't be anything more exciting in the world than teaching the Bible, preaching, counseling, and seeing lives transformed by Christ day in and day out. I told my parents I wanted to be a minister when I was in the second grade. At that time, my mother was not altogether thrilled to hear her daughter say she'd like to be a minister, but my dad was tentatively pleased. I occasionally talked about it through my third-, fourth-, and fifth-grade years—there was nothing else I wanted to do when I grew up. I began to collect sermon illustrations in a card file box, and, in fact, put together and preached my own little sermon to my mom and dad (about loneliness) when I was in the sixth grade.

My mom continued to be somewhat reserved, but my dad's enthusiasm grew. In his denomination, he knew some women pastors who had a feminist agenda. Consequently, he was eager to encourage women who were well grounded in the Bible, with a strong commitment to the gospel, to do ministry alongside him. He was thrilled at the prospect that we might work side by side in his denomination.

In addition, various experiences reinforced my sense of calling. I helped organize a student-led Scripture and prayer meeting before classes began at our public junior high and high schools. I counseled friends and acquaintances, some of whom had very painful lives, with one provision—I told them that I had to be able to tell my dad about the situations if it was too much for me to handle. I loved to study the Bible, to memorize it, and to share it. I led small discipleship groups with junior high girls when I was in high school, and I served on a youth evangelism team. Throughout my four years in high school I helped to lead worship services in Cincinnati and on a two-week national tour each summer with about fifty other teens in a singing group called Young Folk.

I began my college years excited about the possibilities of being a pastor. Many people confirmed that this was God's call on my life, including my parents, since they recognized the gifts for ministry.

In my third year of college, however, several friends asked me one question I had never asked myself: Does the Bible support the idea of women being ordained as pastors? I didn't know that this was a hotly debated issue in a number of denominations. Once I realized that I didn't know what the Scriptures revealed on this issue, I knew I had to study to be sure my sense of call from God was truly from him. No matter what my feelings about being called to ministry were, if the Scriptures didn't allow women to be ordained, God could not be calling me to ordained ministry. (As a Protestant, Scripture was the only authority to which I appealed. Later study, as a Catholic, revealed a rich Church tradition on the interpretation of Scripture that shed even more light on the issue.)

Jesus' Ministry Enhanced by Women

When I looked at Jesus, I saw him as the Liberator—a man who was not bound by his culture, for he was not only a man, but God. (God is not limited by time, space, or culture!) For example, he demonstrated respect toward women, unlike the culture in which he was born. Also, he spoke to women in public, such as the Samaritan woman at the well (see Jn 4:7-26), the woman caught in adultery (see Jn 8:3-11), and even a Canaanite woman (see Mt 15:21-28). Further, he healed women, like Peter's mother-in-law (see Mk 1:29-32), the woman with the flow of blood who merely touched his garment (see Mk 5:25-34), and the little girl whom he raised from the dead (see Mk 5: 21-24, 35-43).

On numerous occasions, he enjoyed the hospitality of Mary and Martha, the sisters of his dear friend Lazarus. He taught women, and, in the case of Martha's sister Mary, he affirmed her choice to sit at his feet rather than busy herself with the more mundane tasks of hospitality, while she had the opportunity (see Lk 10:38-42).

Jesus welcomed women as companions in ministry. He allowed women to travel with him (see Mt 27:55-56). Furthermore, they were the ones who were faithful to the bitter end at the foot of the cross, when everyone else, except John, abandoned our Lord.

Some women were watching from a distance.

Among them were Mary Magdalene, Mary the mother of James the younger and of Joses and Salome. In Galilee these women had followed him and cared for his needs. Many other women who had come up with him to Jerusalem were also there.

MARK 15:40-41

Jesus gave these women the honor of being the very first to greet him when he rose from the dead.

One woman in particular received honor and respect from Jesus—his Mother. First, Jesus demonstrated love for thirty years for Mary in their "hidden" life together in Nazareth before he began his public ministry. Then, his first miracle was at the request of his Mother at the wedding at Cana (see Jn 2:1-11). Not only did Jesus preach the importance of obeying the law, including honoring father and mother, but he also lived what he preached in regard to his heavenly Father and his earthly mother (see Mk 7:10; 10:20). When his mother and relatives joined him in the midst of ministry, he heard a woman praise his mother for bearing her Son. Jesus responded by stating what was even more praiseworthy—more significant than her physically bearing him—was her faith-filled obedience, which included bearing him and *so* much more (see Lk 11:27-28). Finally, from the cross, he gave her to the Beloved Disciple (see Jn 19:26-27), caring for her needs to the end of his life.

As much love and respect as Jesus showed women, however, he chose only men when he chose the twelve disciples. Maybe he was following the pattern for leadership in the Old Covenant, where all priests were male. Perhaps he chose men for convenience, because it could be dangerous for two women to travel together, or because it could look immoral if a woman and a man traveled together. However, *nowhere else did Jesus simply capitulate to his culture*. His reason for selecting only men had a definite purpose. It was not simply to avoid scandalizing others. Pope John Paul II says:

> In calling only men as his Apostles, Christ acted in a completely free and sovereign manner. In doing so, he exercised the same freedom with which, in all his behavior, he emphasized the dignity and the vocation of women, without conforming to the prevailing customs and to the traditions sanctioned by the legislation of the time.[2]

In everything, Jesus' work was united to his heavenly Father's will (see Jn 5:30), so the Father and the Son must have known it was best for the apostles to all be men.

The Example of the Early Church

Each time a new leader was selected in the early Church, those in authority laid hands on him to confer ordination, and each time, the new leader was a man, following Jesus' example. For instance, while the disciples awaited the gift of the Holy Spirit in the Upper Room, they selected Matthias to replace Judas (see Acts 1:15-26), so that Judas's office would be filled. Later, the disciples chose seven Grecian Jews (all men) to assist them in ministry: "They presented these men to the apostles, who prayed and laid their hands on them" (Acts 6:6).

Throughout the New Testament, men were the ones consecrated to serve the Church as pastors. For example, Paul referred to Timothy's ordination through the laying on of hands: "Until I come, devote yourself to the public reading of Scripture, to preaching and to teaching. Do not neglect your gift, which was given you through a prophetic message when the body of elders laid their hands on you" (1 Tm 4:13-14).

In the context of public worship, Paul reminds the Corinthian church about the principle of headship: "But I want you to understand that the head of every man is Christ, the head of a woman is her husband, and the head of Christ is God" (1 Cor 11:3). Paul is speaking about the order of authority, established before Creation (God is the head of Christ) and during Creation (the husband is the head of the wife, since the woman was made from the man [see 1 Cor 11:8]). He is preparing the Corinthian Christians for a later section in his letter to them, in which he establishes the structure of Church authority.

Paul clearly teaches that women should not be permitted to "teach or have authority over men" (see 1 Tm 3:15; 1 Tm 2: 11-14; Ti 2:4) in the official capacity of pastor in the Church. His reasons transcend his culture—the order of Creation, the order of the Fall, the angels, nature, the Law, the teaching of an apostle, and the command of the Lord. If Paul wanted to demonstrate that his teaching was for all

Christians for all time in all places, to what other authority could he appeal?

At first I was offended—weren't women good enough to serve God as pastors? Several friends contributed their thoughts on Paul. Maybe he had had a bad relationship with his mother and just didn't like women. Maybe he was caught up in his culture's mores and couldn't see the possibilities that Jesus would have seen in the same circumstance. Maybe women in that day weren't educated well enough to do a good job teaching, and, since it's different today, his admonition would apply to only the church Timothy was pastoring.

Regardless of whatever sins Paul had, the Holy Spirit did not permit him to translate a dislike for women or a distrust of their abilities or education into a maxim for Church leadership. After all, this was Paul writing, under the direction of God, the authoritative Word of God. This wasn't just a man down the block writing an article for the local newspaper!

Besides, he grounded his arguments in timeless, rather than timebound, truths. As to his feelings about women, he urged the believers in Rome to give a special greeting to particular *co-workers*, including Phoebe, Priscilla, Mary, Junias, Tryphena, Tryphosa, Persis, Rufus' mother, and others (see Rom 16:1-3, 6-7, 12-13). These women worked *alongside him as valued partners in ministry.*

Could God Be the One Who's Slighting Women?

Not a chance.

God is the One who thought of us in the first place. He's the One who created us, male and female, in his image and likeness (see Gn 1:26-28). Dr. Alice von Hildebrand asks, tongue in cheek, if creation is going from the lowest form of life to the highest, what does that say about woman being created after man? Separately, man and woman have different gifts and they reflect the image of God differently. Together, man and woman are called to exercise dominion over the creation.

Pope John Paul II, in his *Letter to Women* (June 29, 1995), refers to the "genius of women" as created by God. "Perhaps more than men, women acknowledge the person, because they see persons with their hearts. They see them independently of various ideological or political systems. They see others in their greatness and limitations; they try to go out to them and help them."[3] Though tainted by sin, this "genius" needs to be "accepted and appreciated" for the good of the Church and society.

God has redeemed us equally, male and female, to be "joint heirs of the grace of life" (1 Pt 3:7).

Gospel "equality," the "equality" of women and men in regard to the "mighty works of God"—manifested so clearly in the words and deeds of Jesus of Nazareth—constitutes the most obvious basis for the dignity and vocation of women in the Church and in the world. Every vocation has a profoundly personal and prophetic meaning. In "vocation," understood in this way, what is personally feminine reaches a new dimension: the dimension of the "mighty works of God," of which the woman becomes the living subject and an irreplaceable witness.[4]

Women *are* different from men, thank God, but we are no less valuable.

Would God Call Me to a Vocation I Could Not Fulfill?

At this point in my study, I felt confused. All my life I had *thought* that God was preparing me to be an ordained minister. I felt like I had the gifts—and the desire—to serve him that way. Yet I had to submit my heart to my understanding of his will, as revealed in Scripture. The dream of my life was called into question. So, after much prayer and not a few tears, I said "yes" to God's plan for my life, and that plan no longer included being ordained a pastor.

It was difficult to yield but good to trust my heavenly Father to lead me in a new direction. My parents expressed disappointment, though they supported me in my decision. Their greater concern was for me to develop my intellect theologically so that I could serve the Lord however he wanted. A year after I married Scott, my parents financed my Master of Arts degree in theology from Gordon-Conwell Theological Seminary.

I did not study theology in order to become ordained. (That's actually a different degree.) Rather, Scott and I wanted to study together so that I could better serve the Lord alongside Scott. Friends were incredulous when I happily shared the news that we were expecting our first child and that, following graduation, I would be a stay-at-home mom. "What was all of the time, expense and effort worth if I wasn't going to earn a paycheck from my degree?" they asked. (Friends asked, though my parents never did—they knew the value of the degree went far beyond a paycheck and encouraged me to stay home to serve my family.)

On the one hand, I was not called to be an ordained pastor, because Scripture prohibited it. On the other hand, I still had gifts, abilities, and desires to serve the Lord. At that time, the question was how I could best serve the Lord in my vocation of marriage to Scott, motherhood to our first child, and service as a pastor's wife, in that order.[5]

A Question of Authority

As a Protestant, I didn't have access to Magisterial teachings or to Church tradition when I was grappling with the question of the ordination of women, since Protestants believe the Bible is the only source of authoritative teaching. I wasn't even aware of male-only priesthood from the apostles to the present. One of the blessings for me, in the midst of my struggle with many of the doctrines of the Catholic faith, was discovering that the issue of women's ordination had already been settled in the Catholic Church. I looked at this enormous, multicultural Church with amazement—for two millennia she had stood firm for truth in the area of women's ordination. As I studied what the Catholic Church taught about ordination, my appreciation deepened.

Pope John Paul II has reiterated the Church's stance:

> Wherefore, in order that all doubt may be removed regarding a matter of great importance, a matter which pertains to the Church's divine constitution itself, in virtue of my ministry of confirming the brethren (cf. Luke 22:32) I declare that the Church has no authority whatsoever to confer priestly ordination on women and that this judgment is to be definitively held by all the Church's faithful.[6]

The teaching authority of the Church can declare only what she knows to be the will of God.

All believers—men and women—are called to be Christ-like. However, an ordained priest is not only called to imitate Christ; he acts in the place of Christ—*in persona Christi*. "It is the Eucharist above all that expressed the redemptive act of Christ the Bridegroom toward the Church the Bride. This is clear and unambiguous when the sacramental ministry of the Eucharist, in which the priest acts 'in persona Christi,' is performed by a man."[7] Though God is neither male nor female, the Second Person of the Godhead, the Son, took on human flesh as a male; hence, there needs to be a male human reflection of Christ in the priest.

The Church—Political Structure or Family of God?

Recently a critique of the Catholic Church's stance for men-only ordination included a reference to the National Council of Catholic Bishops as the last all-male club in America. Some women are adamant that men continue to promote an all-male priesthood as a way to retain power over women. They feel disenfranchised—"men wrote the Bible and then men interpret the Bible to keep themselves in power."

Men—and women—can desire power in a sinful way, to lord it over others. Yet Scripture, primarily authored and interpreted by the Holy Spirit in the Church, can teach only truth. The Second Vatican Council reiterates this traditional understanding of Scripture, repeating what the Church has always taught. Though the human authors were fallible men, when they wrote Sacred Scripture, they were preserved from error. That's essential—we stake our whole lives and our future on it.

How we view the Church makes all the difference in our response to the Church's teaching, which is the command of the Lord, on this issue. If we see the Church as a political structure, fraught with power struggles, then as a woman I'd say: "The power structure of the Church is cardinals, then bishops, then priests. If I can't be any of these, then I have no power within the Church."

However, the Church is not a democracy, influenced by opinion polls and ruled by a majority. Rather, the Church is God's family, which he has established. He is our Father, who is raising up many fathers, our priests, under him to reflect his self-donative, sacrificial love toward his children. When we see the Church as God's family, then we realize that the call to priesthood is not about a political power struggle at all. It is about sacrificial love and service.

In the Church, we use family language to describe ourselves—priests are fathers, men religious are brothers, women religious are mothers or sisters, and the laity are brothers and sisters in Christ. We use the language of family because that's what the Church is, in Her essence—the family of God. This is simply God's plan for how he will care for his children through the ministry of his Son.

In our natural families we reflect an image of the Trinity as family. In a family we don't make ultimatums—"If I can't have power, then I don't have a place in this family!" Rather, we demonstrate our place in the family through service. Likewise, in the family of God, the Church, we do not demand a position of power. Instead, we ask, "How do you want me to serve, Lord?" Please remember, it's not a matter of being worthy of ordination—neither men nor women are worthy of ordination. It's not a right for anybody. Yet God, in his mercy, calls particular men to embrace a vow of poverty, chastity, and obedience in the vocation of priesthood. It is a divine call (see Heb 5:1-4).

The Example of Mary

Mary certainly is an important example for us. She spent thirty years of her life with Jesus. Who knew her Son's thoughts better than Mary did? She observes him begin his ministry by collecting his apostles. Can you imagine the humility it took for her not to pull rank? "Jesus, if you're going to pick twelve, why don't you pick eleven and then put me on the team?" Here's a ragtag collection of sinful men, including one who is going to betray him, and the sinless mother of God. Yet, in her humility, she (seemingly) takes a backseat.

Mary chooses to be known primarily as a mother. I've had people say to me, "Don't lose your identity just to be known as someone's mom!" Really? Tell that to Mary. Pope John Paul II says that motherhood *is* her highest call:

From the first moment of her divine motherhood, of her union with the Son whom "the Father sent into the world, that the world might be saved through him" (cf. Jn 3:17), Mary takes her place within Christ's messianic service. It is precisely this service which constitutes the very foundation of that Kingdom in which "to serve ... means to reign" (Second Vatican Council, Dogmatic Constitution on the Church, *Lumen Gentium* n.36).[8]

Though she was never ordained, Mary's is a wonderful example of a life of service that has everlasting value for the sons and daughters of God. Her titles include Queen of Heaven, Queen of the Universe, Queen of Apostles, Queen of Martyrs, Queen of Confessors.... Can you imagine her complaining to Jesus that there was no place in the kingdom for her, just because she was never ordained?

Our political culture tends to frame the question of the value of a woman in terms of what official capacity a woman may have in Church structure. Therefore, if a woman cannot be ordained a priest, she cannot make a difference in the Church. As Christian women, we need to help reframe the question of the value of a woman within the Church in familial terms: Christian women are called to serve within the family of God, the Church, with all that it means to be a woman.

Women are not called to priestly ordination; they *are* called to offer the genius of womanhood in whatever means of service according to their respective vocation, state in life, gifts, abilities, education, and desire for the greater glory of God and the upbuilding of the Church. Rather than focusing on what we cannot do as women, let's examine some of the possible roles that express the dignity and vocation of women in the Church. And let's keep in mind the example of Christ. "Christ, the 'Servant of the Lord,' will show all people the royal dignity of service, the dignity which is joined in the closest possible way to the vocation of every person."[9]

Mature Womanhood

Whether or not a woman marries, I believe mature womanhood involves spousal commitment and motherhood. When I first had Hannah, I was still a Protestant. I was torn in my heart because I knew that with Scott's fervent Catholic faith, Hannah might be drawn to religious life. I had no interest in becoming a Catholic—nor did I want Hannah to become a nun—but I didn't want to get in the way of God's plan for her life.

When I prayed about my concerns, the Lord spoke to my heart. "Kimberly, if you teach her how to be a faithful wife and a good mother, you will have prepared her for whatever mission I have."

The call to consecrated life, after all, is *not* a call to be neuter for Christ. It is not a call to set aside femininity or the power of sexuality and suddenly to cease being a complete woman. Rather, the call to consecrated life, for a man or a woman, is a call to harness the energies of sexuality and, in great sacrifice, to serve our Lord and his Church with the single-minded devotion that is only possible as a single person for the Lord. As Paul says:

I want you to be free from anxieties. The unmarried man is anxious about the affairs of the Lord, how to please the Lord. But the married man is anxious about worldly affairs, how to please his wife. And his interests are divided. And the unmarried woman or girl is anxious about the affairs of the Lord, how to be holy in body and spirit. But the married woman is anxious about worldly affairs, how to please her husband. I say this for your own benefit, not to lay any restraint upon you, but to promote good order and to secure your undivided devotion to the Lord.

1 CORINTHIANS 7:32-35

So many details of life—so many interruptions—can be set aside so that the person who is single for the Lord can serve him.

A woman's embrace of singleness, even temporarily, is much more than a holding pattern until the right guy comes along. "This cannot be compared to remaining simply unmarried or single, because virginity is not restricted to a mere 'no,' but contains a profound 'yes' in the spousal order: the gift of self for love in a total and undivided manner."[10]

This spousal commitment to the Lord means you give the Lord the honor and the respect that he is due, just as you would give any spouse. You love him, honor him, and respond to his love for you.

Spiritual motherhood requires being generous—generous in fruitfulness. You nurture the souls that are in your care with the virtues that flow from femininity. Every woman is called to be a spiritual mother to those around her. For instance, Paul admonishes the older women to teach the younger women to be reverent toward God and loving toward their spouse and children (see Ti 2:3-5). Young women—those of you who are in high school or junior high school—can spiritually mother the little ones who are younger than you. Reach out to them, guide them, encourage them to come with you to Mass, or to pray and to study the Bible with you.

Mary is such a wonderful model for all of us because she is both consecrated and married; she is a fruitful mother spiritually and physically. We see in Mary a model for virgins who commit the gift of their sexuality in sacrifice to God through consecrated, single-minded devotion to the Lord. We also see in Mary a model for wives and mothers who are sanctified through faithfulness to their vocation of marriage. "For in the mystery of the Church, which itself is rightly called mother and virgin, the Blessed Virgin stands out in eminent and singular fashion as exemplar both of virgin and mother."[11]

Objectively, consecrated life is God's highest call; subjectively, for many of us, marriage is God's highest call. None of us have a second-rate vocation. Since I am married, I know that is God's best for me—

I haven't missed the call of God. If you are married, then you also know God's vocation for your life.

Some of you are single, and you think that your vocation may be marriage. In the interim, don't lose the wonder of this time in worrying about whether or not you're going to get married. Use this time well—it may be much shorter than you think. Consecrate this time to God in a special way, perhaps doing apostolic work that you could not do if you were married. Perhaps, take that short-term mission to Spain, or do special traveling, especially with a ministry orientation. Maybe take that extra course at the university. This time of singleness is a great blessing, even if it's brief. Please don't waste the time being single for yourself. It isn't worth it. Be single for the Lord, but not for yourself.

To Serve Is to Reign

The very core of our being is stamped with either masculinity or femininity. We celebrate it as God's good gift, for that's how God has made us. The question we should ask is, "What can we do with it to strengthen the family of God?"

We must think God's way, instead of the world's way, about what it means to be a woman of God. Pope John Paul II declares that Mary's service is directly linked to her queenly reign:

> Putting herself at God's service, she also put herself at the service of others: a service of love. Precisely through this service Mary was able to experience in her life a mysterious, but authentic "reign." ... This is the way in which authority needs to be understood, both in the family and in society and the Church.[12]

Likewise, Jesus said, "Whoever saves his life will lose it; but whoever loses his life for my sake will find it" (Lk 9:24).

Married women can't put worldly affairs over the service of Christ, yet much of our service to Christ is in the midst of worldly affairs. We have so many demands on our time that it's hard to get in prayer time; however, we still have the obligation to pray. It's not enough for us to say, "If I were in a monastery, I would pray." We have to make sure that Christ is always first in our life. Our path to sanctity wends its way through many competing needs and desires, pulling us away from intimacy with God. We must learn how to balance time commitments so that God is preeminent even in the midst of so many distractions. We need to consecrate our many duties to God so that even the mundane activities of care for family and home become a prayer.

Saint Thérèse of Lisieux's prayer can be ours—I may not be able to do great things for God, but "let me do little things with great love." Never underestimate the small things. If you pick up your distraught child as you would pick up the Christ child, you have communicated love. If you tie your toddler's shoes with love, you have done something valuable for the Lord. If you hand a Coke to your teen, you have offered refreshment to the Lord. It's the little things that help us become like him.

Through our life of service, we are called to have dominion as co-regents with our spouses. Our homes are not cages where we are trapped—they are potential sanctuaries wherein we bring a sense of order, peace, and harmony. We imitate the Holy Spirit as we bring order out of chaos. Our children are works of art in the making. As we nurture them, physically and spiritually, we help mold them more fully into the image of God, which they are. And, yes, it's challenging. As G.K. Chesterton said, "I will pity Mrs. Jones for the hugeness of her task; I will never pity her for its smallness."[13]

The Priesthood of All Believers

All believers are called a kingdom of priests, participating in the priestly service of Christ as he offers himself in heaven to the Father (see Rv 1:6). We who have been baptized into Christ have been placed within the mantle of his priesthood. We are called to respond to his service, love, and sacrifice for us: to serve as he served, to love as he loved, and to lay down our lives in sacrifice as he did.

> In the context of the "great mystery" of Christ and of the Church, all are called to respond—as a bride—with the gift of their lives to the inexpressible gift of the love of Christ, who alone, as the Redeemer of the world, is the Church's Bridegroom. The "royal priesthood," which is universal, at the same time expresses the gift of the Bride.[14]

This is an important message of the Second Vatican Council—God calls us as lay people to help strengthen the body of Christ. Can we do valuable service apart from being ordained? Yes! If we allow the Holy Spirit to do his creative work within us, helping us to be living sacrifices, we will be of indispensable value.

How can we offer ourselves as a Christ-like sacrifice? Look at Romans 12:2:

> Do not be conformed to this world, but be transformed by the renewal of your mind that you may prove what is the will of God, what is good and acceptable and perfect.

This world shouts to us continually what it means to be a woman or a man, what marriage is, and what the act of marriage means. In many ways, we are so much a part of our culture, we are not even aware of the influences expressed on us by the world. We need to discern the influences of the world and their impact upon us regarding our thoughts on what a priest *is* and *does*, and what authority the Church should have in our lives.

God has created men and women for very special reasons. We need to be thankful that God made us as we are and allow him to transform our thinking so that we look at men, women, marriage, priesthood, and the Church as *he* does, rather than believing the world's lies.

"Be transformed by the renewal of your mind"—for what purpose? This will enable us to live the good, acceptable, and perfect will of God. If we allow him to transform our minds, Christ-like actions will flow from Christ-like thinking.

A Gift Greater than Priesthood—The Gift of Holiness

God is working powerfully in our midst—in your lives and in mine—and he is drawing us on, saying, "I want you to be everything I have called you to be." That call will never be less for women. Jesus himself said, "The Son of Man did not come to be served but to serve and to give his life as a ransom for many" (Mt 20:28). We are called to do nothing less than imitate our Lord and Savior Jesus Christ.

While there is growing awareness in the Church of the valuable contributions women can make, there is the ongoing challenge for us to distinguish between our genuine call from God to serve him, and the enticement of our culture to demand power in the hierarchical structure of the Church.

The presence and the role of women in the life and mission of the Church, although not linked to the ministerial priesthood, remain absolutely necessary and irreplaceable. As the Declaration *Inter Insigniores* points out, "the Church desires that Christian women should become fully aware of the greatness of their mission: today their role is of capital importance both for the renewal and humanization of society and for the rediscovery by believers of the true face of the Church."15

A woman's unique gift of femininity is needed in our Church as well as our world.

In this vast domain of service, the Church's two thousand year history, for all its historical conditioning, has truly experienced the "genius of woman"; from the heart of the Church there have emerged women of the highest caliber who have left an impressive and beneficial mark in history. I think of the great line of martyrs, saints and famous mystics.16

The gift of these great women of faith leads us to recognize a calling greater than the priesthood—the call to holiness.

God calls some men to be priests in order to father his people in holiness. Moreover, it is to the holiness of the faithful that the hierarchical structure of the Church is totally ordered. For this reason, the Declaration *Inter Insigniores* recalls: "the only better gift, which can and must be desired, is love (cf. 1 Corinthians 12 and 13). The greatest in the Kingdom of Heaven are not the ministers but the saints."17

The *most important role* to have in the Church is *not to be a priest but to be a saint.*

By defending the dignity of women and their vocation, the Church has shown honor and gratitude for those women who—faithful to the Gospel—have shared in every age in the apostolic mission of the whole People of God. They are the holy martyrs, virgins and mothers of families, who bravely bore witness to their faith and passed on the Church's faith and tradition by bringing up their children in the spirit of the Gospel.[18]

These role models help us to understand how we can best serve our Lord and his Church.

Come and serve—serve God and serve those whom he brings to you. Your apostolic work may not go farther than your front door. It might be focusing on your family and those who come in for hospitality. That is a wonderful ministry. God may have other plans for you that will involve leaving your job or your hometown, even going to another country. Give him your heart. Give him everything you have and say, "Lord, I want to serve. Like you, like Mary, show me the place that you have for me to serve in your Church and I will do it."

Remember Mary's response to the Lord when the angel announced the Lord's plan for her life. She did not say, "You picked the right girl. I can do it, no problem. I am sufficient for the job." Rather, she said, "Behold, the handmaid of the Lord. Be it done unto me according to *thy* Word." In other words, "I'm available to do *your* will. Help me to do it."

That's what our Lord asks from each of us. We cannot even imagine the wonderful things that the Lord wants to do in and through us. He asks for our availability, right where we are, and our willingness to serve him for the good of his Church.

Doors Open for Apostolic Work

When Scott and I prepared to move from Milwaukee, Wisconsin, in 1987, I went to lunch with a friend, who was a prominent Protestant author and speaker, to say good-bye. I shared with her the difficulties Scott and I had gone through due to his spiritual odyssey into the Catholic Church. At that time my heart was open to a sincere exploration of the faith in a new way.

When I shared that I was beginning to study Catholic theology seriously, she gave me a solemn warning. If I remained a Protestant, she could open doors of ministry for me all over the country. However, if I became a Catholic, those doors would slam shut for me for good. That would leave me no outlet for ministry, given that I was a woman, inside or outside of the Catholic Church.

Her comments showed me that she didn't know me very well. I would not have made the decision to study the Catholic faith based on whether or not *I* would have opportunities for ministry. Either that faith was true or it was false, and I would trust God with what would follow. Scott and I had already experienced a kind of death of dreams when he became a Catholic—he would never be a pastor; I would never be a pastor's wife. In our Catholic-Protestant marriage, we couldn't share our faith together in a ministry in talks, articles, or books with others. Earlier, I had had to table my hopes and dreams for being a pastor while I explored the Scriptures on women's ordination. Now I had to put on hold my desire to serve the Lord with Scott as a speaker or author until important theological issues were settled about the Church.

Thanks be to God, in his mercy, I studied the faith intensively for three years and, at the Easter Vigil, 1990, I was received into the Catholic Church. Since that time, not only has our family been restored in worship, receiving the Eucharist together, but the dreams we had shared before we wed have been restored superabundantly.

Ironically, the Lord has opened *many* doors for me to serve him within the Catholic Church. I began a weekly Bible study for women in my home after our move to Steubenville, Ohio, in 1990. I have spoken with Scott all over our country, and in England, Ireland, Israel, and Italy, about the Catholic faith and Catholic family life.[19]

Every day, I am grateful for the mercy of God that called me into the Catholic Church, no matter how painful the journey has been at points. I am thankful for the sacraments of the Eucharist and Confession, and for the assistance of regular spiritual direction that our Lord provides through those men he has called into service through the priesthood. I am amazed at the privilege I have to be the wife of Scott Hahn and mother to Michael, Gabriel, Hannah, Jeremiah, Joseph, and David, and godmother to Andrew, Christopher, Thomas, Michael, and Jackie Joy.

I am living proof—neither you nor I can outgive God. Give him everything you have, no matter what the cost. When he gives it back to you, it may be in a form different than you expect, just as he has given me opportunities to serve him unlike what I ever imagined when I was in college. However, it will be *his* direction for your life, which is what you desire most anyway. Join me in the prayer that my dad taught me—a beautiful reflection of what the holy women of God have lived:

> Lord, I will go wherever you want me to go
> Do whatever you want me to do
> Say whatever you want me to say
> And give away whatever you want me to give away
> To the greater glory of God. Amen.[20]

Chapter 9

A Deeper Purpose

MAUREEN ROACH

May the flowers never lose their meaning—may you find your purpose in life and know you matter.

Child Number Thirteen

I was born May 11, 1940, in Los Angeles, California. I realize now the great honor I received sharing in the month of our May Queen, Mother Mary, and the birth-month of our beloved Pope John Paul II, the 263rd Bishop of Rome and Vicar of Christ.

My name, Maureen, means "little Mary," and I was child number thirteen.

As a young woman, my mother was told she could never have children. This prognosis was given due to a severe blow she had received to her abdomen in a streetcar accident. This trauma left her with bouts of weakness in her ninety-pound frame and kept her confined to bed for long periods of time. Needless to say, she never menstruated, so how could she ever conceive?

My father, Wilfred, encountered his own tragic blow. While working on the railroad at the age of nineteen, a train rolled over his leg and severed it above the knee. His Irish pride nearly convinced him he could never be a fit husband or a good provider, and in those seconds his hopes and dreams of marrying my mother were dashed. My mother, being French-Irish with a lot of determined German, would not allow this wonderful man to succumb to the "poor-me's." She convinced him, with her unconditional love, that nothing had changed. He was still her Prince Charming, and together they would make it! And that they did.

At the age of sixteen my mother married and with the grace and mercy of God had her first blessing a year later. The rest of us are history. He takes the barren and makes them fruitful. "[F]or nothing is impossible for God" (Lk 1:37). I like to think of myself as a miracle, but of course, isn't that what we all are? As Genesis 18:14 reads, "Is anything too marvelous for the Lord to do?"

Growing up in a large family was a real joy. One of the perks was that I always had a friend to play with. It doesn't mean everything was perfect. We had our share of family squabbles and hardships. Yet, through it all, we learned a lot about sharing, forgiveness, and loyalty. The *decision to love* was the key that was always held out for us to use. My parents' example of Christian charity is something I will always treasure. I often think about that now when I read the scripture passage: "I was a stranger and you took me in" (Mt 25:35). We lived down the street from the police station. Our McNeil family was well known by many.

Our home was a refuge for many who needed comfort and validation. At times my mother would get a phone call from the sergeant at the police station and hold her breath for fear it was one of her own rambunctious boys acting up, but then the police would ask if we could house a child until other arrangements could be made. One request turned into many more. Each of them was a child of God, and we were reminded of this with the statement, "Do unto others as you want others to do unto you." Today I find myself echoing this statement to my own children.

I consider myself very fortunate. I inherited my Catholic faith from my parents the day I was born. Fourteen days later they brought me to the waters of baptism to be filled with God's special grace that truly gave life by making me his child. That day was the beginning of my Christian journey. In time I would come to understand this was also the day I was baptized into his death, a calling to die to self and truly live life in the New Covenant.

I was taught Catholic tradition and values at a very young age. Our home was visibly Catholic. Rooms were adorned with pictures of the Sacred Heart of Jesus, and many images of the Blessed Virgin Mary graced the tabletops. Rosaries and medals were tucked into drawers. Our scapular and holy cards were a constant reminder of which church we belonged to. We all attended Catholic school. Looking back, I can appreciate all the sacrifices my parents made for us. Mom helped offset the tuition by cooking for the nuns and working in the cafeteria. A common sight was seeing a couple of her little ones sandwiched between milk bottles and lunch trays while she went about her chores. Her babies received lots of smiles, coos, and love from the nuns and others.

We all were given the names of saints. Often, we would chuckle at my Irish brother with his title, Michael Lawrence Lugenio Pacellio. Of course, he was quick to remind us, "I am not only an angel of a saint, but also an important pope." I thought about that a couple years ago when he died, and I prayed that his namesakes were there to intercede for him and lead him to the arms of his Maker.

Growing Pains

Nativity plays, May Crownings, adopting "pagan" babies with my nickels and dimes, and Lenten sacrifices that restricted me from my candy, bubble gum, and television, were all part of my Catholic childhood. I will never forget those Holy Thursday nights during Lent when my father would leave and not return until the next day. I often wondered where he slipped off to. With time, I learned he had gone to spend the night with Jesus, kneeling before him in adoration, wooden leg and all. How can I not value this beautiful example of faith and the importance of self-sacrifice?

This dear, sweet man was called home when I was sixteen years old. When he died, part of me did, too, for the loss was so great. He was my protector and confidant. I wanted so badly for him to see me graduate and someday meet my husband and hold my children as he did me. However, this dream was gone forever.

Before Dad died he raised his arms to all gathered around his bed and with a smile I will always remember, demonstrated the last act of faith. His eyes seemed to tell us, "It's time to go with my Maker, I love you all, 'be not afraid.'" It was obvious we were not the only ones present, for I sensed the presence of Jesus there, too. The reality of life after death truly took root in me that day. Being present and experiencing the spiritual birthing of my father, as painful as it was to say good-bye, has led me into my own journey of letting go of the things and people of this life. Death has touched me many times since, and a river of tears has been shed along the way, but with each death experience a clearer vision is given that helps me see death as a new beginning, not an end.

The Blessings of Marriage

Besides the beautiful examples of faith I received from my parents, I have been graced by many others who have had an impact on my life and helped my formation.

My husband is a combination of Saint Paul and Saint Joseph who has taught me a great deal about conversion and humility. It was important that I should marry a Catholic, and when God sent this man into my life, I was overwhelmed with attraction and thankfulness to discover he was Catholic too.

For us, there was no question in our minds that we would be married any other way than by a priest. In March 1961, in Greely, Colorado, before a Catholic priest, I pledged myself to my husband, and became Mrs. Richard Roach.

The first three years of marriage were spent in Germany due to my husband's military assignment. God knew we needed this time to mold, bond, and depend solely on each other. "Ye shall leave father and mother and the two shall become one" (Mt 19:5). Looking back I now see the fruit of this time and the foundation that was laid to strengthen us in our call to be interdependent. While in Germany, we were blessed with two fine sons. In 1964, with our two children, we arrived back on American soil. We moved to northern California filled with hopes and expectations and anxious to begin our quest for the American dream. Slowly but surely, our once secure savings dwindled down to a mere twenty-eight dollars. The dream that we searched to fulfill started to look more like a nightmare. Self-doubts, crushed pride, and a sense of failure started to thrive like cancer.

Why does one wait for the chips to fall before crying, "Help us Lord"? Over the journey of life I have come to echo this cry many times and have had to learn to trust in his response, "I will never forget you" (Is 49:15), or leave you orphaned. God is so faithful. He sent a dear friend to offer encouragement and direction, and he suggested my husband try the real estate field.

We learned a lot during these tough times, mainly how to do without and still feel blessed. We also developed a deeper respect and compassion for the so-called underdog, the poor, outcast, and destitute. The years that followed were work-work-work and not much play.

On Sundays, we made sure we were ready for Mass. By this time our family had grown to six. We were blessed not only with our two boys but also now with two girls.

Catholic schooling for our children was a real hardship financially but we felt it was very important. We had both been given the gift of a Catholic education and now that we were parents, we felt responsible for helping to guide our children in their spiritual walk. Their baptisms, first communions, and confirmations always brought a tear of pride. The sacraments were providing a survival kit of the true spiritual food that would help sustain our children through the toughest elements of life. I believe that when we receive the sacraments, the graces that come through to us are used all throughout life. The graces that were given our children were irreplaceable.

In time, my husband became a very successful realtor. Our financial status improved greatly. The days of pork and bean dinners soon became a vague memory. Now it was cocktail parties, fancy hors d'oeuvres, and rich desserts. We never forgot, though, where we once were, and our hearts have always remained with the less fortunate, due to walking in those shoes ourselves and knowing the struggle we had just to make ends meet.

We also found that with success came more responsibility, and in the process of climbing the ladder we had to keep reevaluating and correcting newfound worldly values. One of the habits that got picked up along the climb was overindulging in alcohol. It seemed that the more functions we attended, the more easily available and acceptable the "booze" was. How blinded one can become in serving the ways of the world. During this time other things came into play, which challenged us to look more deeply into our faith.

Growth in the Sacrament Together

Loneliness, lack of communication, misunderstandings, and false assumptions overtook us. After thirteen years of marriage the focus of our togetherness shifted for the worse. We always thought we knew each other so well, but at times we seemed like strangers. We didn't use many harsh words with one another, but we did engage in many nights of grieving, cold war. The silent treatment can pack a lot of venom, and create a storehouse of self-pity. I usually found at these down times that it was easier to dwell on the negative then to accentuate the positive. I fell into the trap of tearing, comparing, and judging other marriages around me. I would then look back on ours and think to myself, "Is this all there is?"

The evil one would have loved to have answered this with a big "yes," and continued to undermine what "God had joined together." How clever his tactics are as he gets one focused on that apple of independence and whispers his deceitful lies that you deserve more than being "just" a housewife and a mom. He works on negative self-image and supposed lack of intelligence, and drives you out into the world in search of yourself, to compete for self-fulfillment and recognition in other areas. I know during those times when I felt dull, boring, and of little importance, how flattered I became when others would notice my beauty, charm, and talents. How pleasing it felt being praised. Little did I realize, though, that I was being swept out of my home at the expense of my loved ones. I tried hard to cover the bases, but there were not enough hours in the day. Something, or rather some "ones" had to suffer.

However, God had his hand ready to reach out and pull me back into focus. The void and hunger I was trying to fill within would not be filled by simply being "active." The Lord would soon point out the true source of nourishment. An old college friend called one day to share with my husband and me about a weekend he and his wife had recently attended. Joe was excited, and his enthusiasm was intriguing. A "Marriage Encounter" was being given. We both agreed to go. We hoped this time away together would help refocus our direction and improve our communication. Much to my surprise, within the first session I sensed the Lord speaking to my heart by gently saying, "Maureen, turn your head, here I am." There, as I turned to look, sitting beside me was my husband. My eyes immediately filled with tears. I then realized that for a long time I had been looking for God's love and fulfillment in all sorts of activities and good works and discounting his loving presence in this man sitting right next to me. It is strange how after a few years of marriage one can lose sight of the treasure in front of one. A profound teaching about the value and depth of our sacrament of marriage was given to me.

The circle of marital love involves not two but *three.* The Sacrament of Marriage that God instituted gives us the grace to look beyond the struggles and demands of life. Marriage is working to bring forth the best in my husband, not with bitter words or cold wars, nor by proving my self-worth or pushing my agenda, or trying to compete by making sure I am getting my 50 percent. "Submission" doesn't mean stupidity, abuse, or wimpiness. It does mean being sent to build respect and love with a servant's heart and to move beyond the "issues" to the person behind them. God is present in a powerful way in the sacrament of our marriage, and it is our responsibility to see him and turn to him in all the phases of life, including romance, disillusionment, and the joys of everyday moments. We are to help each other attain holiness.

From that weekend back in 1976, our life has not been the same. My husband and I felt a definite calling then to be more active in our faith. God placed us in various capacities of ministry. Together from that time forward he strengthened us and has used us to help other couples discover his self- revealing love and tangible presence in their own sacrament. Over the ten years that we have presented Marriage Encounter weekends, we have seen repeatedly the walls of indifference, staleness, and loneliness crumble and be rebuilt with abiding love and renewed purpose between husband and wife.

The call to serve God in each other has become very clear, along with the realization that each family is meant to be like a little church, a "Domestic Church," reflecting God's presence and love. In our world today it is distressing to see the number of families that are being attacked and undermined by the illusions of the modern world. The false messages that ring with the "I, me, mine," mentality are hardening hearts. Individuals are becoming so self-focused in their pursuit of fun, fame, and fortune that soon they believe that it is important to be number one at all costs. This polluted thinking has become like a disease. It eats away at the inner heart of mankind, and weakens the person's desire to serve in committed love. The antidote and answer to this dilemma is *Jesus*. He died for us out of love, and we, in turn, are called to die to self in order to be more "life-giving" to others.

I thank God for Marriage Encounter and the tools that were given that helped us develop the vision of God's love for each other. We understand more clearly that true freedom (and identity) is found in the giving of self. This understanding is the very foundation of our Catholic faith and therefore our marriage as well. It means making the decision to love even when you don't feel like it, for love is a decision, not a feeling! We know that it's not the one with the most toys who wins; materialism is something we must always keep in check, if we are to lead with our hearts.

Beyond Ourselves

Several years ago my husband and I were asked to join the R.C.I.A. team at our parish. We looked at this as an opportunity to share the gift of our Catholicism, and to help others find the treasures of the Church that we ourselves to this day are still uncovering. The first thing we made clear to ourselves and others is the fact that the Church is made up of imperfect people! Through this acknowledgment and acceptance, one is given the grace then to move on and heal some of the wounds of past grudges and hurts. It was an eye-opener to hear of some of the misconceptions other denominations and faiths had about our Catholic Church. More troublesome were the many Catholics who walked away from the Church due to unresolved misunderstandings, a confessor who turned them off, or a doctrine that was too difficult to follow. Our Catholic journey is not easy! Much is expected of its members: obedience, fidelity, and sacrifice.

We all came with our stories of one kind or another. What rang out loud and clear was the need to belong to the family of God. The fact remains that our Church *is* the family of God, the mystical body of Christ, and it is comprised of the People of God, striving to grow in the virtues of faith, hope, and love. There are members with whom we don't always agree, and rules that seem hard to understand. However, we discovered that we must not turn our back on our faith or walk out of each other's lives. All one must do is look at the cross to see what reward came to us through his fidelity. He did not give up on us, the very ones who crucified him.

Participating as a sponsor and team member in the R.C.I.A. program has helped me appreciate more deeply my Catholic faith. I rejoice with those members who are returning to their church family. I am privileged to stand on this holy ground where the Lord is present in the Eucharist, in the Word, and in his people the Church.

The Eucharist, Our Greatest Gift

Back in 1987, the air was permeated with excitement and much anticipation. Our Holy Father, John Paul II, was coming to California, and going to say Mass in the Monterey Diocese. The news of his coming threw many into joy and panic. Preparations upon preparations were in full swing. Each parish was to select a certain number of Eucharistic ministers to help distribute communion at the Laguna Seca Raceway, where our pope was scheduled to celebrate the Holy Mass. How privileged I felt being one of the commissioned. I will always treasure the memory of that day. It was laced with many blessings and also a mixture of intense feelings. It all began to unfold in the early dawn, when we arrived at our designated area. Clearing security, I was then given an apron that read, "Eucharistic Minister." How humbled and proud I felt being part of such an awesome event and being given the gift of distributing the Body of Christ.

The morning was enveloped in thick fog and there was great concern that the poor visibility would prevent the landing of the papal helicopter. Great relief and joyous shouts abounded as we watched the fog quickly being swept away. Witnessing our Holy Father's arrival was a miracle in itself. The scene will always be embedded in my memory. Experiencing our Church in the multitude spread out on the hillsides recaptured once again the Gospel account in Mark 6:30 of Jesus feeding his people.

Thousands upon thousands of us were fed! The Spirit of the Lord was very much alive and visible in all those gathered. It was hard to hold back the tears as I looked out on the sea of faces and the hungry hearts that came to receive the Bread of Life. It was obvious then, as it is today, the important role our Holy Father plays in unifying God's Church and elevating our awareness of the sanctity of the Holy Mass. Being a eucharistic minister at the Holy Father's Mass has led me into a deeper understanding of this.

Another ministry that has become an important part of my life is the ministry to shut-ins. Every Sunday my husband and I go from Mass down to the rest home in our town to be with the elderly. We have been given the great privilege of bringing Jesus to them, not only in the Scriptures but also in Communion. We are an extension of the church family that brings living hope in the Eucharist. How their faces light up when they see us coming!

When I first started going into these homes, I was overwhelmed by the smell, the outbursts, and the eyes of loneliness. Many times, I would leave in tears with a feeling of great sadness. It's not always easy to expose ourselves to this side of life, and it is frightening to come into contact with places such as these, for it quickly makes us think of the reality of our own mortality. The material things we strive toward, protect, hoard, and sacrifice for mean nothing as one gets to this advanced stage in life.

We soon begin to see that the most important lasting treasure is another person's love, caring, and concern. Many of these people are forgotten, considered out of touch and useless. I quiver when I hear the verbiage on euthanasia and the apathetic way this topic is presented. The natural course of each person's God-given life is being threatened today as some strive to persuade society to justify and legalize this sinful act in the name of so-called compassion. We cannot play God, nor should we interfere with his divine plan for our lives. His timing for life and death must always remain in his hands. It saddens me to think that I or others would ever be deprived of the privilege to walk the end of life's journey with these precious ones.

I will always treasure this gift of being involved with ministry to the shut-ins. What grace I receive when I look into their eyes and experience Jesus in the flesh before me in the disguise of these valuable, often overlooked people. In serving them, I am serving God. I can't be a Mother Teresa, but I can be an extension of her in my own town, and in my own small way. I call it "The Gift of Love" ministry. Over the years, we have said good-bye to many of these saints. I like to believe that those we have touched with God's love are now interceding for us in their heavenly home. The promised place, where there is no more sickness, tears, pain, or loneliness, just pure joy. Thank you, Lord, for allowing us, like Veronica, to wipe your face in the suffering, lonely, and forgotten!

The Treasure of the Rosary

Twenty-five years ago, a dear friend, Pat, and I started praying the rosary together. This was at a time when many Catholics had put their beads aside and begun to regard them as obsolete. There was a strong inner call to dust off our rosaries and join our Blessed Mother in prayer. Each week, without fail, we would come together to pray for our family, friends, the lost, lonely, and suffering among those we knew. We soon began to extend our prayers to the concerns we heard on the news or read about in the newspaper. Over the years others have joined our group.

The power of prayer extends far and wide. For instance, during the Middle East crisis, our group offered encouragement by writing letters and sending rosaries to our service people. Some wrote back in gratitude for the support and strength they received. It is known that through the powerful prayer of the rosary, wars have been ended and others prevented. What tremendous hope this offers, not only for those wars on the battlefield, but also for those wars that go on within our own daily lives. What better "weapon" to have than the instrument of healing and mercy that our Blessed Mother holds out to us in the gift of the rosary. Today, the rosary remains an integral part of my daily prayer life; and yes, Pat and I still meet to pray it together!

Our Blessed Mother calls out to each of us, especially to her daughters of today through her example to be reconcilers, to lift up and not to tear down—to refrain from the desires to compete, and instead be facilitators of Christ's peace to all those with whom we come into contact, at home, in our neighborhoods, and in our communities. We are called to be reconcilers not only with others, but with ourselves too. Women must recognize the wounded hearts they harbor, and ask for God's love and mercy to heal the anger, resentment, and rebellion that lie deep within. I would encourage the women of today to be reconciled unto God.

Holy, Anointing Spirit

Several years ago I had the wonderful opportunity to attend a "Life in the Spirit" seminar. This came at a time in my life when I felt a void, a hunger within that just couldn't be satisfied. If you asked me if I knew God personally then, I would have had to honestly answer "not really." I loved him, however, with a reverence I was taught from my childhood, but I didn't know how to take him into my everyday life.

I wasn't familiar with the God I could turn to any time of the day. I did not truly know the inner companion who would speak to my heart and be with me in my joys and sorrows like a "daddy"; a God who strengthens me in my role as wife, mother, daughter, and friend. I was not aware that our Lord wanted to guide me in all my decisions and help me find my true purpose in life. On an everyday, personal level I thought this kind of God did not exist. How wrong I was! At the Life in the Spirit Seminar, something happened that stirred my spirit and left me with an inner glow and a hunger to delve more deeply into the Word of God.

The Holy Spirit came upon Our Lady and the apostles in the Upper Room, filling them with the power that set them free from fear, doubt, and confusion (see Acts 2). He breathed purpose and vision into them. He gave them new eyes, and a new heart with which to love. They were baptized with the Holy Spirit, filled with power to change and accept God's love for them. God's Word and truth were embedded in their hearts. No more luke-warmness, but strong convictions were instilled to know, love, and serve God by being servants and proclaiming his message of love.

This time was another beginning for me, too. I wasn't, of course, in that Upper Room, but I recognized the need to ask for a release of the Holy Spirit in my life. The indwelling of the Holy Spirit came through my baptism and confirmation, but I didn't fully understand his presence. I needed to be reawakened with his powerful spirit and to learn more about the Third Person of the Blessed Trinity, who moves and breathes and has his being within me.

Reawakening to the presence of the Holy Spirit in me, I began to use more fully the gifts he had given me. I also came to realize that he is the Paraclete, the Helper who brings all my life's experiences and their subsequent lessons into focus. He is the inner voice that urges me to turn the other cheek, the one that leads me to a sick friend's side. He is that source that lifts the heaviness of grief, the light of truth that sets me free. He is the Love between the Father and Son that runs deep within my soul. Yes, I heard with new ears our Lord's command to "go forth and be fishers of men" (Mt 5:19).

I find the Holy Spirit is *the source* of strength. It seems when I forget this important ingredient and start building on my own power I soon begin to lose stability and quickly sway with the tide of life. He is the love of the Father and the Son who awakens my faith and purpose and helps me grow in spiritual maturity. "I cannot confess Jesus is Lord unless I am guided by the Holy Spirit" (1 Cor 12:3), who continually reveals his majesty in my life.

Since I have been growing in the Spirit, my prayer life has become increasingly important to me. I rise early in the morning while the house is still quiet, and I begin my day in praise and thanksgiving for another day of life. I offer God, Our Father, my day, work, and play. I ask him to bless and protect all my loved ones, and to strengthen us for the day's journey, that it be in accord with his holy will, bringing him honor and glory in all that we do.

Communion of Saints

I often think of the saints and martyrs, and the roads of life they have helped open up through their hard work, dedication, and examples. When I read their life stories, I find a ray of hope that speaks to my own fallen nature. I can't help but be inspired by their sacrifice and ongoing conversions.

Saint Monica is an example of motherly persistence. She reminds me that through prayer God hears a mother's cry. Saint Monica was a mother on a mission who never gave up her purpose of bringing forth true life. For years she pleaded for God's intervention in the life of her son, Augustine. She repeatedly stepped out in faith, powerfully demonstrating the persuasive influence of her womanhood. Saint Augustine is now known as one of the greatest doctors of the church, his conversion story being intimately linked with the prayers of his mother. As a mother, I have come to call upon the faith of Saint Monica, and to ask for her help when I feel threatened by seeing my own children being uprooted in the ways of the world.

Another woman whom I love very much is Saint Anne. She is Mary's mother and my grandmother—at least I like to think of her this way. I have the privilege to have her name attached to mine: "Maureen Ann." Over the years many mothers have turned to Saint Anne with many different requests. I join my voice with theirs. Saint Anne was the grandmother to the King of Kings. Though not much is known about her interaction with her divine grandson, I would like to believe Saint Anne was very much a part of Jesus' life. Grandmothers play a very special role in the family. Their wisdom, experience, and faith are very important, especially in this day and age, when the family is being attacked on so many fronts. Situations like divorce, abortion, drugs, and suicide throw a family into total pain. A grandmother can be like a beacon that helps provide direction for the confused and lost. I will always hold Saint Anne in high esteem.

One needs strength, grace, perseverance, and a dying to self to help span the troubled highways of life. The saints weren't always saints, and their lives weren't always lived with heroic perfection. While on earth they were saints *in the making,* and so too are we. The rich testimonies of the saints' lives continue to inspire me to follow more closely in their path, asking for their help and intercession as I try to pick up the crosses in my life and bridge the road for the good of others.

The Catholic Woman of God

The teachings of the Church give a source of direction that help me stay focused. There are many false messages out there today that come packaged in varied forms. No one can dispute that mankind has adopted values and standards contrary to those of God. "Woe unto them that call evil good and good evil: that put darkness for light, and light for darkness, that put bitter for sweet and sweet for bitter" (Is 5:20). This passage from Isaiah speaks to my heart of the times in which we are living today.

Hands that shed innocent blood and call it "a woman's right." The arts, the media, and the movie industry, which portray fornication, adultery, murder, pornography, and violence in the guise of compassion, commonality, and entertainment—it frightens me to think of what's coming next when I hear of statements like "death with dignity," "depopulation," "cloning," "organ harvesting," and "earth worship." I can understand why there are so many apparitions taking place around the world. The darkness of our times needs the power of God's grace and mercy to fill this land and help purify our senses. Mary, the new Eve, is sent to lead us away from sin and destruction, and point us heavenward. Our Lady is ever mindful of the great dangers and evils that threaten to overpower mankind in our time. She continues to remind us with the words she once gave to the servants at Cana: "Do whatever he tells you" (Jn 2:5). For us this means being children of the Light who is Christ, and turning away from the darkness of the world. When the Virgin of Nazareth gave her yes to bring Christ into the world for our salvation, her yes was also meant to be inscribed into our hearts. By her example of submission we are taught to also echo our "yes" in proclaiming how our soul magnifies the Lord, and how our spirit rejoices in God our Savior. Being a Catholic woman of God in the twenty-first century is a challenge.

There is much talk about equality, rights, and liberation. There seems to be a contagious chant that echoes throughout this land: "I will not serve." We live in very turbulent times, and it's sad to see the brainwashing women are getting with today's modern depiction of what it means to be a fully "liberated woman." This leaves many terribly confused about their identity, and their need to prove their self-importance.

Many women think that to be a modern, intelligent, and "together" woman, one must battle the male sex, be independent, and find comfort in "female victimization." The extra baggage that is being carried is a pity. I know, I have carried a bit of this baggage myself, especially in those times I thought I wasn't being heard, understood, or valued. More honestly, I carried that baggage when I didn't accept myself for who I was, and fought against our God-made differences, and allowed pride to block humility.

Understanding Our Dignity and Vocation

As you have followed me through this chapter I have shared the different ministries in which I have been privileged to participate, and the ways in which God has called me to serve him. The last one I will share with you is a ministry for Catholic women called *Magnificat*. I am honored to be a part of such a wonderful group of liberated women who silently chant, "I will serve." Through *Magnificat*, women are guided by hope, peace, and joy instead of distrust, defiance, and despair. *Magnificat* helps women renew their minds by sorting out false doctrines of women's spirituality that tend to de-Christianize and repaganize. Through *Magnificat*, women are discovering their true nature and genuine femininity.

We are not about male bashing, or seeking the limelight, or undermining the pope and the Magisterium of the Church. We firmly uphold the papacy and submit to his God-given authority. We are about prayer, sharing the Good News, growing in the Spirit, and bearing the light of Christ, as Mary did in the visitation with Elizabeth. When women come together in this way, great things happen! The mystery of Christ grows in each one of us. There is a transforming power in one who bears the Lord. His light "shines" from within us the radiance of his love to each other. The Scriptural story of the Visitation clarifies our understanding of what it means to be a woman impregnated with the light of the Lord. Since I became an active participant in the ministry of *Magnificat,* I have grown so much more in love with life, with my husband, my family, my church, and my community. I keep discovering more about myself, and the wonderful way God made women. We are a special design.

In fashioning the woman, God said that she would be a "helpmate, suitable for man" (Gn 2:18). I understand this to mean that I am given as my husband's companion, not as his *possession.* This doesn't mean that woman is inferior to man, or created merely to *serve him.* God made woman and man equal. Vastly different in body structure yet with the same dignity. Their diversity in unity is a fuller reflection of the image of God, and in no way can male or female attain fulfillment apart from this image and likeness, whether one is married, single, priest, or religious.

Our Holy Father has stated this so beautifully in his Apostolic Letter, *Mulieris Dignitatem* (On the dignity and vocation of women). It is a rich and innovative document that holds great spiritual enlightenment. Pope John Paul II is very forthright in discussing issues that concern the rights of women. He adamantly upholds their dignity in his words and deeds, emphasizing the unique qualities that all women possess in the eyes of God. In this document, the Holy Father challenges women to discover their true identity and vocation in the "order of love." Unfortunately, this challenge is not being heard by everyone. We see the radical feminists striving to change the feminine identity. This is largely due to the misunderstanding of their own dignity and feminine genius. Sadly, they set themselves and other women up to relinquish their specific gifts of feminine insight, compassion, and understanding, in exchange for a falsified sense of "empowerment."

The Teaching of John Paul II

I am strengthened by our Holy Father's position:

> The church gives thanks for each and every woman: for mothers, for sisters, for wives; for women consecrated in virginity; for women dedicated to the many human beings who await the gratuitous love for another; for women who watch over persons in the family, which is the fundamental sign of the human community; for women who work professionally, and who at times are burdened by a great social responsibility; for "perfect" women and for "weak" women—for all women as they have come forth from the heart of God in all the beauty and richness of their femininity; as they have been embraced by His eternal love; as, together with men, they are the pilgrims on this earth, which is the temporal "homeland" of all people and is transformed sometimes into a "valley of tears"; as they assume, together with men, a common responsibility for the destiny of humanity according to daily necessities and according to that definitive destiny which the human family has in God himself, in the bosom of the ineffable Trinity.
>
> The Church gives thanks for all the manifestations of the feminine "genius" which have appeared in the course of history, in the midst of all people and nations; she gives thanks for all the charisma which the Holy Spirit distributes to women in the history of the people of God, for all the victories which she owes to their faith, hope and charity: she gives thanks for all the fruits of feminine holiness.

The church asks at the same time that these invaluable "manifestations of the spirit" (cf. 1 Corinthians 12:4 ff.), which with great generosity are poured forth upon the "daughters" of the eternal Jerusalem, may be recognized and appreciated so that they may return for the common good of the church and of humanity, especially in our times. Meditating on the biblical mystery of the "woman," the church prays that in this mystery all women may discover themselves and their supreme vocation.[1]

After reading this document, how could anyone doubt the love and sincerity of this beautiful man, our Holy Father? He is certainly not out of touch with the role of women in the Church and world. Pope John Paul is a magnet, a global leader who continues to help reshape our deformed world. He has experienced the death of loved ones and tasted the dangers and hardships of survival himself. He understands what it means to be oppressed, for he lived under the tyranny of Hitler during the Second World War and later the Communist regime. He comes to us with a wealth of knowledge and wisdom that makes him unafraid to speak out and challenge world leaders on issues of human dignity and social justice. No other pope has brought the Vatican out to the world as Pope John Paul II has done, especially to the youth of the world. We must not forget his mission.

The Eternal Jerusalem

Being Catholic is a privilege. Jesus established the "One, Holy, Catholic, and Apostolic Church." It is awesome to realize this is the Church to which I belong, the church family that has lasted over two thousand years. I rejoice in the promise of Jesus that even the gates of hell shall not prevail against it. Over the years I have come to understand that Catholicism is not something to know only with my mind, but instead it must be a religion of the heart that directs my daily life. The joy for all Catholic Christians is putting our Eucharistic Lord at the center of our lives with enthusiasm, for only "He is the Way, the Truth, and the Life."

This world is like a vast garden. Each person is planted in the soil of life. No matter where we are positioned on this planet, we are meant to bloom and bring forth the fragrance of his love. I am thankful for the words that were given to me in a dream, "May the flowers never lose their meaning—and may you find your purpose in life and know that you matter."

I have come to realize that I am that flower in God's garden that is meant to bloom fully. I am finding my purpose by knowing, loving, and serving God, as his beloved and in my calling to love and serve others as a wife, mother, grandmother, and friend. In giving of myself I am discovering more fully my true strength as a woman and the deeper significance of my femininity. I know that I matter, that I have purpose and meaning, according to the perfect plan of God.

Just as God made manifest his wonders in Mary, he continues to work them in us. I truly believe we all make a difference in the Church and, through the Church, in the world. My prayer is simply this, "Help me, Holy Spirit, always to imitate Mary, your spouse, in *my Fiat—my Magnificat.*"

PART FOUR

The Call to Love: Vessels of Mercy

"He has come to the help of his servant Israel
for he has remembered his promise of mercy,
the promise he made to our fathers,
to Abraham and his children forever."

To believe means *to abandon oneself* to the truth of the word of the living God, knowing and humbly recognizing "How inscrutable are his judgments and how unsearchable his ways" (Rom 11:33). Mary, who by the eternal will of the Most High stands, one might say, at the very center of those "inscrutable ways" and "unsearchable judgments" of God, conforms herself to them in the dim light of faith, accepting fully and with a ready heart everything that is decreed in the divine plan.[1]

We are called to be people of faith. Set before us, giving us example, is the presence of Our Lady. Mary *believes*, she *abandons* herself! In this manner, she becomes a living Vessel of Mercy.

The fullness of truth, *the Word* of the living God, is Jesus Christ himself. The Blessed Virgin embodied the greatest of faiths, even greater than that of Abraham. She accepted completely the Truth, who was conceived by the Holy Spirit within her. Abandoned to God most fully, she conformed her will to fulfill God's will, and the Word of God "became flesh and dwelt among us" as a result. In the words of her *Magnificat,* Mary reminds us of the genesis of the covenant relationship between God and Abraham. The promise of mercy made to our fathers will be fulfilled in and through her. Because of this, the inheritance of David will manifest itself in and through her Son. A new kingdom is "at hand":

When at the Annunciation Mary hears of the Son whose Mother she is to become and to whom "she will give the name Jesus" (= Savior), she also learns that "the Lord God will give to him the throne of his father David," and that, "he will reign over the house of Jacob for ever and of his kingdom there will be no end" (Luke 1:32-33). The hope of the whole of Israel was directed toward this. The promised Messiah is to be "great," and the heavenly messenger also announces that *"he will be great"*—great both by bearing the name of *Son of the Most High* and by the fact that he is to assume the *inheritance of David.* He is therefore to be a king, he is to reign "over the house of Jacob." Mary had grown up in the midst of these expectations of her people....[2]

In this newly inaugurated kingdom, Mary would be a servant-queen. Bearing the fulfillment of this promise of mercy who is Jesus the Savior within her, Mary becomes the Queen of Mercy; the *servant* of Merciful Love. As Queen of Mercy, she is intent on consoling her children, not in rendering justice. Therefore, her love invokes confidence. The mercy of God is transmitted through the heart of a young virgin; the promise of God is fulfilled after generations of waiting and is translated by the blood of her Son into the new and everlasting covenant. Mary, the figure of the biblical "woman," stands at the threshold of hope, the dawn of the messianic age. She recognizes herself to be a daughter of Abraham through whom the faithfulness of God is manifest in a most miraculous conception. She sees the promise now extending to "his children forever," and will, in time, accept "his children" as *her own.*

She is conscious that the promise made to the fathers, first of all "to Abraham and to his posterity forever," is being fulfilled in herself. She is aware that concentrated within herself as the Mother of Christ *is the whole of salvific economy,* in which "from age to age" is manifested he, who as the God of the Covenant, "remembers his mercy."[3]

In the life of Mary we reach the summit of the call to holiness: union with God. In this union, she is the model of perfect love, a model for all humanity. Finally, she exemplifies the gift of femininity in the area of life-giving love. She dwells for all eternity in the heart of God and as the New Eve, mother of all the living, she longs for us to share eternal life with God. This longing for the salvation of souls is the culminating point of the initial conversion experience; for Our Lady, it is intimately connected to her role as "Theotókos." Mary's motherhood is not limited to the biological process of giving birth, for in giving birth to Christ, who is the head of his mystical body, the Church, she gives birth to the members of the body as well. As spiritual mother, she loves us all with the love of God. "God is love," proclaims the New Testament, "and whoever remains in love, remains in God and God in him.... Let us love, then, because he has loved us first" (1 Jn 4:16, 19). So, she leads the way for us, giving birth to *the Way*.

The chapters in this section demonstrate the great gift and capacity for love with which women are endowed. Recognizing their heritage as daughters of Abraham, these women have trusted in the unchanging promise of God, even if their own lives have taken many turns. They have lived lives of faith, seeking the truth. Inspired by Our Lady, they have accepted the call to abandonment to divine love. In loving, they, too, have given "birth," and their spiritual children are many. Together they rejoice in the fulfillment of the expectations of generations passed; together they look forward in intercessory prayer and transmit God's mercy to "his children forever."

Chapter 10

Marika's Story

MARIKA GUBASCI

I Have Called You by Name

Thus says Yahweh: "Do not be afraid for I have redeemed you: I have called you by your name, you are mine. Should you pass through the sea, I will be with you; or through rivers, they will not swallow you up. Should you walk through fire, you will not be scorched and the flames will not burn you. For I am Yahweh, your God, the Holy One of Israel, your Saviour."

ISAIAH 43:1-2

I never was a very good sleeper; I am used to waking up in the early hours of the morning. It is a special time for me, enjoying the peace and serenity around me and getting in touch with my inner self and my Maker.

On one particular morning in early February 1977, I was lying in bed wide awake when I suddenly heard a voice, a man's voice in a clear Hungarian accent, calling out my name, "Marika ...!"

I sat up in bed and turned to my husband, Miklos, who was fast asleep beside me, "Did you call me?" I asked. Half awake, he said, "No," and went straight back to sleep. I lay down again, thinking over the experience, and feeling a certain peace flowing through me. I stayed like that for a while, then later I got up, started my work for the day, and life went on as usual.

Then, about a week later, exactly the same thing happened. I remember praying, asking God, "Lord, if this is you, please identify yourself, reveal yourself to me!"

Another week passed; another morning came, when I heard the same voice calling: "Marika ...!" I sat up in bed, alert, listening with expectant faith, and the voice called again, "I have called you by your name ...!"

For a moment I was paralyzed. The voice was strong and clear and I was filled with the Holy Spirit. Joy and peace swept over my soul and I started crying. "Thank you, Lord, praise you, Jesus. Glory to you for calling me and for whatever it is you want me to do, I say, *'Yes, yes, yes, O Lord....'"*

I think I had wanted to say "yes" to Jesus from the time I was a very young child but I did not know how. My first acquaintance with Jesus came when I was five years old. You could say he first called me by name then when I was baptized "Marika," in the Franciscan church next to my home in Budapest. This event, under the careful tutelage of these saintly men of the Order of Saint Francis, was a divine turning point for me.

My parents were Jews—not practicing Jews; perhaps they were agnostic. In that year, 1938, Hitler was planning to invade Hungary. My father was an engineer and owned a large factory. My mother was a well-known opera singer who traveled much of the year, singing with the finest voices, Gigli and others, at La Scala and other famous opera houses. I was a lonely child, left mainly in the care of a governess in a luxurious sixth-floor apartment in Budapest. From the age of two and a half I had also been a sick child after a careless nanny had left me frozen and wet in the snow one day so that I developed a kidney disease and spent three years in a hospital.

Well aware of what the Nazis were doing to Jews in Germany, my parents were frightened of what could happen in Hungary. They reasoned that if they could take on a Christian religion they would be safe. So, not being at all particular about the religious aspect of what they were doing, they started shopping around for a minister, priest, or religion who would take them on immediately and give them a certificate without really studying. They felt the matter was too urgent for any delay.

A Franciscan friary was practically next door to our apartment block, and the parish priest agreed to receive the family into the Catholic Church after a crash course in the faith. I first learned about it when my Catholic nanny was dressing me in my best blue silk dress and black patent leather shoes. She tried to tell me in a few words what was going to happen before I was taken down to the church where I had never been before.

Once inside, I was absolutely enchanted by the beauty around me—the statues, the golden decorations, the whole atmosphere of the place. I think the delight must have shone in my eyes, as afterward the priest encouraged me to visit him with my nanny. He also visited our home very often, and then, a year later, when I joined the school, he was my religion teacher. He talked so beautifully about Jesus to me that I fell in love with Jesus and the whole Catholic religion. He prepared me for first Holy Communion and not long after that he was sent away to the missions to Africa—the Belgian Congo—and on his tenth day there he was killed by the Africans. I have never forgotten him as the first one to introduce God to me and me to God.

My childish attraction to the beauty of the Church was to grow with the years. The Catholic tradition still speaks to my senses and especially in its Liturgy and rituals, which express the deepest feelings of our nature. As a child I grew to love the Liturgy of the Holy Mass, and now as I grow older this love has deepened.

The Star of David

After four years of primary school, my parents sent me to an exclusive Catholic school, Saint Margaret's. I had hardly been there a year when my life changed dramatically. By this time the Germans were in control of Hungary and Jews were obliged to wear a large yellow star. I remember the day the Germans came to our home. From our apartment window I saw them coming up the street in little carts with boxlike seats on top. They gave each of us a yellow Star of David to wear, and we were told that we had to wear it all the time. It was my first impression of being a Jew, and I hated it. I would not wear the star, I was so embarrassed.

At school one day in 1943, three German SS troopers stormed into our classroom with their guns drawn. They asked for me by name. They told Sister that I was a Jew—a Jewess—hiding from the Germans and that they wanted to take me away. They quickly stuck the Star of David, cut out of yellow vinyl or linen, on my dress, and pulled me out of the bench to the front of the room. I'll never forget the Sister saying, "You dirty pig! You never told us you were a Jew!" and how the kids in the class, all ten-year-olds, started pointing their fingers at me and spitting at me, "You dirty Jew!" That was the first encounter in my life where I suddenly met the agonizing question: What am I? Am I a Jewess, or am I a Christian? The sister did not let the Germans take me away. The principal came in and said she would take the necessary steps. When they had gone, she rang my parents and they collected me. We changed our address, moving to Pest for a while, into a little one-room apartment. One day a friend of my father rang him and said urgently, "Don't ask questions. Just get out. Now. Don't ask questions. *Go. Now!*" Soup was bubbling on the stove for dinner and we left it there as we ran out, just as we were, down the steps. As we ran down the stairs the Gestapo were riding up in the lift! For the next two years I was in hiding with my parents.

My parents were very bitter that despite a change of religion they were still considered Jews by the Germans and the Hungarian government. Of course they decided they would have nothing further to do with the Catholic faith. However, I decided to stay with it. I was a

Christian and I was going to persevere with a Christian life from then on. I treasured an ebony crucifix that my godmother gave me when I was baptized. I accidentally left it behind as our flight from death continued.

We had so many different hiding places. A Unitarian minister, who was a friend of my aunt, who had married a gentile, helped us. We hid anywhere we could—in workshops, under a stage, and finally in a hospital. The Germans were leaving as the Russians were coming in. The hospital was bombed and operated mainly underground. My father pretended to be a Red Cross worker, and by a sheer miracle, and the confusion around at the time, he was accepted and we were given a small room to ourselves. One night while I was alone, there was an air raid and the lights went out. I fumbled, feeling my way along a wall until I found a door. I opened it and went in. The door slammed behind me and, still trying to feel my way, I discovered I must have been in the hospital morgue, along with the broken, limbless bodies of air-raid victims. I was there for nine hours before I was found. I spent much of the time praying.

Refugees, Again

When the Russians took over, initially there was more freedom. Our first home had been bombed out but we were able to go back to our apartment in Pest, which since we had left had been used by about sixty other Jews. First of all, though, it had to be cleaned. Excrement was thick on the small balcony from the time the sewage system broke down, but in it I found my godmother's crucifix! All the furniture had been burnt and the ebony cross was gone, but the metal body was still there. My mother told me not to touch it but I rescued the body, washed it in snow, and later put it on a new wooden cross, and I still have it with me. Members of my godmother's family were jewelers, from whose shop my father had bought beautiful jewelry for my mother. When he knew the Germans were coming, my father had collected money and the jewels and put them in two jars. He took me to the cemetery and, selecting an old grave, buried the jars there. He made sure I would remember where it was. We found them still safely there after the war. Our lives had been spared by God's grace, and we tentatively started them again.

Gradually, after 1945, daily life took on some normalcy. Father reopened his factory and built it up. I went back to school. However, as soon as school started, persecution began again. The Christians did not want to take me in because I was a Jew, and the Jews did not want me because I had left my faith. The more persecution I went through, the more I loved Jesus, and the more I wanted to serve him with all my heart and all my soul and all my life.

My love for Jesus was growing. I spent as much time as possible in my parish church, which was run by Carmelite priests. I felt the need to be near Jesus in the Blessed Sacrament. I decided that I would join the Carmelite convent in Budapest and I would give my life to him in full. About this time, however, the Communists were growing increasingly strong in Budapest, and one day, when I was in the second year of my novitiate, they took over the convent by force and we had one hour to leave. God had other plans for my vocation. This time in the convent, however, would seal in my heart a love of prayer.

So here I was out in the world again, this time persecuted by the Russians. At school I had learned typing and shorthand, and I was able to get work at the University of Budapest as secretary to the chancellor. I also studied there while I was working. I stayed at the university until I left Hungary five years later. I met my husband, Michael, whom I had known when I was six years old. He was a gentile, a Presbyterian, and had been very good to us while we were in hiding. He is ten years older than I am and he had always loved the little Jewish Christian girl. My father gave me money to pay our way over the border. We needed a guide to avoid the guards in the towers and to find a place where the barbed wire barriers were down.

We left two days before Christmas 1956. We hid and slept in the daytime and crawled through the snow at night. Our guide left us before we knew we were through, and it was not until I heard German voices that I knew we had made it. By this time I was bleeding. I was frozen. I had no clothes but the ones I stood up in. I spent my first days of freedom in Vienna in the camp hospital. There were a hundred thousand refugees in Vienna then. Michael got work as a butcher in the city and I as an interpreter at the Canadian Embassy, as I could speak Hungarian, German, and English.

First of all, though, we were married. Three other couples were married with us in Saint Stephen's Cathedral in Vienna by a refugee Franciscan priest. Once again, Saint Francis was with me through this humble servant of the Church. It was a very poor little ceremony, but as we came out of the church a woman came up to us with some flowers and gave each bride a flower. "It is not fitting for a bride not to have a flower on her wedding day," she said. It was a happy symbol for our new life. We planned to emigrate. My father had always liked Australia, although he had never been there. He did not know it had been called on the old maps the "Land of the Holy Spirit." I did not know this either, but I was to find there a new revelation of life in the Spirit that would profoundly change the way I lived.

I was determined my marriage would be a completely new beginning for me. I would leave off the old things and especially my Jewish background. With the New Year of 1957, we went to the civil registrar in Vienna as soon as it opened on January 2. The law required a civil marriage service before a religious one, and in filling out official papers I changed my Jewish identity as far as I could. Sadly, I felt only shame in thinking of my Jewish heritage. I will return to this point later, however.

In a sense I felt I was reborn. The next thing was to find a new country. We knew we could not stay in Austria, although I spoke German and could have easily fit into life there. Austria had too many refugees there already, so we had to look elsewhere. We put our names down for countries of the New World—Canada, South Africa, America, and Australia, and we would have to go to whichever one agreed to take us first.

The Land of the Holy Spirit

On May 1, 1957, we arrived at night at the Wagga Wagga migrant camp in Australia. The next morning we saw a utility truck outside and found it was going to Melbourne, so we asked the driver to take us, too. The driver took us aboard and we shivered in the back of his truck while he drove all through the night and left us next morning in front of the Melbourne Town Hall. We stood there looking at the traffic and realized there was a whole new world in front of us.

Once again my life changed, however, as I became pregnant shortly after our arrival. I struggled with pregnancy, ill health, and the difficulties of establishing ourselves in our new country on only one small income. As for my faith life, it was a struggle too. After leaving Hungary and getting married, our lives centered on the physical effort of survival. We made another move, this time from Melbourne to Sydney. After a year, we were able to buy a delicatessen shop and residence.

The shop entailed working long hours, seven days a week. Then I had another baby, the next year I had a miscarriage, and after that another pregnancy. There was no time, I felt now, even to go to Mass, and I was worried about the Church's teaching on birth control. A non-Catholic spouse cannot always understand the Catholic position and does not always encourage it. I was in a spiritual desert, which lasted for about eighteen years. I acknowledged the authority of the Church and accepted its guidelines, but at this time I thought them irrelevant to my life and ignored them. This is different from becoming one's own authority in opposition to that of the Church. I think that once we lose respect for the authority of the Church it is very easy to lose faith altogether. I never quite did that. My faith was at a low ebb, however. I would say it was in abeyance, "on hold." Yet God was moving in my spirit and took drastic measures to "get my attention."

The Call to Follow Him

In 1970 I had two children, and was pregnant again. I was then involved in a car accident that left me almost totally disabled. For the next five years I had different medical and surgical treatments that included an operation to fuse my spine and physical therapy five days a week. I could only sit in the shop while my condition gradually worsened. After five years I could endure it no longer and we decided to sell the business. With the proceeds we put a deposit on a house and took a trip to Hungary to visit Michael's family.

I remember that on the plane going over, I had a strange sensation. The words of the hymn "Nearer My God to Thee" kept running through my head as I looked out at the sky. I thought it was funny to think I was nearer to God, being nearer to the sky, but the words persisted, as did the idea that God was calling me again to follow him more closely. While in Hungary I found an old confessor whom I had known years before, and I went to Confession and Communion for the first time in years. I was so happy! I was uplifted, and once again, on the plane returning to Australia, I had the feeling of getting closer to God.

Back in Sydney, we moved into our new house and Michael started his wholesale butcher business. I could no longer work, with the state of my back, but I could go to Mass in my new Franciscan parish church. It was 1975 and I started going to weekday Mass with renewed fervor. The words of the doxology, "Through him, with him, and in him, in the unity of the Holy Spirit ..." struck deeply into my soul as I committed myself to a deeper spiritual life. I was aware of the significance of being again in a Franciscan parish as I had been when I was first baptized. It was a Franciscan priest who had officiated at our marriage, and here again there were Franciscans to help me. A young Irish Franciscan befriended the family and often visited our home. He was there one night when I could hardly sit still for the pain in my back, and I asked him, *as he knew everything,* did he know of a way I could be cured of my back problem? I had tried all that the doctors could do.

"Yes," he said. "I do know a way."

"Tell me," I said. Yet he answered,

"You will have to find it out yourself."

I was not so pleased with this cryptic answer but he would say no more, until some time later he was again visiting our house while the family was watching television. I suddenly thought to ask him what he thought of the charismatic movement. He looked closely at me and said,

"Why do you ask?"

"I don't know. I have never heard the word before and I don't know what it means."

He was visibly moved and said, "I have been praying for a year that you would ask me that question." He said that he met with a prayer group weekly.

"Today is its day. Can you get ready and come now?"

So we went with him: my mother (now living with me), my three children, and I. I entered into the room hardly able to move. We were greeted warmly by a nun. About twenty people were there, and I thought as I heard them praying how strange they all looked. I had never seen anything like it. People had their hands up, while some had their mouths open. There was a priest praying, another Franciscan, and he said, "Somebody is here who was injured in a car accident, and God wants to heal her. Would you please put your hand up?"

I looked around. No hands were up, but I knew I had been injured in a car accident, so I put one finger up. The priest came over to me and put his hand on my head and prayed in a strange language. I know now it was in tongues, the language of the Holy Spirit. All I could think of was, "How soon can we get out of this stupid place?" I then realized something was happening in my back. The priest looked at me and said, "In the name of Jesus, get up."

Incredibly, I stood up!

"In the name of Jesus, touch your toes."

This was getting more absurd. I had not been able to do that in years. "I can't do that," I said. Yet he replied,

"I said, in the name of Jesus, touch your toes."

I bent down and touched my toes. It did not hurt. And once again, I stood straight up!

"Once more."

I did it again. And again. Then I went up and down, like a yo-yo. I could *not believe* I had *no pain*. I could move freely. My mother and my children were as excited as I was. It was the feast of Saint Clare, August 11, 1976.

I could hardly believe I had been healed, even when I got out of bed the next morning and my husband saw me moving without pain. I decided I would take my little five-year-old daughter for a quiet walk on the beach, where I could test my newfound freedom. On the beach she danced ahead of me then turned to run back toward me. "Lord," I said as she rushed to me, "if I can lift her up all right I'll know I'm healed." I grabbed her and lifted her up. I felt no pain and I knew God had healed me. The pain has not returned in over twenty years.

The priest who prayed for me came the next day to ask how I was. "Perfect," was all I could say.

He said that when God touches someone in such a special way it can mean that he is giving that person a work to do—perhaps in my case, even a gift of healing. He asked if I would like to join him in his healing ministry as a member of a prayer team. Of course, I was happy to join him. So began a most incredible time for me, as I witnessed extraordinary healings at the prayer meetings and elsewhere. Then my parish priest asked if I would like to work in the Franciscan friary. I cooked for the friars as well as looking after the office and telephone. It was about this time that I woke one morning and heard my name being called, "Marika..."

A Life of Prayer—A Ministry of Healing

After my own healing I *did* feel called to pray for the healing of others, and I joined in with the members of the prayer group who had prayed for me. As time passed, the demand for prayers for healing increased to such an extent that we decided to hold regular morning meetings on Thursdays between 10:00 A.M. and 12:00 noon.

At the first meeting only about ten people came, and the priest who prayed with us arrived late. He apologized for this. He explained that he had been so busy that he had not yet had time to say Mass that day.

Would the people mind if he said Mass and prayed separately with them afterward? Of course, we all were delighted with his suggestion. During the elevation of the chalice a man cried out, "Oh, my back is healed! I have no pain!" He had had cancer of the spine.

The next week there were about twenty people in attendance. Once again there was Mass, and again someone spontaneously cried out, "I am healed!" The physical healings that took place during the celebration of the Holy Mass were spontaneous, instantaneous, and complete. We were in awe of God's mercy.

The next week there were about forty people there, and more people claimed healing. We realized that people were healed just by being at the Mass; however, the tremendous healing power in the Eucharist was brought home to us in a concrete manner. Although each and every Mass brings healing, for us that was the start of our regular masses together, and the people called them *"healing masses."* Those of us in attendance soon came to realize the power for healing in *all the sacraments,* and especially in the Sacrament of Reconciliation.

Increasingly I felt the need for my own reconciliation. There was a blockage within myself that prevented my total surrender to God. I prayed that what this was would be revealed to me. Some months later I felt that the Lord was taking me by the hand back to the time of my baptism when I was five years old. I felt he was saying to me, "I am the light, the eternal light; follow the light. I want you to come out from hiding. I want to set you free. Step out in faith and confess the truth and the truth will set you free." It was a very strong message and I had no doubt that the Lord was talking to me. I could not sleep all night, and I kept asking the Lord to show me what he wanted me to do, but he just kept repeating, "Confess the truth."

The next day I went to my priest friend and confessed that I had concealed my Jewish background because I was ashamed of it. Later the members of the prayer group prayed for me for deliverance from this spirit of shame. Immediately I felt relief and release in the knowledge that God loved me just as I was. Later, alone in the church, I felt the Lord was talking to me, taking me further on:

I want to pour my gift of love upon you.... You did not choose me; I have chosen you. You have suffered persecution and humiliation while only a child because your blood is the same as my blood.... I want you to pray with people, people with broken hearts and people with problems similar to those you have had, and I will give them a new heart, like I have given you a new heart today.... I want you to have all the blessings and gifts of the first Christians. They were converts, too.... My own people crucified me, but you were not there.... Punish yourself no more for the sins of your fathers. I give you today the grace to accept your identity. Rejoice within your heart, my child.

I felt free, *truly free,* for the first time in my life. I could rejoice wholeheartedly with the people who attended the "Healing Masses," which were now a regular weekly feature at the church. The ten people at the first Mass grew at their peak to hundreds, even thousands, so that police were called to control the traffic on the street outside.

Priests came from all over Sydney to concelebrate, and the concept of "Healing Masses" spread not only through the Sydney diocese but also throughout the world. Today hardly a parish in Sydney is without a Healing Mass once a month. It is a Mass that designates the extra time needed for specific prayer requests for the healing of those in attendance. One priest from Westminster Cathedral in London came with his sister and young nephew, who was sick and needed prayer. The boy was healed and the priest returned to London and celebrated the first Healing Mass there.

As my healing ministry began I believed God was expecting me to do for others what he had done for me. My ministry relied on the charismatic gift of the *Word of Knowledge,* by which I was able to grasp *how* to pray for people. I felt inwardly directed to know how, when, and for what to pray.

Often people do not come straight out and ask for their real need for prayer. Priests say the same thing happens in the confessional. People do not at first bring out their real problems. This is especially true with sexual problems. It takes a good confessor, with care and discernment applied, so that people do not go away dissatisfied with "Three Hail Mary's" and "God bless you."

One day when I was not long into my ministry, I was cooking lunch for the friars and up to my elbows in hamburger and dough when the doorbell rang. People were at the front door, wanting the priest to pray for a paralyzed man. They had come a long distance and were not very happy when I had to tell them the priest was away but if they liked I would pray for him. Reluctantly they accepted my offer and carried the man, wrapped in a gray army blanket, into the church and put him on the back pew. The man had had an accident at his workplace and was now paralyzed. He had been engaged to be married but the girl had since entered a convent. He was now alone and miserable and unable to pursue what he believed was his true vocation. I sat beside him and suggested he offer his loss to God, and I prayed that God would take his offering, bless it, and give it back to him. The man suddenly said, "Move over, I want to get out." As I moved he pushed himself to the end of the seat and slowly started walking, down the aisle toward the altar. He was shouting; he kept repeating, "I can walk, I can walk!"

Just then, the parish priest came into the church, looking for me to give me a message. He was astonished to see what was happening before his eyes. After these people left, the priest and I went back to the friary and he took me into the parlor.

I could see he was deeply moved. He was, and had been, very much against the Charismatic Renewal, in general, and unfavorable toward our prayer team, specifically.

"How can you forgive me?" he said, "I have been so much against this healing ministry."

I forgave him immediately.

From that moment on, he became my greatest support. He would hear confessions every Thursday as people queued from 7:00 A.M. to 11:00 P.M., sitting there, all day, every week. People would arrive at the church as early as 7:00 A.M. to get a seat for the 10:30 A.M. Mass.

In the Name of Jesus, Get Up and Walk

There is an important link between the Sacrament of Reconciliation and healing. Jesus demonstrated this for us, as he said to the man lowered down from the roof, "Your sins are forgiven," before he followed it through with, "Get up and walk." Through this sacrament sins are forgiven and there is no brick wall between the person and God; healing can get through. We emphasize this fact. People go first to the confessional and then come up for healing prayer. Some people haven't been to confession for twenty or thirty years. Even if we pray for deliverance, we always ask people to go to this sacrament *first*. The healing in this sacrament, in all sacraments, is fantastic! It is being realized more than ever that there is a strong link between our physical, emotional, and spiritual welfare. Very often psychological problems will manifest in physical pain. The greatest link we have seen occurs between emotions like hatred, resentment, and unforgivenness. As a result of prayer, people are able to forgive and surrender their pain to God. Receiving God's grace through reconciliation is essential for this process of healing to begin and continue. Often, their physical ills, even cancer, are healed. We have seen it many times.

Some people say that all this is just emotionalism, or that perhaps people were not really physically sick before they claimed physical healing. Yet we are emotional people. Our emotions can need healing as much as anything else. Who is to say which is the greater gift of healing?

Our Healing Masses continued for about two and a half years and, as I said, the crowds were phenomenal. The healing power of the gospel was being renewed and experienced right before our eyes. Priests and people took this message back to their parishes, not only in Australia but around the world. I was part of the original prayer team and witnessed so many beautiful things happen. All this unfolded in my life after I heard myself being called by God, "Marika..."

Only one other time did I hear what I believed was God's voice speaking to me. Early one Sunday morning, as I lay in bed, after the Masses had been going for about two years, I heard a voice say,

"Tell him to get up and walk."

I turned to my husband and asked, "Did you say something?"

As on the previous occasion, he said "No," and went back to sleep. I was puzzled and wondered what the message could mean. That afternoon I went to a healing service at a nearby parish and had to pick up a couple of priests on the way. In the car I mentioned what I'd heard that morning. One of the priests said,

"Just keep it in your spiritual pantry. You never know when you might use it."

When we arrived at the church we found it packed. As we stood at the front we saw a young man in a wheelchair being pushed by a nurse in a white uniform. She brought him right up to us, in front of everybody. One of the priests nudged me,

"Say what you shared with us this morning."

"How can I? What if it doesn't happen?"

"Don't forget that if you trust God, he never makes a fool of you."

(This may not *always* be the case!) Nonetheless, at the encouragement of this priest, who believed in the authenticity of the word of knowledge I had received earlier, I went over to the young man and said,

"In the name of Jesus, get up and walk."

The congregation went quiet as the man struggled to get out of his chair. It took about half an hour before he got really moving. First he slowly moved his fingers, then his hands and his arms. He pushed himself up and out of the chair and started walking, jerking, like the Tin Man from Oz. Everyone else now seemed paralyzed, and the whole church was absolutely still as we watched. Finally the man was walking, up and down then freely backward and forward in front of the altar. Two days later he was discharged from the hospital.

The prayer ministry team working today consists of people with their own healing stories, not unlike my own. They feel the desire to give something back to God, and they are the best witnesses.

It was not long after that that the Healing Masses stopped, as the priest who had started them was transferred. Their message was spreading through the diocese and the world. We realized there was still work to be done.

Our Lady of Good Counsel

One night I had a phone call from the parish priest of the church where the healing of the young man in the wheelchair had taken place. He had heard of the closure of the Masses and he wondered if I would be interested in looking at a possible new site. We drove over to a lonely little place on the shores of Yarra Bay, and I saw for the first time this little church in terrible need of repair. Like San Damiano, the church Saint Francis of Assisi had repaired, it was near ruin. We looked inside and saw that the ceiling had fallen onto the pews. "I hate to see a church closed," the priest said. "Could you use this place?"

"Me?

"Yes. You might be able to continue the Healing Masses here."

"How? I am a laywoman."

"What about the priests who used to concelebrate? Can't you call on them? There would be no rent. Only keep it in order ..."

He gave me the keys, one for the front door and one for the side, and then he left me. I sat there and prayed for an hour among the ruins.

"I am a laywoman ..."

I have never had the slightest desire to be a priest. As a woman I have found more than enough to do in the Church. My only sorrow is that I have not time to do more. There are things that women can do that men can't, and things that men can do that women can't. We do not have to take each other's roles, but we do need to support them. The Church is opening more and more doors to women as lay ministries expand. Why did Jesus choose only twelve men to be his leaders? Was he sexist, or did he realize that women have their own important things to do? I think the special gifts of the average woman are needed in the Church today as they have never been needed before! The world needs to be loved and cared for in the daily business of life, and I think this is a unique charism of women. As I prayed in the church that day I realized there was further work that I was called to do.

I contacted one of our most faithful priest supporters, and with his encouragement I called in the prayer team. Within two weeks the church of Our Lady of Good Counsel at Yarra Bay was back in working order. The ceiling was up, the church was painted, and the altar was restored. Everything was supplied, including a set of vestments made by a friend who was a tailor. On January 23, 1980, the church was rededicated. At the first Healing Mass, celebrated a few days later, I recalled the message that had come to me while I prayed among the ruins: "Consecrate yourselves to me and dedicate yourselves to the needs of others." This message became the one upon which I based my ministry, as did the members of the prayer team who adopted my calling and my wish to follow this special invitation. We recalled also the words from John 15:9-16:

As the Father has loved me, so I have loved you. Remain in my love. You did not choose me, no, I chose you: and I commissioned you to go out and to bear fruit, fruit that will last.

Now every Tuesday morning we celebrate a Mass for healing. We celebrate with song. Joyfully we try to help one another, receiving strength and blessings. Our aim is "*just to be there*" for anyone who needs love, care, an ear to listen, or a shoulder on which to cry.

Some people call this little church at Yarra Bay an "Oasis in the Desert."

There is an atmosphere of peace, love, and joy within the church. It is a special place where we can be ourselves, without having to pretend. Those who come here can show that they are hurt, wounded people who are suffering from pain, loneliness, and rejection. We don't have to fight back our tears, because we are accepted and loved the way we are, as the persons we are, even in the midst of experiencing the Cross.

After Mass and healing prayers, we share fellowship together over a cup of tea. There is much healing in sharing and fellowship. Countless friendships have started as a result of our life-sharing experiences. Indeed, we experience the Resurrection together as well as the Cross.

The Lord's calling to me has never weakened in my ministry over the last twenty-plus years. I realize more than ever the support of the Franciscan spirit from the time I was baptized to the time of my work at Our Lady of Great Counsel. As a Secular Franciscan I am trying to live the gospel life simply and joyfully. As the vice president of the Holy Spirit Fraternity I am glad to see the great numbers of "regulars" at the Healing Masses.

Consecrate Yourself to Me

I have been asked, "What is the goal of Yarra Bay; what do you want to achieve?" I feel *God wants us just to be there*. Not just for the hour of the Masses but to encourage those who come in any way. If people come for counseling, if we feel it is beyond our ability and they need professional help, then we refer them to those whom we think can give it. We work with the Sisters of Charity, Saint Vincent's Outreach, Centre-care, or Catholic and other institutions where further counseling or advice on physical care, housing, or whatever might be needed can be given.

The people feel that coming to this little church is like coming home. In my own spiritual journey, it seems as if all the searching in my life came to fulfillment in Yarra Bay through our healing ministry and fellowship. The people coming to Our Lady of Good Counsel have also had a great effect on my life, especially those in the prayer team and core group as we try to carry out the dedication of our lives.

When we have suggestions for what we might do in the future, we consider, "Is it serving God; is it helping us to dedicate ourselves to others?" These are the directions we must always follow. In this ministry we have discovered that it is essential to keep these two points in the forefront of our minds.

I have been asked in the past if I am a feminist. I am not. I do not like some of the things this movement attempts to accomplish in the Church. If the Church says there are to be no women priests, I am quite happy with that. I was brought up to respect authority, and I respect the pope and the authority of the Church. I believe the pope is the Vicar of Christ. We simply have to accept him and believe Christ is speaking through him in union with the college of bishops. If a member of the hierarchy were to come to me tomorrow and say, "Sorry, we have to close Yarra Bay," I would probably carry on a bit but would say, "Yes. Thank you Lord. This must be your will," as I believe God uses his Church to direct her members.

I suppose I could best describe myself as conservative, always looking for the middle way and no extremes. I love the beauty of the Liturgy. I do not like the way the fabric of the Mass in many cases has been changed, even torn, to accommodate this or that popular trend. The Holy Mass is so beautiful as it is, priests need just to present it and the laity need only to participate with reverential prayer.

Christ established *his* Church. Even if our human nature brings in faults, sins, and mistakes, it is still a God-centered place. I am not a theologian. I am just an average woman with a little tertiary education. I can only speak from my heart. I know God in his great mercy has entrusted me with something beautiful. Because of this, I feel a great sense of responsibility about the ministry in which I am called to serve.

I rejoice that God has given me the wonderful gifts of being a wife and mother and also allowed me to work in a particular area of the Church. I have never missed ordination or felt the need for it in my life. I feel I can work as much as I like and reach out with compassion to others without wearing priestly garb or acting with a clerical "authority." My natural reaction to life is to rejoice in my womanhood. I rejoice in the opportunity of being able to have children and grandchildren and still serve the People of God. I am a happy Catholic. I experienced a taste of religious life when I was in the convent for two years. I loved religious life dearly and left over from those days is my deep love for the Office of the Church. In this daily prayer we are united with the whole Catholic world. It is the Church's official prayer, and we can't have better prayer than that.

Today the ministry of healing through the masses at Yarra Bay is continuing. Prayerfully, with God's help, we might carry on for some years yet. But the future is in his hands. If he calls me tomorrow then I have had the most beautiful, fulfilling life, despite the tragedies of its early years. At Our Lady of Good Council, people still are touched and healed by God. People refer to the little church as "a power house," and it is. Here, God's call can be heard more clearly and we answer as best we can. We acknowledge the words of the prophet Isaiah and are grateful to know that "God called me before I was born, from my mother's womb he pronounced my name" (Is 49:1). Glory to you for calling me, and for whatever it is you want me to do, I say, "Yes, yes, yes, O Lord...."

Chapter 11

God Writes Straight on Crooked Lines

JOY SHIROI

This Heavenly Enterprise

*I*n the many years that have passed since 1968, when Our Lord began to show me the road leading to a new life, to a new and valid reason for living, I have been taught that he provides the guiding star to lead us to him. I have been taught by him through joys and sorrows, through the reading of his Word and the faith of friends. All his lessons have shown me, without doubt, that he knows our deepest needs better than we know them ourselves. Each of us is unique in his sight, and he has reserved a way that is tailored for us.

I did not always take up this "heavenly enterprise" of following his way. Many were the times when I shrank away from his will because of my fear. I feared the unknown and what I might find myself committed to. This lack of faith and trust has been the greatest barrier to my accepting Our Lord. In essence, my doubt prevented me from taking him at his word.

My conversion took place in 1964, and my subsequent return to the Church occurred in 1969. In Cardinal Suenen's book *A New Pentecost?* I found an echo of my thoughts:

The Holy Spirit does not arrive unexpectedly from outside to perfect his work, putting finishing touches here and there. The Holy Spirit is an abiding gift; it is for us to let him work in us, "both the will and the action." It is we ourselves, who, in a mysterious interaction of grace and freedom, make it possible for him to perform a new action, to take a deeper possession of us and to overcome the hindrances and obstacles caused by our sins, our stubbornness, our hesitation. "Do not *extinguish* the Spirit, do not *sadden* the Spirit"—these are the imperatives of the Christian life. When the action of the Holy Spirit becomes more effective in us, it is not that the Spirit has suddenly awakened like some dormant volcano come to life. It is *we* who are awakened to his presence by a combined movement of his grace, a deeper faith, a more living hope, a more burning love....[1]

I can easily remember the many times when Our Lord has tried to open me up to his Spirit. Religion "came to life" for me when I was fifteen years old. This came about as a result of World War II, when I was evacuated to a convent school in Wales, far from my home, friends, and school close to London.

My home at that time was in Surrey, outside London, and the general expectation was that this part of England would become a direct route for German bombers aiming to destroy the City of London. This proved to be true. My mother, though not Welsh, was brought up in Wales, where she attended a Wesleyan chapel. My father was an Anglican. They were both lovely people. They had a sure faith but I cannot remember being taken very regularly to church by them. My mother did not want to send me to a Catholic school, but during that time of war she had no choice. They seemed to have a great horror that someone would turn me into a nun and then they would lose me forever. Nonetheless, a friend of hers who had an Anglican daughter at the convent school encouraged her to send me.

Previous to this time (of study in the convent school), I had never met a nun and found these strangely dressed ladies—who rattled as they walked—something very hard to understand. As I came to know and love them, the sound of their rosary beads and the swish of their long skirts was comforting as we settled down to make new friends and to pass our exams, trying not to think too much about the bombs falling in other parts of our country.

Non-Catholic children were given the opportunity to attend religious services off the school grounds. Thus, each Sunday we were marched off two by two to the Anglican church in the town. On Friday evenings, however, there was a mysterious service called "Benediction" to which we were allowed to go. I have never forgotten my first meeting with Jesus in the Blessed Sacrament—it was to prove to be the beginning of a love that has been a part of my life ever since. At fifteen years old I knew that in that small convent chapel something very special was happening—something I needed to know about and to understand. I knew that what I was seeing in my first contact with Catholicism was faith in action. It was alive. These nuns had given their lives to their faith, to Jesus. At fifteen years old, for someone without a particularly strong religious background at home, this was all very impressive and beautiful. For me Our Lord made it into a change of direction and a revelation that changed my life.

And so it all started, and I believe that my whole life has been a battling with—a running away from—this God and his Spirit. I had found a very dear, loving God, who gave me flashes and glimpses of the wonder of a life lived just for him. Yet he could not break through the huge barriers I put up and enter into the depths of my heart, bringing the courage I needed to truly follow him. Keeping him a bit at arm's length, I would never let him come "too" close.

At nineteen—thanks to the last remaining graces from my two years at the convent—I managed, in spite of very tough parental opposition and heartbreak, to get myself received into the Church. My instruction was scanty, with no follow-up at all. We were in the middle of a war, which prevented the opportunity for thorough catechism. I can remember thinking very clearly, after my reception into the Church, which I knew I loved so much, "There *must* be more to it than this."

I landed on a kind of hair-raising spiritual seesaw, knowing deep down that what I had done was right for me but also knowing that I was failing miserably to be what I considered, in my ignorance, a "true Catholic." It is very hard with no Catholic background, no spiritual direction, and very few Catholic friends to be a convert. It is hard even when one does have support!

After five years on this spiritual seesaw, I decided that this highly spiritual "thing"—this Catholicism—had all been a big mistake. I doubted my inspiration to join the Church, seeing it as only the result of a teenage mirage. I ran away from my spiritual seesaw to a new start in marriage. My husband-to-be was an Anglican, and so we were married in the Anglican church near my home. I looked forward to our life together in Portugal, where his work brought us.

Learning to Pray

My husband's international contacts, through his business, gave us an exciting and varied social calendar. It was a busy and rewarding time for us. I loved our family life and interesting social life. I tried to give to my children what appeared to me (then!) to be a good "education" in religious matters. "When they are old enough," I thought, in my selfishness and pride, "they can decide for themselves about God and a church." We had nineteen years of a good, happy marriage, a lovely home, and a son and a daughter who were our pride and joy.

During this time, one of my dearest friends lost her husband after a long illness and another good friend had the incredible pain of losing a nineteen-year-old daughter, who committed suicide. These tragedies made me pray deeply for the first time in many years, and I realized that, in spite of all the happy times, there was something painfully missing in my life. I was totally switched off spiritually and had lost touch with the loving God I had known before my marriage. The Holy Spirit was quite extinguished, this wonderful Spirit I had only briefly met.

Our Lord started to wake up my conscience, to thaw me out of my deep-frozen vacuum. As I learned to pray again, he forced me to look fairly and squarely at the treasure I had thrown away. As the ice melted, I saw just how much light and love I had extinguished. How deeply he loves us. He tries and tries again to give to us a life more closely united to him. For me, God has truly "written straight on very crooked lines." I tried once more to say yes to God, in spite of a tremendous amount of apprehension. Courage came, and God sent his Spirit in to answer my prayers.

Supportive people came into my life at the most difficult moments, and it was at that time of questioning that I met a new friend, a Dominican priest, whose insights into the faith were quite encouraging.

I remember walking for hours with my dogs, thinking to myself, "My marriage will not stand up to this...." Yet the way became clear. I knew that, whatever happened, this time my "Yes" *must* be true—with no strings attached. This time there would be no running away. The months of praying—of popping into lovely old Portuguese churches, where I found and met again my beloved Jesus in the Blessed Sacrament, finally showed me where I would find the strength I needed to sort out my life. This strength would not come from me; it would come from Jesus, truly present in the Eucharist! Even though I could not yet receive Communion, I was, through the spiritual direction of the young and brilliant Dominican priest, rediscovering the wonder of the gift Jesus gave to us at the Last Supper. I answered him, "Dear Lord, I will draw closer to you, but this time *you* will be in control. I put the whole of my life, my heart, into your hands. Just, please, show me my small part."

The walls of these Portuguese churches are soaked in the prayer of centuries of worshippers. I fell in love with Jesus in the Blessed Sacrament there. Our Church is alive with his Presence, a place of love and courage for those who search, as I had searched with all my heart. The Sacrament of the Eucharist is an unbelievable and priceless gift— the gift of Our Lord himself. How often do we realize just exactly *Who* is contained in that small consecrated host? It is God himself truly with us, bringing his grace and his love to our lives, giving sight to our sometimes blind human eyes. The Sacrament of the Eucharist for me has become a meeting with Jesus himself. In times of difficulty and doubt, especially, he is there, sweeping away problems and fears. Even in the deepest darkness I know he is there as I reach out "to touch his garment." I have discovered, of course, that Our Lord is with us wherever we are, but his Real Presence in the Blessed Sacrament is something that we, as Catholics, have been given to keep, to worship, and to adore.

Finally, in the summer of 1968, the day arrived for my reception back into the Church, and for my husband and I to renew our wedding vows. I was there early to go to Confession after nineteen years of absence from this sacrament. It is hard to describe the freedom and deep happiness I found there. Mount Everest was lifted from my shoulders.

I found myself utterly lost in gratitude—amazed at such wonders and full of peace and joy. I was truly knocked over sideways at the experience of such a Love. It is a love, a compassion, and a forgiveness that have given to me my second chance to love and to serve. I can now truly worship—in spirit and in truth—the God whose specialty for me has been to make impossibilities possible. Finally, years of fear were replaced with a strong sense of commitment.

Our Lord has continued to lead me and has shown me that when we turn to him in our weakness, all the failures and faults of the past can be turned into blessings—into growth experiences that he can then use to help other people in their needs, needs that we understand, having "been there already." As Saint Paul said to the Corinthians:

Let us give thanks to the God and Father of Our Lord Jesus Christ, the God from Whom all help comes! He encourages us in all our afflictions so that we are able to encourage those who are in any affliction using the same encouragement that we ourselves have received from God.

2 Corinthians 1:3-4

"Fiat"

One special blessing I came to realize when I became a Catholic that we all have received is the wonderful gift of Mary, Our Blessed Mother. I had not really known this lovely lady until I came back to the Church. Now here I was, meeting Our Lady in Portugal, the small country where Mary is Queen—queen of so many hearts here who cherish her as their very own Mother. To watch the crowds flocking to Fatima, the young, old, sick, and healthy, is to witness a movement of faith that has to be experienced firsthand to be truly understood. It took quite a few years for my heart to be deeply touched by this dear and loving lady and her shrine in Fatima. Even organizing our yearly "English-speaking Pilgrimage" to Fatima did not seem to altogether do the trick. There was a strange lacking in my heart, a strange missing piece in the Catholicism that made me so utterly sure and happy in my faith. I knew that Mary was there, somewhere! But where?

Then one day I read these words and everything came to life—her "Yes," her suffering, her searching, her purity, and her beauty—indeed, the whole glory of her womanhood. And so I quote:

In giving life to him she was giving death. Christ is *Life;* death did not belong to him. In fact, unless Mary would give him death, he could not die.

Unless she would give him the capacity for suffering, he could not suffer.

He could only feel cold and hunger and thirst if she gave him her vulnerability to cold and hunger and thirst.

He could not know the indifference of friends, or treachery, or the bitterness of being betrayed unless she gave him a human mind and a human heart.

That is what it meant for Mary to give human nature to God.

He was invulnerable; she gave to him a body to be wounded.

He was joy itself; she gave him human tears....

The stable at Bethlehem was the first Calvary. The Passion had begun.

Christ was Man, and through the joys and sorrows Mary knew that this little son of hers was God's Son and that he belonged not only to her but to the whole world....[2]

I realized that Mary was utterly one with her Son. The great suffering he would bear, she would bear too. She knew, this young, inexperienced girl, that she was being used in a great movement of salvation for God's people. In that she would play her part—whatever the cost for herself, and for her beloved Son. They were in it together and forever. She would be faithful. She would keep her promises.

No longer could I go to Fatima just to be "on duty," counting heads, counting beds, wheelchairs, and places in the dining room. I, too, was visiting this Queen of Portugal—this Queen of countless hearts—and my own heart was touched deeply as I tried to find words to thank her for the gift of her Son and for her Son's gifts to me.

Mary has become for me an example of womanhood—motherhood—faithfulness—which all women should try to emulate. Everything we go through, everything we try to do in cooperation with God in our lives, we should bring to her. Everything that, as women, we bring to our homes, our families, and our friends should be a small "imitation" of all that Mary gave to her Lord. "I am the handmaid of the Lord," she said, "Let it be done unto me according to his word" (Lk 1:38). A handmaid is always there, always aware, always ready to do the will of the Master out of love and willingness to serve him. This is, for us, a daunting task, and sometimes it seems to be a thankless one. Mary did it quietly and selflessly. We have an English saying that goes like this: "Do your best and God will do the rest." For Mary, at Cana in Galilee, so long ago, these words came true, as her Son turned huge quantities of water into wine.

It breaks my heart today to see so many women caught up in demands that destroy their precious and God-given femininity. We are not like men—we are equal in dignity in his sight but we are not *the same*. We have our own gifts, our own genius for giving, our own way of loving and serving, our own tenderness and compassion. We have responsibilities as homemakers, as mothers and friends and grand-mothers, that *no one* else can undertake for us. We are very different from men, who have, too, their own gifts, their own way of loving and supporting. We are so different but we complement each other well if we have the love and patience to do it! Surely this is the way Our Lord intended it to be?

Our Holy Father has made his compassion, respect, and admiration for women very clear. He has willingly extolled the gift of femininity. He knows the deep and very difficult problems many of us face each day. His message for us is one of hope and love. His tremendous devo-tion to Our Blessed Lady is a tangible and "public" devotion. Countless photographs capture him deep in prayer, as if in intimate conversation with his heavenly Mother. In his book, *Crossing the Threshold of Hope*, Pope John Paul II tells us:

If our century has been characterized in liberal societies by a growing *feminism*, it might be said that this trend is *a reaction to the lack of respect accorded each woman*. Everything that I have written on this theme in *Mulieris Dignitatem* I have felt since I was very young, and, in a certain sense, from infancy. Perhaps I was also influenced by the climate of the time in which I was brought up—it was a time of great respect and consideration for women, especially for women who were mothers.

I think that a certain *contemporary feminism* finds its roots in the absence of true respect for woman. Revealed truth teaches us something different. Respect for woman, amazement at the mystery of womanhood, and finally the nuptial love of God himself and of Christ, as expressed in the Redemption, are all elements that have never been completely absent in the faith and life of the Church. This can be seen in a rich tradition of customs and practices that, regrettably, is nowadays being eroded. In our civilization woman has become, before all else, an object of pleasure.

It is very significant, on the other hand, that in the midst of this very situation the authentic *theology of woman* is being reborn. The spiritual beauty, the particular genius, of women is being rediscovered. The bases for the consolidation of the position of women in life, not only family life but also social and cultural life, are being redefined.

And for this purpose, we must return to the figure of Mary. Mary herself and devotion to Mary, when lived out in all its fullness, become a powerful and creative inspiration.[3]

In Rome, on May 13, 1981, the anniversary of Our Lady's first appearance to the children in Fatima, there was an assassination attempt on the pope's life. In the following year, the pope came to Portugal to be present in Fatima on May 13, to take part in the ceremonies and thank Our Blessed Mother personally for "saving his life." It was widely reported in the media that when he met, in an Italian prison, the man who intended to kill him, the conversation was extraordinary:

"Why are you still alive?" asked the prisoner. "My bullet should have killed you."

"You fired the shot and directed the bullet," the pope replied. "Another hand guided it."

The Holy Father's latest visit to Fatima took place on May 13, 2000, for the beatification of the two little shepherd visionaries, Francisco and Jacinta. His complete faith in Our Lady's power as a heavenly Mother—as an intercessor for us—fills me with admiration and awe. As a mother and a grandmother, I can only pray that a little of Our Lady's "fiat," uttered all those years ago, will be something I successfully emulate.

Come, Holy Spirit

The Convent of Bom Sucesso was founded in 1639, and the Irish Dominican Sisters still run a Portuguese-language school for girls there, with an English-speaking college flourishing closer to Estoril. When in 1834 freemasonry gained power under a new Portuguese government, all religious communities were expelled from their convents and colleges. *Only* the Irish Fathers in Corpo Santo, and the Irish Dominican nuns in Bom Sucesso, were allowed to carry on their work, which they have continued until this day. Over the years I remember many of these friends from Corpo Santo—always available and helpful. After my husband's death in 1994, I started to attend the meetings of the English-speaking Lay Dominican chapter in Lisbon. Slowly I also came to know and to love many of the Sisters. In all of these Dominicans I found a simplicity and depth of faith, a humor and a deep happiness that have truly made a difference in my life and faith. Many friends—truly gifts from God himself—have been given to me amongst these Dominicans, and I shall always appreciate how I have been led by them in dark spiritual moments. After much heart-searching, I became a Lay Dominican myself in January 1997.

To be a Lay Dominican is, I think, to become part of the power-house of prayer in the Church. It enables one to have a structure for one's prayer life—to have a time of study and sharing of Scripture or other documents of the Church. We are a small group, but I know that we have a unity that comes from the roots of the Dominican Order of Preachers. Saint Dominic and Saint Catherine of Siena are our con-stant inspirations.

It was at Bom Sucesso in 1973 that I discovered the work and min-istry that was to fill my life and my heart. I was invited to come along to a prayer meeting. The (then) prior of Corpo Santo said to me, "There is something happening at Bom Sucesso which I think you may enjoy." And so, wondering what this mysterious invitation meant, I went along. We were a small group—perhaps two priests, two lay brothers, two or three sisters, and several lay people. We sang, we prayed, we listened to Scripture. As we prayed so beautifully and so spontaneously from our hearts, the presence of God—of his Holy Spirit—became tangible. Suddenly, I knew that here was a gift that was being offered to us—a gift of love and of deep friendship with God and with each other. It was a gift to be cherished and to be used to spread God's Word and his love far and wide. I knew then that I had been searching for a way in which to serve—to help God's people—and to find deep healing of my own wounds. Loud and clear, once again, the Holy Spirit told me, "This is it!" This time there was no interior battle; I agreed wholeheartedly with him!

I had no idea of the joys and sorrows we were to face—the great complications of trying to follow the lead of the Holy Spirit, in creat-ing our prayer groups, which were watched at the beginning with sus-picion by very many fellow Catholics.

We started to build our groups with the help of Dominican priests and religious. With much prayer and great joy, we found ourselves, and many others who joined us, renewed in the Spirit. Scripture came to life. The sacraments, too, came to life. We entered more fully into relationship with Christ through his Holy Spirit, and our lives were transformed. This was a time of great spiritual growth. My prayer life deepened. My knowledge of Scripture grew. My daily Mass became, if possible, a more wonderful time of closeness to Jesus. My confessions deepened, and sometimes, with the help of the Holy Spirit, became times of true growth in love of God and in self-knowledge.

When I talk about charismatic gifts I am entering a new area—a new dimension of relationship with God. Those of us involved in the Charismatic Renewal know through experience that this new dimension leads us into deeper prayer, a more total trust, a *yielding* to whatever God wishes to give us and for whatever reason. We are "on the receiving end" and not at all in charge of this situation. We know only that these charismatic gifts, such as healing, wisdom, discernment, and words of knowledge, are given to us to use *in the service of others*. These are not "permanent" gifts but God-given moments when the Spirit takes over with a special grace for someone in need. These gifts are not meant for our own emotional satisfaction; they are meant to be used under proper spiritual direction for the building up of the body of believers.

Charismatic gifts are a manifestation of God's power; all to be used *as God wills,* remembering always that all these gifts, as Saint Paul said, are useless if they are not used with charity.

New Horizons

On April 25, 1974, the "bloodless" but nonetheless thorough revolution came about in Portugal. Suddenly we were hearing a great deal of Communist propaganda. Communist leaders, exiled by previous governments, were quickly reappearing—like mushrooms in the night! People flocked to Fatima, and I think there are very few Portuguese who doubt that Portugal's eventual movement into democracy and peace came about as a result of Our Lady's intercession. No Portuguese sovereign has worn the royal crown since the seventeenth century, when the long-standing devotion to Our Lady of the Immaculate Conception was confirmed by her coronation as Queen of Portugal by King Joâo IV.

In the same year as the revolution, the Dominican community at Corpo Santo also elected a new prior, who was to stay with us for ten years. His workload was truly enormous, as he and his community of seven coped with the "fallout" of the revolution. He found time, however, to be with us as we expanded our prayer groups. In 1975, a few of us, along with the prior and one of the sisters from Bom Sucesso, were able to attend the first-ever International Catholic Charismatic Congress, held in Rome. This was a never-to-be-forgotten time of prayer and new experiences. We were still very wary of those very extraordinary gifts of the Spirit about which we had read. One day, on the bus going from Rome out to the conference site, I met a man from London who was at the conference with his whole family, including his wife and three children. We chatted and exchanged addresses and he said to me, "We have a very good prayer meeting in Soho Square. Next time you are in London, do visit us." I was delighted and promised to go. Soon afterward I visited England and while in London went to Soho Square to meet again our new friend. His name is Myles Dempsey. I asked him to come to Portugal as soon as he could to help us with our groups, to teach us how to teach them. He put my card with my name and address into his Bible and said, "We will see what the Holy Spirit has to say about this."

I do not have space to write all that I would like about Myles Dempsey and his ministry. I can only say that he came, he prayed for and with us, and he taught us from his own experience of "life in the Spirit" and of guiding prayer groups. When he prayed for healing, his gifts of discernment and prophecy brought with them the tangible presence of God.

For more than twenty years Myles Dempsey has been for our prayer group and many others our teacher, our healer, and our great friend. Our Lord chooses his time, his instruments, and his places to lead us in his way.

Many years ago Myles said to me, "Your group is fine, but until you are able to integrate with Portuguese groups you are going to remain just a happy group of like-minded people in a 'holy huddle.'" He was right, and even though it has taken time and much patience, we are now, finally, official members of the Portuguese Charismatic Groups in the Diocese of Lisbon.

When my husband was very ill, in 1994, I nursed him at home— something that meant a great deal to both of us. I learned a lot then about being "carried along" by others' prayer. I learned about friendship and I learned a great deal about love. I shall always be grateful to my two children and to all my wonderful friends for their support and for Our Lord's presence and peace when my husband died. He did not become a Catholic but was a deeply committed Christian. We were able to have a beautiful "ecumenical" service for him in the Anglican Church of Saint George in Lisbon. The Anglican Archdeacon—a good friend—took the service and the Dominican prior of our English-speaking parish of Corpo Santo—also a marvelous friend—gave the homily. It was lovely to see that black and white Dominican habit in an Anglican pulpit. The Holy Spirit is opening many doors to people of different denominations, and it is a beautiful experience to be able to "mix" like this, respecting and trying to understand others' beliefs.

Each year on the first Friday of March, a World Day of Prayer is celebrated worldwide. Each year the service, which is for all denominations, is written by the women of a particular country. In 1997 the service was written by the women of South Korea. The English-speaking Catholics at our parish centre in Estoril hosted the event. The Anglican, Scottish, and Catholic Churches take it in turn to do this. This ecumenical service was a wonderful example of people wanting to be together in faith and prayer. People from at least seven denominations were present. As the service progressed, the gospel message of unity and growth in prayer helped us to desire to overcome our theological and traditional differences.

Our centre was filled to overflowing. We had a magnificent Korean gong, which boomed out beautifully, reminding us of our unity with South Korea and the political struggle there. The gong was actually lent by a Welsh member of the Scottish Church, which, again, reminded us of the "grass roots" unity that is desired by so many. As we all chatted, enjoying our coffee in the Portuguese sunshine, it seemed that our service had been filled with graces and friendship as we all gathered "in his name." Doors were opening and there was a great feeling of gratitude in the air! The Holy Spirit will show the way—one day—for us to all "be one." He alone can do this, and in his own good time. We must wait and pray, giving spiritual help and space to ourselves and to others as we travel along to our God. Surely God the Father will answer the prayer of his Son: "Holy Father, keep those you have given me true to your name, so that they may be one, like us" (Jn 17:11). This is the prayer of Christ, and it is our prayer as well as we also read in Pope John Paul's words:

> Among the most fervent petitions which the Church makes to the Lord during this important time, as the eve of the new millennium approaches, is that unity among all Christians of the various confessions will increase until they reach full communion. I pray that the Jubilee will be a promising opportunity for fruitful cooperation in the many areas which unite us; these are unquestionably more numerous than those which divide us....
> In this way the Jubilee will bear witness even more forcefully before the world that the disciples of Christ are fully resolved to reach full unity as soon as possible in the certainty that "nothing is impossible with God."[4]

A Rock and a Refuge

The Roman Catholic Church has been my rock—my refuge. The abiding presence of Our Lord in the Blessed Sacrament is one of the wonders of my world! As a eucharistic minister, I am able to bring Christ to people, both healthy and sick. I am more grateful than words can tell to serve the Church in this manner.

The question of the authority of the office of Peter has been resolved for me. To be a member of a Church that, through its God-given leader, the Holy Father, is able to speak with authority in today's world is something for which I am very thankful. To hear solid teaching— to hear the truth—is to be given a freedom in which to live, to work, and to "have one's being."

Our Holy Father uses his gifts with charity and courage. To see him now, speaking out boldly in the name of Christ, in the name of all humanity, is a very heartwarming experience. He has "entered in" to a suffering and misguided world where his prayer and his presence bring the love of God.

There is a very beautiful ceiling in the Sistine Chapel in the Vatican in Rome. This ceiling, painted by Michelangelo, shows us God the Father reaching out his hand to a man, Adam, who represents our human family. The man, too, reaches out his hand but the two hands do not meet—there is a small gap. The Church supplies us with many "bridges" in its sacraments to fill this gap in our own lives. The Sacrament of Reconciliation is where we meet Our Lord and, through his priest, receive total forgiveness—a new start—a new life. When I came back to the Catholic Church, "going to confession" was a ghastly nightmare—trying to find something to say and then forgetting what it was and being struck dumb—quite literally! I am a very reserved person, but step by step, with a great deal of help and patience from confessors who understood my difficulty and knew me well, I have learned how to bring spirituality to my confession. I did not understand the tremendous power in this sacrament. Now I know that even after the shame of a poor confession, Jesus understands and strengthens me. Gradually I have found the ability, only through him, to stand before him in poverty and sin. This sacrament has been the way to my own personal truth, leading to healing, peace, and freedom.

Then again, those of us who have participated in the Sacrament of Marriage know full well the strength that this sacrament brings to our shared lives. I know from my own experience that this sacrament gave me a grace for my marriage that kept it, in spite of the ups and downs, a special gift of love for both of us. Marriage for me was always an "until death us do part" commitment. How happy I am to have been given the grace to keep this promise to my husband.

The Sacrament of the Anointing of the Sick is no longer a sacrament just for the dying, but one for healing and peace. For many people I have met, this anointing has been a bridge back to God, to full health and happiness in him. Recently I visited a friend who had been seriously ill and was still, I understood, in great pain. It was a privilege for me to pray with him *after* he had received the Anointing of the Sick. His pain had gone, he was filled with great joy in Our Lord's healing power, and we were able to join together in gratitude to God for such wonder and such love.

These three sacraments are examples of how Our Lord has cared for us, strengthening us and providing for our deep spiritual needs.

I am happy to be a woman in the Church in these years of change. I think we have a very special job to do, using our feminine gifts—our love, our womanhood—to bring peace to our families, to our friends, and to our parishes. I pray that just one or two words that I have written may touch a heart in need—a person searching for a closer walk with God. I pray that in God's own time we will learn how to better emulate Our Lady and her "fiat"—that her womanhood will be reflected in ours—and that we shall be used, as she will always be used, to bring Jesus to his people. As I conclude this chapter, it seems fitting that I share a small incident that happened recently. I heard myself saying to someone, "I believe firmly in a God of the impossible." In spite of all my fears and my wobbly faith, God has managed to lead me back to him. He has given me joy and security. I now live a life where, in constant awareness of him, I can at last say, "Yes." He is in the center of my heart. He is still writing straight, as he has been doing for all the many years of my life, on very crooked lines.

Let us take these words to heart:

If we live by the truth and in love, we shall grow completely into Christ, who is the head by whom the whole Body is fitted and joined together, every joint adding its own strength, for each individual part to work according to its function. So the body grows until it has built itself up in love.

EPHESIANS 4:15-16

Chapter 12

Encountering Christ

JO CROISSANT

"The Way, The Truth, and the Life"

I was born in France into a simple Catholic family. My parents felt it was important to pass on their faith and their sound moral values. From as far back as I can remember I was aware of a desire for God within me; turning to God, I sensed that true fulfillment was to be found in him alone. In my teenage years my thirst for God increased, but remained unquenched, as I was unable to find what I needed in my surrounding environment. I was alone with my questions, and my friends did not seem to have the same aspirations as I did. Mum was concerned and thought that I was too preoccupied with spiritual matters. She was also worried about my sister, who said she did not believe in God. Mum would have liked a "happy medium" for both her daughters.

When I left my village to begin high school I met an elderly lady who taught catechism, and we became friends. I went to see her regularly to share what I was living. She did not always know what to say to me, so she would open up the Bible and read me a passage from the Gospels.

I sought after God; I did not know him.

The words, "Jesus is the Way, the Truth, and the Life" were in my heart, but I was still waiting to have a personal encounter with him. While still at school, one of my Protestant friends shared her experiences of God and took me to a Pentecostal Church. I liked listening to her talk about God but he remained a stranger to me. Another

265

friend who is Catholic recently reminded me of the time I went to see her, crying my eyes out and asking what I had to do to have real faith.

I was in my last year at high school when the events of May 1968 took place in France. Everybody talked about changing the world, and everyone had his own ideas; as for me, most of the time I remained silent. These words dwelt in my heart: "You will speak when you will have lived."

I wanted to get married, but I wanted it to be "in God and for God." I did not really know what that meant at the time, but this was how I expressed myself.

Getting to know "L'Arche," a community founded by Lanza del Vasto, turned out to be a decisive event in my life. Here families and celibate members tried to live the gospel by putting everything in common and living by the work of their hands. Life there was tough but also beautiful and full of meaning. It was the first time I had seen people living what they proclaimed, people who did not revel in a lot of words, but the testimony of their life was a powerful word in itself. At L'Arche I understood that it was possible to live by the gospel.

Here I met the person who was to become my husband. Ephraïm was studying Protestant theology and, like me, he was looking for God. Straight away there was a great communion of souls between us, and God showed me that this was the man he had destined for me. I was a Catholic and he a Protestant, but that was not a problem for me. I no longer really knew what it meant to be a Catholic. I called myself a Christian and what I desired was that my husband be a "man of God."

On the day of our marriage, not only did we commit ourselves to one another, but together we gave ourselves to God, without knowing where that would lead us, yet in the certain knowledge that God would remain faithful.

From that day, God's hand has never left us. Two months after our wedding we simultaneously received the baptism in the Holy Spirit during a prayer meeting, an event that was to completely change our lives. From that moment on, the God for whom we had been searching and to whom we had already given ourselves became a living Person. Like the pilgrims on the road to Emmaus, our eyes were opened and we understood the Scriptures. Before, I had read the Bible without understanding what I read, yet suddenly it spoke to my heart and nourished me. We also experienced that the Lord was guiding us, leading us step by step.

This encounter with the Living God and the experience of knowing that the hand of God is in all things—right down to the little details of our lives—made us want to go even further in the gift of our lives to God. It thus became obvious and even imperative that the most radical way of living the gospel, for us, was community life.

So it was that we began living our lives *in community.* In September 1974, with another young Protestant couple, Jean-Marc and Mireille, who had just experienced the same powerful baptism in the Holy Spirit, and following the example of the first Christians, we put everything in common in order to be totally dedicated to prayer.

Receiving a Ministry

Before passing from this world to the Father, Jesus said to his disciples: "When the Spirit comes he will lead you to the complete Truth" (Jn 16:13). This was just what we experienced. At the same time that Ephraïm had the awesome experience of discovering the Catholic Church through Our Lady, the Eucharist, and the apostolic succession, slowly but surely I rediscovered my childhood faith. On the feast of Saint Francis of Assisi, in October 1976, with twenty or so other Protestant brothers and sisters who had come to join our community, Ephraïm entered the Catholic Church. Others would follow later. Ephraïm tells the story of his experience of baptism in the Holy Spirit and the foundation of the Community of the Beatitudes in the book

Rains of the Late Season.

At a time when Catholics were questioning many things concerning their faith, we were just discovering ours. We were like children standing in admiration before a beautiful treasure that was the source of our joy, the same treasure that others found to be old-fashioned, out of style.

We thus went against the prevailing attitudes of the time. The cultural revolution of May 1968 introduced a profound upheaval of values and accelerated the crisis that was to penetrate the very heart of the Church itself. All authority was considered as suspect and judged to be repressive. Freud's theories on sexual liberation and the Oedipus complex became the new bible, which nobody dared to challenge. Everybody wanted to be free, rich, and sexually fulfilled.

While all this was going on, we went in the opposite direction. We were discovering, through experience, the spiritual strength that comes from religious obedience, from fraternal submission and submission of a wife to her husband. We discovered the beauty to be found in poverty, and in chastity that is lived for God, and in God.

As for me, from the time I began to live in community, I had an intuition of the beauty of woman's vocation. I sensed that therein lay a mystery that was beyond me, but that I wanted to fathom. The fact of being men and women, families and celibate members, all living under the same roof, obliged each one of us to discover his or her place in relation to the other, to find the balance that would permit personal fulfillment while respecting the other person's identity.

In 1990 a certain event played a role that was to be catalytic in all my research into the vocation of women. Several members of our community had been invited to appear on a television show that dealt with the problem of homosexuality. In fact, the producers had prepared the show in such a way that the opponents of homosexual behavior would be made to look ridiculous. Nobody could get a word in edgeways; nobody was listening, everybody shouted louder than his or her neighbor in order not to hear what was said and so as not to be challenged. It was the perfect illustration of the words of Scripture:

Woe to those who call what is bad, good, and what is good, bad, who substitute darkness for light and light for darkness, who substitute bitter for sweet and sweet for bitter.

ISAIAH 5:20

I did not have words to describe what I was witnessing, but one thing became clear to me: in this tragedy what is actually being gravely offended is the mystery of the beauty of womanhood and that of the vocation of women.

The following day a publisher friend came to visit us, and as I shared my feelings with him regarding the identity crisis facing our society, he asked me to write a book on the subject. I was amazed because it was something I would never have imagined being asked to do. I spoke to my husband, who duly encouraged me. I thus got down to the job of writing, counting on the help of Our Lady, in whom I confide all things.

A short while later I was asked to give a retreat on the vocation of women. The reaction of the women present confirmed the perspicacity of my intuitions and that what I said had touched them profoundly. During the retreat, among other things, I broached the question of submission, aware that the word was often found to be unacceptable and full of innuendo. In fact, for many, the word alone is enough to open up deep wounds and bring about visceral reactions of rejection because of unhappy family experiences. When the act of submission is not mutual, or lived in a spirit of reverence for Christ (as Saint Paul reminds us in Ephesians 5:21), it turns into an act of domination that is destructive and cannot be received by the other person. I surprised myself in daring to say: "In fact, the temptation for women is to be the one who dominates!" and I was even more surprised when

I saw all the heads nodding in agreement, showing little smiles of approval. I realized in more concrete terms what was actually hidden behind the appearances of "liberated women." I understood that they had not yet found the right path and that deep down they remained unsatisfied, continuing to search for their identity. The modern woman is, in fact, unaware of what her true vocation really is, and she loses her way without realizing it, thinking she is experiencing liberation while in fact she is alienating herself.

I found myself dwelling on the problem of submission, as it is a very touchy subject. At first sight we think that to be in submission is a sign of inferiority. In reality, there is a kind of secret to be discovered in a woman's vocation with regard to man and to God. Submission can be understood as the woman being deeply attentive to what is in man's heart, an attention that does not mean she ignores herself, but forgets self so as to impart life. She is called to reign through gentleness, love, and humility because she is clothed with an interior strength coming from her relationship with God. Receiving her dignity from the Father's gaze resting on her, knowing herself to be infinitely loved, she can therefore give of herself without risk of going astray. Thus she enters into her vocation of giving birth, and this in turn enables man to be himself. In this way, like Adam, man is enabled to see woman as a gift from God, and he, in his turn, can give his life for her.

The interest shown by these women greatly encouraged me in my research. I immersed myself in the study of God's Word, particularly the creation of man and woman in the Book of Genesis, finding nourishment in the rabbinical commentaries, which liberate a whole richness of different meanings from every word.

When the debate on the ordination of women became intense and the Holy Father's position upset those campaigning for equality of the sexes, I felt the urgent need to delve deeper into the whole question of a woman's true identity and her specific mission in the family, in the Church, and in our society. Why should it be necessary, yet again, for women to become like men in order to be accepted? Did they not have their own specific and irreplaceable role? Rather than wanting equality through similitude, was it not necessary to plead that the difference be recognized not as an inferiority but rather as something of great value that allows complementarity and reciprocal fruitfulness?

The book came out, and I was amazed when I heard how it had been received by the women who had read it. Women of all ages and classes were able to identify with these words spoken from the heart and also with the testimonies they read. For many it turned out to be a revelation of the splendor of their identity, the beginning of a process of reconciliation with their femininity. Though the book's title was somewhat provocative: *La Femme Sacerdotale ou Le Sacerdoce du Coeur* (The priestly woman or the priesthood of the heart), its contents are in complete union with the teachings of the Catholic faith. I receive many testimonies from men and women for whom the book has been an occasion to come into a deeper self-awareness. For women specifically, it has been an instrument enabling them to discover their fulfillment in embracing the "grace of being a woman."

On visiting the different houses of our community throughout the five continents, I have had the opportunity of giving retreats and talks in very differing cultures. Each time I was greatly blessed to see how much the truth contained in the Word of God makes one free (see Jn 8:32). I was very aware that the language I was using did not conform to current secularized ways of thinking, that what I said was completely opposed to what they were used to hearing. I should have encountered violent reactions. On the contrary, I found that their hearts were with me.

"It's a clarification for the whole of my life!"

"You've just said exactly what I think but never knew how to express."

These women regained their dignity and the joy and pride of being a woman.

I also studied at length the beautiful custom of dance from the ancient Jewish and early Christian religious traditions. Through conferences given for young people on these types of dance and prayer, I delved deeper into the problem of identity. As the young people learned to dance *under the Father's gaze,* I witnessed many healings in people's identity and saw people being reconciled with their bodies and their femininity. The "tomboys" came into the joy of being a woman, of being beautiful under the gaze of God and in the eyes of others.

As for the young men, they learned manly gestures and entered more fully into their masculine identity.

The Discovery of God

Personally speaking, what radically transformed my spiritual life was the discovery of God the Father.

I was very marked by the anguished scrutiny of my mother, who was anxious that I correspond to what she wanted me to be, and who undoubtedly desired my happiness.

Unsure of myself, I was sometimes paralyzed by the way others looked at me, until the day I had my second conversion experience. It came through an insignificant event, so insignificant that I cannot even remember what it was that triggered off a feeling of shame that pervaded my whole being that day, right up until I entered the chapel for the office of vespers. I was not proud of my inner reactions, and a voice was saying, "What a hypocrite! You come to pray to God and you're capable of feelings like that!"

I wanted to run away. Like Adam, when he realized his sin, I would have liked to hide behind some trees. Yet at the same time I felt drawn toward the Father, as if there were a voice in me saying, "throw yourself into my arms!" Then the fear and shame came back. I do not know how long this inner dilemma went on; these two contradictory forces were equally powerful. Yet, suddenly, God became the more powerful, and I threw myself into his arms like a child. In my heart I could hear the following words, which I will not easily forget: "It is my gaze which purifies you!"

In an instant I understood everything. I understood that I was unique, that I was loved. God did not ask me to be perfect, but to remain unceasingly under his gaze.

It was by living under his gaze that, little by little, I discovered my identity as a woman—that of daughter, spouse, and mother—and I began to marvel at God's plan for men and women. I rejoice every time I bring to mind God's creation of man and woman. The more I explore their respective identities, the more I understand how much they are made one for the other, that they are a gift of God one for the other.

I have a very great desire to communicate this feeling of wonder because I know that therein lies the path to happiness, this happiness that no one can take from us.

When a woman has begun to perceive the beauty of this plan she begins to have peace and has the desire to conform to her real and deepest vocation. She no longer sees her condition as an inferior one, but as a marvelous reality where there will always be more to discover, and which is a treasure for humanity.

In order for this to happen there has to be healing of all false ideas of what a man or a woman should be, and a healing of false images of fatherhood and motherhood that have their origin in a false image of God.

We have been created in God's image and likeness (see Gn 1:26), which means that knowledge of man is given in knowledge of God. It is vain to seek to understand man "outside" of God; one can only end up having a partial and limited knowledge, through which we risk losing our way. Just as a child receives its identity from its father, it is God the Father who gives us our identity as sons and daughters. A consequence of sin is that we have a disfigured idea of God the Father. The Church continues the mission of Christ, who came to reconcile us with the Father, heal us of the fears inscribed within us, and remove our false ideas of fatherhood.

The Church shows us that a woman's liberation is not primarily with regard to man, but with regard to God. It is under the gaze of God that she discovers her beauty, her dignity, her strength, and her radiant influence, and not by comparing herself *to man,* as if seeking her identity *in him,* becoming in this way dependent upon the way he sees her, upon his approval. If she enters into this false behavior pattern she either becomes servile through fear of losing his love, ignores herself to the point of becoming completely out of touch with self, or she decides she has no solution other than to dominate man to escape being dominated herself. Encountering the Living God is the only way out and the only way to freedom—not to be free to do as she likes, satisfying her self-centered needs, but free to love, free to give life. A *face-to-face* relationship is the most difficult one for us. We are more naturally inclined to place ourselves in the role of parent or that of the child, as the one who dominates or the one who is dominated. Yet most people have great difficulty in finding their place in a face-to-face relationship, where man and woman face one another, without fear of being themselves, with their differences. Knowing themselves to be loved by God, they can, quite simply, be themselves, welcoming the other as a gift from God. This knowledge of being loved by God is given in prayer, in the simple dialogue with "Our Father." We begin to be healed when we begin to live under the Father's gaze, allowing him to gaze upon us while we adore him in the Blessed Sacrament, exposing ourselves to Jesus' gaze in his Eucharistic presence. Reading and meditating upon the Word of God reveals his love for us, his goodness, and affirms us in our faith in his all-powerfulness. In this way we can love God and our brothers because he has first loved us (see 1 Jn 4:10).

Promoting Womanhood

It must be recognized that the feminist explosion was a spiritual explosion. The shackles imposed by the narrow-minded spirit of the secularized family structure had become unbearable for those women whose intuition told them they had something more to live: a widening of their horizons, a deployment of their capacity to love, which could not develop freely in what had become the restricted world of the family deprived of its religious foundations. The mistake had been to confuse sexual liberation with women's liberation. Following this there was a devaluation in the values that are proper to women, as much on a biological level as on a spiritual one.

In this way, the women's liberation movement went astray and did not contribute to helping women find their true identity, their mission as prepared for them by God, or to helping them find their rightful place in relation to men. The result has been confusion and a serious identity crisis in today's society, of which we cannot measure the consequences upon the new generations who have lost their points of reference. I have often dreamt of a new women's movement, not feminist but feminine, where the gifts God has given women, gifts so valuable for humanity, may be allowed to develop. Perhaps certain women may receive this calling from God?

With the tragic situations confronting women and the helplessness of their children, who are ever more wounded, they need the means to be able to help one another, because God has put the power of life and resurrection into their hearts, a power that can save the world.

I am a strong believer in the hidden fruitfulness of small things done out of love. Often we want to do great things and change the world, and we get discouraged at the sight of our powerlessness. If first we change our hearts, then the hearts of our husband, children, and those who are dear to us will all be transformed by the power of love. There is one thing alone that we can change in this world, and that is ourselves. When a journalist asked Mother Teresa what was wrong with the world, she replied: "You and me! If the world is in bad shape it's because of our own lack of conversion."

With all my heart I hope that women will come together to support one another in the determination of becoming *women of God,* expecting everything from him, receiving their strength and their courage from their intimate relationship with the Father, and entering fully into their womanhood, fulfilled in all the dimensions of their femininity and maternity.

A Father Who Proclaims the Truth

I am writing these lines as the Holy Father visits France, and I am struck by the stir that has preceded his visit. It is becoming ever more obvious that those reacting to the declarations of the Holy Father and the Magisterium are completely out of touch with the real message. In fact, it is quite evident that all kinds of fears, fantasies, and false images of God are projected onto the pope. How can one otherwise explain the blatant lack of goodwill on the part of all those who, never having read the writings of the Holy Father, dare to give a dishonest interpretation of the pope's message. He is speaking of facts that appertain to the kingdom of God, and they listen to what he says in a completely human way, filtering it through a kind of political analysis. He preaches the cross and it is a scandal for the pagans. The wisdom of this world is folly in the eyes of God, and the wisdom of God is folly for the world. When the spirit of the world enters into the Church, it becomes deaf to the callings of the Holy Spirit, and to be reminded of what the gospel demands becomes intolerable.

This reminds us of Saint Paul's epistle addressed to the Church of Corinth, where the community was divided through not having

understood the true wisdom of God, which is different from the ide-
ologies of the world.

> *Christ ... sent me to preach the gospel, and not by means of wisdom
> of language, wise words which would make the cross of Christ point-
> less. The message of the cross is folly for those who are on the way to
> ruin, but for those of us who are on the road to salvation it is the
> power of God.*
>
> 1 CORINTHIANS 1:17-18

> *Yet we do speak wisdom among those who are mature; a wisdom, how-
> ever, not of this age nor of the rulers of this age, who are passing away.*
>
> 1 CORINTHIANS 2:6

> *Now the Spirit we have received is not the spirit of the world but
> God's own Spirit, so that we may understand the lavish gifts God
> has given us. And these are what we speak of, not in the terms
> learned from human philosophy, but in terms learned from the
> Spirit, fitting spiritual language to spiritual things. The natural per-
> son has no room for the gifts of God's Spirit; to him they are folly; he
> cannot recognize them, because their value can be addressed only in
> the Spirit. The spiritual person on the other hand, can assess the
> value of everything, and that person's value cannot be assessed by
> anybody else.*
>
> 1 CORINTHIANS 2:12-15

Personally I think of our present pope as a wonderful gift from God to
the Church of our day. He is one of the few men who, in this day and
age, are really free. At a time of great confusion on all levels, he remains
like a rock in the midst of the storm, not giving in to pressure or men-
aces, he continues to go forward and to lead us toward the kingdom,
that is to say, toward happiness.

As God the Father, who, after having given the law to his people in the desert, said:

If only their hearts were always so, set on fearing me and on keeping my commandments, so that they and their children might prosper for ever!

Deuteronomy 5:29

And later on, seeing his people choose the way of destruction:

If only my people would listen to me.

Psalm 81

What the pope suffers is what God suffers in his heart when he sees his children bringing unhappiness upon themselves, even though he has given them all they need in order to be happy. The pope continually reminds us of what the gospel demands and which is the condition for our happiness: to proclaim the truth, that is to say, the very words of he who said,

I am the Way, and the Truth, and the Life.

John 14:6

As a woman I feel completely understood and accepted by the Holy Father in the grace that is my own. The way he sees women is extraordinary; he has such a great respect for us that he elevates us and gives us back our dignity, and the joy of receiving the gift God gives us in making of us daughters, sisters, spouses, and mothers. It is because he thinks so highly of women and their irreplaceable mission in the family, in the Church, and in society, that he remains unmoved in the face of his accusers, who are not really concerned with the needs of women but rather want to see the triumph of their own ideological concepts.

The Church declares her opposition to abortion and there are cries of scandal. She is accused of being anti-women. Yet when we see the psychological damage, the disastrous consequences that ensue for the woman, with regards to herself, in her relationship with her husband, and even for her other children, one can see clearly that the Church is a mother who protects her children.

When the Church recommends natural family planning methods, it is once again so that the woman's body be respected in the mystery of its fertility. She wishes to invite man to better understand his wife and to love her in an unconditional, wholehearted way, so that she would not be an object of pleasure continually at his disposition, but that he would listen to her, so that together they would both grow in love. A woman is not satisfied by sexual relationship alone; she grows through receiving the gaze and the tenderness of her husband in relationship to his whole person.

Having said that, it is certain that there is a lack of provision in the Church to help the faithful incarnate the teachings of the Magisterium in their daily lives. The faithful frequently find themselves helpless in the face of life's difficulties, and do not always find the listening ear and the necessary understanding within the Church that would allow them to continue to advance in the ways of Christian living. They thus think that they are confronted by a *law that only* makes them feel guilty, because it is impossible to observe, and that they find rigid and implacable.

One would certainly desire to see a growth in the number of self-help and sharing groups where Christians can find an understanding ear and be met where they are in order to progress in the spiritual life and receive the necessary graces enabling them to live their faith.

A Loving Gaze Upon the Mystery of the Woman

I am touched to see the great respect that John Paul II has for women, and how much he senses the greatness of their mission.

When I started to write my book, I discovered John Paul II's Apostolic Letter, *Mulieris Dignitatem* (On the dignity and vocation of women). It was a wonderful confirmation for me. I found, almost word for word, what God had put on my heart.

The love, the great devotion—in the noble sense of the word—that the Holy Father has for Our Lady, renders him, more than any other person, sensitive to the mystery of woman. His familiarity with Mary, blessed among women, prototype of the woman who is accomplished in all the dimensions of her being, gives him an extraordinarily high regard for women, for the grace of femininity, of maternity, their identity, and their mission. In their misunderstanding of Mary, feminists perceive her as an inaccessible goddess, an unattainable role model, a purely sentimental figure to be rejected, incompatible with their idea of a liberated woman. John Paul II returns to the source, using the Word of God, making us rediscover the vocation of man and woman in the divine plan. In this way he gives the Church and the faithful the necessary remedies to heal our generation, sick and wounded after having been sapped at its foundations.

He writes:

> A woman's dignity is closely connected with the love which she receives by the very reason of her femininity; it is likewise connected with the love she gives in return.... Woman can only find herself by giving love to others.[1]

The Holy Father demonstrates that in marriage, as in religious life, a woman finds fulfillment in the unrestricted gift of self. It is here that she can deploy the full power of her love. The woman who allows God to fill her heart will become a fertile source, a treasure for her husband, for her children, and for the Church.

It is in being fully spouse that a woman becomes fully mother. Maternity does not exist without espousal, without the union in the gift of self and the welcoming of the other, whether on a natural or a supernatural level. How admirable is the mystery hidden in the body and the heart of a woman, in the receptivity of her very being where the power of life and love is deployed. This is why the devil is much more jealous of women than of men, because a woman's mission is first to *be life*, to give life, to give birth, and in this way participate most intimately in God's plans. The serpent knows that to obstruct God's plans he must attack the woman in order to reduce her potential as a giver of life.

In this way, in touching her in her maternity, he touches her in the depths of her identity, in the very heart of the mystery that is hers, and thus he plunges humanity into sterility. It is true that one cannot give life without giving one's life, and to give one's life is to shed one's blood, to renounce everything, accept all sacrifices, all sufferings.

John Paul has perceived that there is a mysterious relationship between suffering and giving birth, and this not only in physical maternity but also in spiritual maternity. The relationship between suffering and giving birth is the sign of a maternity that is much deeper and is part of woman's very being and that she shares with God in order to bring man to birth into divine life.

The actions that man exercises upon the world in a visible way and that are "outside" of himself, the woman accomplishes within herself, in an invisible way, in the same way as the child is formed within her own flesh. Her offering is an interior one; she offers herself, she offers the suffering of her heart. It is her suffering that becomes the bread of sacrifice and that, through an admirable exchange, God transforms into the source of life. It is in this that the woman is priestly by nature, through her capacity to suffer and to offer herself up, to die to self in order to give life. She is naturally disposed toward "priesthood of the heart," because the spirit of sacrifice, so natural in her, is an integral part of the spirit of priesthood. Her vocation is truly accomplished in the highest degree of love, which is the offering of her whole being to the point of the total gift of her life.

A Father in the Image of the Father

More so than his teaching, which reestablishes us in what is just and causes us to pass from the spirit of the world to the contemplation of divine wisdom, what touches me most about John Paul is what he communicates to us through being what he is. He is the icon of Christ, his representative on earth, the testimony of the incarnation of the Word, of this God who took upon himself our human condition with all our burdens and lived our sufferings and agonies. The Holy Father lives in his flesh something of the mystery of Christ the suffering servant, rejected, misunderstood, slandered, put to death, and even so continuing to give his life for us, continuing to exhort us, to proclaim the truth, whether it is popular or not, tirelessly, like Saint Paul.

Amidst all the slanderous campaigns against him, I could not help thinking of these words of Saint Paul to the Corinthians:

> *By using the weapons of uprightness for attack and for defense: in times of honor or disgrace, blame or praise; taken for impostors and yet we are genuine ... dying and yet here we are alive; scourged but not executed; in pain yet always full of joy....*
>
> 2 CORINTHIANS 6:7-10

John Paul II maintains in his person the graces of his two patron saints: Saint John, the disciple Jesus loved, resting like a child on the heart of his master, confided to Mary, resting on the heart of the "Mother," totally given (*totus tuus*); Saint Paul, traveling the earth to announce the gospel; John the mystic and Paul the apostle of the nations.

We can all see ourselves as his children—those who are active in the world, contemplatives, theologians, Bible scholars, worshippers, charity workers, missionaries, and lovers of Mary.

In this way the Holy Father is the image of God the Father for us. As Jesus said to Philip:

Anyone who has seen me has seen the Father.

JOHN 14:9

Thus, for me, John Paul is the living icon of our heavenly Father. On seeing him I so understand the Father's love and tenderness, the way God made himself vulnerable for us. "My God and my Father, power and tenderness," sings Father Labaky. We proclaim him similarly in the Creed, "We believe in one God, the Father, the Almighty."

An almighty God who was not a father would be terrifying, and a father who was not almighty would be totally ineffective in saving us. Our Holy Father is this image of strength and tenderness, of kindness, a father who is both demanding and merciful. This is really what we need today in order to be reconciled to God, to be healed of our fears, and to rediscover the trust and audacity of children who dare to ask all of their father. Ephraïm, my husband, often says that God gives in to our caprices because he has a soft spot for us, but he never gives in on what is essential for us, and when he wants to lead us to the place where we will be completely fulfilled, he does not mind us not understanding his way of doing things. The pope is not a politician or a demagogue; he is a father, and he does not allow himself to be overawed by our childlike cries of fear of what will be asked of us. A father wants to help his child to grow, and it is his tender firmness that reassures us, that allows us to believe that everything is possible, even the things that seem difficult to us.

Another thing that touches me deeply about John Paul II is the power of his prayer. The first time I had the joy of participating in one of his private masses in the little chapel in the Vatican, I was captured by the intensity of his prayer. It was as if I were drawn upward by his prayer and plunged into God with him, interceding for the Church and the world. I cannot help but think of Jesus, who withdrew from the crowd to converse with the Father. John Paul possesses an amazing capacity to withdraw into prayer wherever he finds himself. One feels that he is inhabited by the Presence, and lives in the very heart of the Trinity. As soon as he arrives somewhere, one immediately feels the radiance of God's presence in him, the intensity of this presence. One feels irradiated.

He does not content himself with thinking, acting, he "is," and he "is" intensely because God lives in him.

It is no longer I, but Christ living in me.

GALATIANS 2:20

Belonging to a Universal Family

It is a great privilege for me to be able to share my joy in belonging to the Catholic Church. First of all, because it is a family, and as in all families, everyone has his place, even the unruly child.

I love the Church because she is catholic, that is to say, universal, and the most diverse cultures, with the most opposing sensibilities, can find themselves at home there, like children of the same mother. The Holy Father, as Christ's representative upon earth, is the head, the principle of unity that allows all the diversities, the expression of all the differences, to exist, without putting the whole body in danger. It is just the opposite in sects and totalitarian regimes, which demand total uniformity, where being different is not possible without being considered as a dissident or being forced to cut oneself off from the group to create a new one.

I love this infinite richness that is expressed through the existence of the different spiritual families in the heart of the Church. Everyone can find the nourishment and the expression of faith that suits him or her without being rejected, while at the same time feel he or she is a fully committed member of the body. Thus, her members also enrich the Church by their own charisms, and not just as consumers, but also as collaborators, participating in the edification and sanctification of the Church.

The Catholic Church does not limit herself to what we see on earth. She leads us into contemplation of the heavenly Church, the Church triumphant, the saints, the martyrs, all those who have preceded us in faith, who have shown us the way, and who, through the communion of saints, are present among us to support us, help us in the tough combat of the faith that we have to live. They are also the beacons that guide us through the night of this world. The example of the saints encourages us, and we are fortified by their testimony. They reveal the beauty of the world to come, and they communicate to us the graces that were theirs during their pilgrimage upon this earth, the treasures that they amassed for us through the gift of their lives and the offering of their suffering, through the strength of their faith, capable of moving mountains.

All these treasures are ours within the Church. It is up to us to seize them and to make them bear fruit. "Take possession of the country which I have given you" (see Dt 9:23), God said to Moses. We must trust in the goodness of our heavenly Father, and obey his Word for us.

God freely gives us the gifts of his kingdom, but it is up to us to take them. We can die of thirst next to a well if we do not take the trouble of lowering the bucket in order to fill it with water. In the same way we can pass alongside all these riches if we do not decide to take possession of our heritage. God does not force us, the Church does not force us. Yet, if we want it, then everything belongs to us, and we can enter into the fullness of the world to come. Does Jesus not tell us? "To you is granted to understand the mysteries of the kingdom of heaven" (Mt 13:11).

Jesus is the one who takes the initiative, and it is within the Church that these mysteries are revealed.

Was it not to Peter that Jesus confided the keys to the kingdom of Heaven? This means that the fullness of the kingdom is given within the Church; in her is the fullness of Revelation.

> *So I now say to you: You are Peter and on this rock I will build my Church. And the gates of the underworld can never overpower it. I will give you the keys of the Kingdom of heaven; whatever you bind on earth will be bound in Heaven; whatever you loose on earth will be loosed in Heaven.*
>
> MATTHEW 16:18-19

God created me a woman, and I rejoice in his handiwork. Today, I praise him for the gift of his Church, for through this great sacrament I have come to encounter Christ. May you likewise be blessed.

Daughters of Abraham: Women of the New and Everlasting Covenant

*Glory be to the Father, and
to the Son and to the Holy Spirit:
as it was in the beginning, is now, and
will be forever. Amen.*

*I*t is always a bit miraculous for a Christian to live out his life in faith, and quite thought-provoking, if not disconcerting, for the nonbeliever to witness this life. A Christian realizes the imminent truth of Genesis 2:7, "the Lord God formed man out of the clay of the ground," and knows full well he shall return to that clay. Simultaneously, the Christian finds transcendent meaning in the reality of Christ, the God-man, through whom he can "do all things," for "nothing is impossible to those who believe."

This bold, living truth echoes across the centuries in the very life of the Mother of Christ, the first Christian and disciple of our Savior. Most poignantly, the simple words of Our Lady's "Magnificat" reflect a model exemplar for all people in acknowledgment of the gift of salvation through Christ. First and foremost, her prayer is a spontaneous response of humility and deep joy, based on her profound sense of gratitude. Mary, in her gratitude is appreciative of the gift she has received. She also views her life within the perspective of the history of salvation, uniting all of humanity and most especially the line of Abraham to herself in prayer and praise. She bears great witness to the fundamental starting point of understanding who we are as persons and, equally important, she bears witness to who we are not. As Saint Teresa Benedicta of the Cross (Edith Stein) noted before her entrance into Carmel, "Only someone who regards himself as nothing, who no longer finds in himself anything worth defending or asserting, only in such a person is there room for God's boundless action."

This is not a reference to self-annihilation. It is in union with the Scriptural understanding that one must lay down one's life in order to find it. As Catherine Doherty noted, "To love with the heart of God, we must empty ourselves totally of self, to allow Christ to love through us. Without him we cannot love anything or anyone, not even ourselves." Christ taught us this supreme truth through his Incarnation, for even though he was "divine, he did not deem his divinity something to be grasped at," but gave himself up to be crushed as a seed for the Tree of Life to rise. In the encyclical letter *Fides et Ratio* we learn that "It is precisely this philosophy in the Bible which allows man to discover Jesus Christ who is *the reference point for understanding the enigma of human existence*."[1] "The Truth is that only in the mystery of the Incarnate Word does the mystery of man take on light.... Christ, the new Adam, in the very revelation of the mystery of the Father and of his love, fully reveals man to himself and brings to light his most high calling."[2]

This concept of "kenosis," or self-emptying, is completely antithetical to the "modern" cultural mantras of self-actualization and personal empowerment. "Women, no less than men, are fulfilled 'in a sincere giving of self.'"[3] However, today, it is widely believed that in order to find oneself, a person must perpetually seek the fulfillment of his or her ego and in doing so gain "power" to move about the world in a self-satisfying manner. Hence, a popular bumper sticker in America reads, "He who dies with the most toys wins." Whatever the cost, the "I" must come first! Strangely, people find themselves living amidst much social chaos and materialism resulting from this so-called enlightened approach to living; its inhabitants are desperate for *emotional intimacy, order, and peace*. The search for meaningful relationships is at a fevered pitch, while simultaneously the focus on "self" has never been more pronounced. Where does this lead us? If "I need" and "I want" is the starting premise of my adult existence, then "I must" and "I will" do anything to satisfy myself. "After all," one may justify, "I am entitled to have all my needs met now, and I'm the master of my own world, right?" This ridiculous example screams out for a sane reply.

All one must do is take an honest, open-eyed look (especially in the "first-world" countries) at the society in which we live, and the problem of this unrealistic assertion is evident. This modus operandi lands one square in the middle of an isolated "unreality." When one's whole being is centered primarily on the self, a culture of death is fostered.

We, as human beings, are created to live in relationship with one another and in relationship with God according to the divine ordering of reality. Living in the image and likeness of God involves us all in the co-creative activity of developing a "culture of life." This creative responsibility necessitates our free-will cooperation. We are brought into eternal life by living as we were created to live. Mankind, having been fashioned in the image and likeness of God the Most Holy Trinity, will naturally reflect this divine community of persons. This community of persons is love itself. The nature of love, or "agape," is to see everything in the goodness of the beloved while desiring the greatest good *for* the beloved. The person of Jesus Christ is the principal reference point for understanding the nature of human "being," that is to say, "the truth about man" and the reason for his existence. Living *in* Christ brings us to see each person we meet as beloved, and his grace maintains for us a life of true emotional intimacy, order, and peace with each other. Jesus Christ, who said to his disciples, "Remain in my love," demonstrated that he is the way to enter into relationship with the triune community of divine love. In order to be fully alive, in order to be fully human, we must all experience this intimacy and *share this with each other.* "In order to be a teacher of peace, a woman must first of all nurture peace within herself. Inner peace comes from knowing that one is loved by God and from the desire to respond to his love."[4]

God's plan from all eternity is unfolding this minute for you and me. This plan is to bring each one of us into the fullness of the covenant relationship of the Most Holy Trinity.

Be not afraid; for I bring you good news of great joy which will come to all the people; for to you is born this day in the city of David a Savior, who is Christ the Lord.

LUKE 2:10-11

Two thousand years ago, the angel spoke these words to the witnesses of the arrival of Christ the King. While Our Lady gave birth in a manger, those who heard the angels singing ran to share in the joy.

Christ himself told his disciples, "Be not afraid." Still today, another man echoes them:

> *At the end of the second millennium, we need, perhaps more than ever,* the words of the Risen Christ: "Be not afraid!" Man ... needs to hear these words.... Peoples and nations of the entire world need to hear these words. *Their conscience needs to grow in the certainty that Someone exists who holds in his hands the destiny of this passing world; Someone who holds the keys to death and the netherworld* (cf. Rev 1:18); *Someone who is the Alpha and the Omega of human history* (cf. Rev 22:13)—be it the individual or collective history. And this Someone is Love (cf. 1 Jn 4:8, 16)—Love that became man, Love crucified and risen, Love unceasingly present among men. It is Eucharistic Love. It is the infinite source of communion. He alone can give the ultimate assurance when he says, "Be not afraid!"[5]

Who better than Our Lady demonstrates for us both *how to listen and how to respond* to the Living Word of God? It is Mary whom God chose as Mediatrix of all Grace, the "Woman" of Scripture, who even now "labors to bring forth her Son" (see Rv 12:1-2). At the end of this book, we focus on the transmission of God's grace as the ultimate work of Mercy. Mary, as Mother of God, Mother of Fairest Love, is *the* presence in salvation history that establishes for us the measure of holiness in conjunction with her Son, to which we must all strive:

> In bringing my reflections to a conclusion, I cannot fail to mention the Blessed Virgin Mother who reveals the Church's mission in an unparalleled manner. She, more than any creature, shows

us that the *perfection of love* is the only goal that matters, that it alone is the measure of holiness and the way to perfect communion with the Father, the Son and the Holy Spirit. Her state in life was that of a laywoman, and she is at the same time the Mother of God, the Mother of the Church, our Mother in the order of grace.

The Council concluded the *Dogmatic Constitution on the Church* with an exhortation on the Blessed Virgin. In doing so, the Council expressed the Church's ancient sentiments of love and devotion to Mary. Let us ... make our own these sentiments imploring her to intercede for us with her Son, for the glory of the Holy and Undivided Trinity (cf. *Lumen Gentium,* n.69).[6]

In the *Magnificat* of Mary, which we have used to frame the testimonies in this book, we reflect with her upon the exultation she expressed at the Annunciation. She responds to the Divine Initiative with her free will self-offering, her unreserved, "Fiat." [*"Fiat mihi secundum verbum tuum"*—"Let it be done unto me as you say" (see Lk 1:38).] Throughout her life, she continued to say yes to the Father, Son, and Spirit, in perfect imitation of her Son. She followed him *for us* to his cross and welcomed his resurrection in her heart with faith-filled joy.

It is precisely in this Paschal Mystery that the "great things"— which God who is mighty has done for Mary—find their *perfect fulfillment,* not only for her, but for all of us and for all of humanity. It is precisely at the foot of the cross that the promise is fulfilled, which God once made to Abraham and to his descendants, the People of the Old Covenant. It is also at the foot of the cross that there is an overflow of *the mercy* shown to humanity from generation to generation by him whose name is holy.

Yes, at the foot of the cross, the "humility of the Lord's servant"— the one upon whom "God has looked" (cf. Luke 1:48)—reaches its full measure together with the absolute humiliation of the Son of God. But from that same spot the "blessing" of Mary by "all ages to come" also begins.[7]

In the pilgrimage of faith, Mary precedes even the apostolic witness and causes us to ponder much over God's predilection toward her. The role of *the Woman,* and thus all women in salvation history, should not be underestimated:

> The whole ecclesial movement of women can and should reflect the light of Gospel revelation, according to which a woman, as the representative of the human race, was called to give her consent to the Incarnation of the Word. It is the account of the Annunciation that suggests this truth when it tells that only after the "fiat" of Mary, who consented to be the Mother of the Messiah did "the angel depart from her" (Lk 1:38). The angel had completed his mission: he could bring to God humanity's "yes," spoken by Mary of Nazareth.[8]

Mary continues to encourage, through her example, all men and women to *respond* to God's call throughout their lives:

> One must accept the call, one must listen, one must receive, one must measure one's strength, and answer, "Yes, yes." Fear not, fear not, for you have found grace; do not fear life, do not fear your maternity, do not fear your marriage, do not fear your priesthood, for you have grace. This certainty, this consciousness helps us as it helped Mary. "Earth and paradise await your 'yes,' O Virgin most pure." These are the words of Saint Bernard, famous most beautiful words. They await your "yes," Mary. They await your "yes," O Mother who must give birth. A man who must take on a personal,

family, social responsibility awaits your "yes"....

Here is Mary's response, here is the answer given by a mother, here is the reply of a young woman, a "yes" that suffices for a whole life.[9]

The *Magnificat* prayer should become our own:

We will be able to sing the *Magnificat* with interior exultation of Spirit if we have within us Mary's sentiments; her faith, her humility, her purity.[10]

Perhaps today, more than ever before, it is the age of the "woman." Women especially must take this reality into their hearts:

This Marian dimension of Christian life takes on special importance in relation to women and their status. In fact, femininity has a *unique relationship* with the Mother of the Redeemer.... Here I simply wish to note that the figure of Mary of Nazareth sheds light on *womanhood as such* by the very fact that God in the sublime event of the Incarnation of his Son, entrusted himself to the ministry, *and* the free and active ministry of a woman. It can thus be said that women, by looking at Mary, find in her the secret of living their femininity with dignity and of achieving their own true advancement.[11]

In the fullness of time, God brought forth a Son, born of a woman. That fullness of time continues to unfold today, and to bear forth the grace of God through the fruitful gift of femininity.

In the light of Mary, the Church sees in the face of women the reflection of a beauty which mirrors the loftiest sentiments of which the human heart is capable; the self-offering totality of love; the strength that is capable of bearing the greatest sorrows, limitless fidelity and tireless devotion to work; the ability to combine penetrating intuition with words of support and encouragement.[12]

How do we respond to God's invitation?

Mother Teresa, our beloved saint of the "poorest of the poor," reported that she saw the face of Christ on those she cared for, literally! She understood that it was her Savior *in her brother* who drew her out of herself and encouraged her to love in such a sacrificial manner. Her work often brought her into the homes of Hindu and Christian alike. She noted, "The joy of loving is in the joy of sharing and it is something so beautiful that *love* begins at home and that can spread like a burning fire from house to house. In this way, it will spread throughout the world. Peace, joy, unity and love." It is not a coincidence that several hundred years before Mother Teresa consoled the dying of Calcutta there lived a heroic predecessor who also ministered in the homes of those she was called to serve. This woman, Saint Catherine of Siena, wrote, "If you are what you should be, you will set the world on fire." Christ, who did everything for the glory of his Father, came to light a fire upon the earth. The greatest of saints understood this. They demonstrate, then as now, that the fire of Christ continues to burn through the pouring out of the oil of our lives.

History is filled with marvelous examples of women who, sustained by this knowledge (that they are loved by God), have been able successfully to deal with difficult situations of exploitation, discrimination, violence, and war.

Nevertheless, many women, especially as a result of social and cultural conditioning, do not become fully aware of their dignity. Others are victims of a materialistic and hedonistic outlook which views them as mere objects of pleasure and does not hesitate to organize the exploitation of women, even of young girls, into a despicable trade. Special concern needs to be shown for these women, particularly by other women who, thanks to their own upbringing and sensitivity, are able to help them discover their own inner worth and resources. Women need to help women and to find support in the valuable and effective contributions which associations, movements, and groups, many of them of a religious character, have proved capable of making in this regard.[13]

The Word Incarnate coming from the heart of God answers the essential question in the depths of every person. In this respect, then, this concept of living comes from the heart and nature of God himself. It is a sharing in the very life of God, whose indwelling Presence then radiates throughout all humanity in what Pope John Paul II continually refers to as the "civilization of love." Jesus Christ came to announce that "the Kingdom of God is near." Through Christ, it is as near to us now as the beating of our hearts.

How many self-styled answers has mankind attempted to provide in order to satisfy the aching in his heart? In the face of today's pervasive secular humanistic approach to life, a philosophy that is incapable of fortifying any genuine social stability and provides no ultimate fulfillment of the individual, the Church responds with wisdom and charity. In the teachings of Pope John Paul II, a science that enables us to better understand the nature of human existence has been pioneered: a *Christian humanism*, with its philosophical foundations rooted in Sacred Scripture. The focus of his pontificate has been the "human person" himself, *as revealed in the light of Christ.* This "personalism" of John Paul II, coupled with a "more adequate anthropology," which includes the "Theology of the Body," is so rich in its mystical beauty and so profound in its philosophical depth that we are, some twenty years after their initial publication, just beginning to see an inkling of localized, practical applications, and teachings.[14] This philosophical approach of the Holy Father will bring great healing to mankind. I am thrilled to be alive to see its beginnings.

In relationship to this Scriptural, philosophical, anthropological, and theological understanding of who we are as human beings, the Holy Father urges us to meditate upon Our Lady to enhance our understanding of ourselves:

> One can already perceive the immense dignity of women by the sole fact that God's eternal Son chose, in the fullness of time, to be born of a woman, the Virgin of Nazareth, the mirror and measure of femininity. May Mary herself help men and women to perceive and to live the mystery dwelling within them, by mutually recognizing one another without discrimination as living "images" of God![15]

In Mary's life, the Holy Father sees the example that enlightens Christian humanism and encourages us to go beyond the knowledge of *why* we were created and move forward into the awareness of *how* one must live as a "new creation in Christ."

The Church has always seen in Mary the foundation of hope, giving her the title of Mother of Hope, who is, especially now in this new millennium, leading her children into a fresh springtime, a new Pentecost. In reality, Mary's "fiat" inaugurated this new creation in us, effectively solidifying her role in salvation history as the missing link between a broken humanity and redemption and reunion with the Most Holy Trinity. When you or I say "yes" to God today, he hears in our voice the sweet reverberations of her agreement spoken two thousand years ago in the name of all the human family. A new humanity springs forth from her, while being accomplished *in* her. Through her the most delicate presence of God reached down to us, presented first in the form of the tiny conception of the King of the Universe in the throne room of her womb. In that instance in which the gate of heaven opened, the angels witnessed the dawning of that day which will have no end. The words from a sermon by Saint Anselm, Bishop, taken from the Office of Readings for December 8, the Feast of the Immaculate Conception, beautifully articulate this point:

Virgin Mary, all nature is blessed in you. Blessed Lady, sky and stars, earth and rivers, day and night, everything ... rejoices that through you they are in some sense restored to their lost beauty and are endowed with inexpressible new grace. The world, contrary to its true destiny was corrupted and tainted by the acts of men ... now all creation has been restored to life and rejoices ... the universe rejoices with new and indefinable loveliness. Not only does it feel the unseen presence of God himself, its Creator, it sees him openly, working and making it holy. These great blessings spring from the fruit of Mary's womb.... Lady, full and overflowing with grace, all creation receives new life from your abundance. Virgin blessed above all creatures, through your blessing, all creation is blessed, and not only creation from its creator, but the creator himself has been blessed by the creation.

To Mary God gave his only begotten Son, whom he loved as himself. Through Mary, God made himself a Son, not different, but the same, by nature Son of God and Son of Mary. The whole universe was created by God, and God was born of Mary. God created all things, and Mary gave birth to God. The God who made all things gave himself form through Mary, and thus he made his own creation. He who could create all things from nothing would not remake his ruined creation without Mary.

God, then, is the Father of the created world and Mary the mother of the recreated world. God is the Father by whom all things were given new life. For God begot the Son, through whom all things were made, and Mary gave birth to him as the Savior of the world. Without God's Son, nothing could exist, without Mary's Son, nothing could be redeemed. Truly the Lord is with you, to whom the Lord granted that all nature should owe as much to you as to himself.

Mary highlights the importance of the dignity of the human person, and illumines the gift of the feminine nature for the life of the human family as well as the Church while assisting in our greater understanding of the mission of women in the proclamation of the gospel and their role in salvation history. Let us look at the arrival of the "woman" from the biblical beginning. The Genesis account of the creation of the human race takes place according to a precise plan. Man, while alive in the midst of a world full of creatures, finds himself "alone." This "original solitude," as the Holy Father describes it, is deemed "not good," thus God intervenes and makes him a fit helper. John Paul notes that, from the outset, the creation of mankind is marked "by the principle of help, not one-sided, but mutual." Help not merely in acting but also in *being*. Womanhood and manhood are complementary not only from the physical and psychological points of view, but also from the ontological. It is only through the duality of the "masculine" and "feminine" that the "human" finds full realization:

> Indeed, from the very first pages of the Bible, God's plan is marvelously expressed: He willed that there should be a relationship of profound communion between man and woman, in a perfect reciprocity of knowledge and of the giving of self. In woman, man finds a partner with whom he can dialogue in complete equality. This desire for dialogue, which was not satisfied by any other living creature, explains the man's spontaneous cry of wonder when the woman, according to the evocative symbolism of the Bible, was created from one of his ribs: "This is bone of my bones and flesh of my flesh" (Genesis 2:23). This was the first cry of love to resound on the earth!

Even though man and woman are made for each other, this does not mean that God created them incomplete. God "created them to be a communion of persons, in which each can be a 'helpmate' to the other, for they are equal as persons ('bone of my bone') and complementary as masculine and feminine" (cf. *Catechism of the Catholic Church*, n.371). Reciprocity and complementarity are the two fundamental characteristics of the human couple.

Sadly, a long history of sin has disturbed and continues to disturb God's original plan for the couple, for the male and the female, thus standing in the way of its complete fulfillment. We need to return to this plan, to proclaim it forcefully, so that women in particular—who have suffered more from its failure to be fulfilled—can finally give full expression to their womanhood and their dignity.[16]

God then calls the man and woman to "fill the earth and subdue it" (Gn 1:28), thus designating to humanity the responsible use of the resources of his gift of the earth and a mutual caring for the gift of procreation. In this activity, too, the mutual complementarity signifies equality and dignity without "sameness." The impact upon the world would be significantly marred if there were an absence of either the male or the female. To paraphrase the teachings of our Holy Father, man is created as a free and intelligent being who is given the earth as a gift. He is called into a co-creative activity with God in the newly created world. He is called to transform the world as he interacts with it. This is essentially the task of "culture." Together, in this work, man and woman share equal responsibility. Therefore, not only do they participate in the divine transmission of life through procreation, together the man and woman are responsible for the creation of history itself.

In the initial creation of mankind and in the subsequent creation of culture and history, the presence of women in the process is intended by God to be a "gift." All that she is facilitates God's blessing of humanity. This subsequent blessing of humanity and the divine ordering of mankind in relationship to all other creatures occurs only *after* the creation of the woman: "God blessed them saying, 'Be fertile and multiply; fill the earth and subdue it. Have dominion ... over all the living things that move on the earth.' And so it happened. God looked at everything he had made, and he found it very good" (Gn 1:28-31).

The concept of seeing women as a "gift" is clarified for us through the pastoral application of this biblical instruction by John Paul II:

> When women are able fully to share their gifts with the whole community, the very way in which society understands and organizes itself is improved and comes to reflect in a better way the substantial unity of the human family. Here we see the most important condition of authentic peace. The growing presence of women in social, economic, and political life at the local, national and international levels is thus a very positive development. Women have a full right to become actively involved in all areas of life, and this right must be affirmed and guaranteed where necessary, through appropriate legislation.
>
> This acknowledgment of the public role of women should not, however, detract from their unique role within the family. Here their contribution to the welfare and progress of society, even if its importance is not sufficiently appreciated, is truly incalculable. In this regard I will continue to ask that more decisive steps be taken in order to recognize and promote this very important reality.[17]

Where are we today in this understanding of the gift of femininity and the knowledge of God-given equality and dignity of men and women? It is a temptation of a hedonistic, consumer-driven society, such as that of contemporary culture, to reduce all things to a commodity. The phenomenon of the Internet has given us an exaggerated example of this fact in the recently reported scandal of twin adopted infants being "sold" and "resold" to the highest-bidding parents through a website. Likewise, the equally appalling scandal of the adolescent sex-slave trading rings exists as further proof of the powerful and pervasive draw of the sin of exploitation on a global level. In this model of living where even human life is a commodity, there is no reciprocity, no mutual complementarity as in the image of the life-giving communion of the Trinity.

Our progress as a human family must not be based solely on scientific and material advancement. It must also include the social and ethical dimension. Here we are dealing specifically with human "spiritual values and relations." Very often, these areas of life develop quite inconspicuously, beginning with the daily relationships between people, especially within the Domestic Church—the family. Thus, the Holy Father is quick to point out, "society" as it exists owes much to the genius of women. In the area of interpersonal relationships, women are uniquely gifted to positively influence life. The Church, while it recognizes the important timing of this active participation, does not limit this "gift" to one social sphere.

> Women have the right to insist that their dignity be respected. At the same time, they have the duty to work for the promotion of the dignity of all persons, men as well as women.... In view of this, I express the hope that ... many international initiatives ... of which some will be devoted specifically to women ... will provide a significant opportunity for making interpersonal and social relationships even more human, under the banner of peace.[18]

How do we work for the promotion of the dignity of all persons? How do we as a people of God come to understand his plan for us as a human family? How do we as women respond to our calling to actively participate in the plan of God? By embracing the very call, life, and work of the Church.

A central theme of the pontificate of John Paul II lends insight into the answer to these important questions. He writes in the Encyclical Letter *Fides et Ratio* (Faith and reason), (n.2), "Among the different services that the Church must offer humanity, there is one she is responsible for in a very particular way: the cause of Truth...."[19] The fullness of truth is revealed in the person of Christ, who is the Truth.

With this understanding we are able to conclude with John Paul that only "Jesus Christ reveals man to mankind," and therefore the Church and her members must see as their primary responsibility the presentation of Jesus Christ to the world. The primary mode of presenting Christ to the world begins first with the conversion of our own hearts. The life of Christ is transmitted through his love, given to us first. We must love him in return, with our whole mind, heart, and soul, and cling to him intensely. We must live, breathe, move, and have our very being rooted in the grace and life of God, the Most Holy Trinity. When we live in him and he in us then we witness the love of Christ to the world without saying a word! It is his love that changes the world, one heart at a time. As we move in his love, we promote the dignity of all persons and better understand his plan for us.

This collection of personal testimonies has been assembled to serve as an instrument to accomplish this fundamental goal of presenting Christ to the world, while highlighting, through example, the mission of women in the Church and the special gift of the feminine genius for humanity.

> The decision to choose this "feminine" model of holiness is particularly significant within the context of the providential tendency in the Church and society of our time to recognize ever more clearly the dignity and specific gifts of women.[20]

Inspired by the example and direction of our Holy Father, this collection has intended to witness *from the heart* the personal experience of each woman as she was touched by Christ and chose to *remain in his love.*

The lives of these particular women have specific significance for our times. Twenty centuries of heroic labor on behalf of Christ and his Church have allowed them the opportunities they have today. This fact, coupled with their personal, daily decision for holiness, allows the divine prerogative given to women to manifest itself in a myriad of beautiful and remarkable ways. How blessed are we to have a pontiff whose many special charisms have enabled him to present this gift of femininity to the world!

> The Church has not failed from her very origins to acknowledge the role and mission of women, even if at times she was conditioned by a culture which did not always show due consideration to women. But the Christian community has progressively matured also in this regard, and here the role of holiness has proved to be decisive. A constant impulse has come from the icon of Mary, the "ideal woman," Mother of Christ and Mother of the Church. But also the courage of women martyrs who faced the cruelest torments with astounding fortitude, the witness of women exemplary for their radical commitment to the ascetic life, the daily dedication of countless wives and mothers in that "domestic Church" which is the family, and the charisms of the many women mystics who have also contributed to the growth of theological understanding, offering the Church invaluable guidance in grasping fully God's plan for women.
>
> This plan is already unmistakably expressed in certain pages of Scripture and, in particular, in Christ's own attitude as testified to by the Gospel. The decision to declare Saint Bridget of Sweden, Saint Catherine of Siena, and Saint Teresa Benedicta of the Cross Co-Patronesses of Europe follows upon all of this.[21]

Indeed, women have shaped and will continue to form the lives of generations. The women in this book are a wonderful example of this. Drawing close to the person of Jesus Christ, they have come to understand his ever-present love for them. They know the gospel vision of women through personal experience, which has led them into an interior freedom and given them an impelling desire to imitate Christ in his obedience to the Father. Far from feeling enslaved by and resentful of their God-given nature as women, they demonstrate a special willingness to pour themselves out in emulation of Our Lady, and, like Mary, in their serving they are blessed.

We are living in a time in the world when women are gaining a God-given authority that is intimately linked to the overall plan of salvation history:

> It is a "sign of the times" that woman's role is increasingly recognized, not only in the family circle, but also in the wider context of all social activities. Without the contribution of women, society is less alive, culture impoverished, and peace less stable. Situations where women are prevented from developing their full potential and from offering the wealth of their gifts should therefore be considered profoundly unjust, not only to women themselves but to society as a whole.... In fact, woman has a genius all her own, which is vitally essential to both society and the Church.[22]

The Holy Father has outlined as well as inaugurated an "intelligent campaign for the promotion of women," based on the witness of Christ:

> In his (Jesus') time women were weighed down by an inherited mentality in which they were deeply discriminated. The Lord's attitude was a "consistent protest against whatever offends the

dignity of women" (*Mulieris Dignitatem*, n. 15). Indeed, he established a relationship with women, which was distinguished by great freedom and friendship. Even if he did not assign the Apostles' role to them, he nevertheless made them the first witnesses of his Resurrection and utilized them in proclaiming and spreading God's kingdom. In his teaching, women truly find "their own subjectivity and dignity" (*Mulieris Dignitetam*, n. 14). In the footprints of her divine Founder, the Church becomes the convinced bearer of this message. If down the centuries some of her children have at times not lived it with the same consistency, this is a reason for deep regret. The gospel message about women, however, has lost none of its timeliness. This is why I wanted to present it once again with all its richness in the apostolic letter *Mulieris Dignitatem*, which I published on the occasion of the Marian Year.[23]

John Paul continues to write numerous encyclicals, exhortations, and letters that specifically address the topic of women. He has raised two women saints to the position of Doctor of the Church (one of whom died at the young age of twenty-four!) and has encouraged international conferences for women and the family. Along with calling for a special Marian Year, he inaugurated a new "Day of the Woman" (March 8), where he expressed the "wish that this celebration be the occasion for renewed reflection on the dignity of the woman's role in the family, in civil society, and in the ecclesial community." This pope has opened up the essential issue of the dignity, role, vocation, and rights of women today as seen in the light of the Word of God like no other leader in the history of the Catholic faith.

Just as Jesus spoke to women and requested his disciples to allow the children to come to him, so, too, has this pontiff encouraged a naturalness in relationship to women. As is noted in a recent book, *When a Pope Asks Forgiveness*:

The statements of the Pope are a manifestation of his particular affection for women in the Church. He gives expression to his tenderness with great freedom and in so doing, he radically revises the traditional papal attitude. Popes have never before been seen (but we hope henceforth to see it regularly) to kiss little girls, hug them, take them by the hand or almost dance with them. Even this change of behavior has been, in its own way a revision of history.[24]

John Paul II stands as a sign of solidarity and gratitude to women. In a critical evaluation of the Church, he has asked us to forgive those people in the history of Christian civilization who did not respect the position and presence of women and subsequently abused them in relationship to all they had to offer. In recognition of this painful reality he says:

Unfortunately, we are heirs to a history which has conditioned us to a remarkable extent. In every time and place, this conditioning has been an obstacle to the progress of women. Women's dignity has often been unacknowledged and their prerogatives misrepresented; they have often been relegated to the margins of society and even reduced to servitude.... And if objective blame, especially in particular historical contexts, has belonged to not just a few members of the Church, for this I am truly sorry. May this regret be transformed, on the part of the whole Church, into a renewed commitment of fidelity to the Gospel vision.[25]

He has urged us all to take up the task of acting upon the message of Christ regarding the dignity and role of women in salvation history anew:

When it comes to setting women free from every kind of exploitation and domination, the Gospel contains an ever relevant message which goes back to the attitude of Jesus Christ himself. Transcending the established norms of his own culture, Jesus treated women with openness, respect, acceptance and tenderness. In this way, he honored the dignity which women have always possessed according to God's plan and in his love. As we look to Christ ... it is natural to ask ourselves how much of his message has been heard and acted upon.[26]

Finally, he has motivated the Church to open wide the opportunities for women in all areas, as is tactfully noted, again, by Luigi Accattoli:

Here is demonstrated the novelty and the extent of the Pope's attitude toward women in the Church. He realizes that women should be more highly appreciated, thus admitting that the situation is defective; nevertheless, he does not see any need to correct the situation by means of a reform. Rather, he advises the full use of the ample resources that are already available:

"Today I appeal to the whole Church community to be willing to foster feminine participation in every way in its internal life.... The Church is increasingly aware of the need for enhancing their role.... The 1987 Synod on the laity expressed precisely the need and asked 'without discrimination women should be participants in the life of the Church and also in consultation and the process of coming to decisions' (Propositio 47: cf. *Christifideles Laici*, 51).

This is the way to be courageously taken. To a large extent, it is a question of making full use of the ample room for a lay and feminine presence recognized by the Church's law. I am thinking, for example, of theological teaching, the forms of the liturgical ministry permitted, including service at the altar, pastoral and administrative councils, diocesan synods and particular councils, various ecclesial institutions, Curias, and ecclesiastical tribunals, many pastoral activities, including the new forms of participation in the care of parishes when there is a shortage of clergy, except for those tasks that belong properly to the priest. Who can imagine the great advantages to pastoral care and the new beauty that the Church's face will assume, when the feminine genius is fully involved in the various areas of her life?" (Sunday Angelus, September 3, 1995).[27]

We are entering a new springtime for humanity and a renewal of the global culture is not impossible. "On the threshold of the third millennium, ... the Church intends to proclaim God's plan in a positive way, so that a culture may develop that respects and welcomes 'femininity.'"[28] As the natural world comes alive in spring, shall we not unite in a joyful response of praise and gratitude ourselves in this, the Church's new springtime?

The Holy Father has specified a game plan:

In union with all those who favor a culture of life over a culture of death, Catholics must continue to make their voices heard in the formulation of cultural ... projects which, with respect for all ... will contribute to the building of a society in which the dignity of each person is recognized and the lives of all are defended and enhanced.[29]

God's Call to Women is a living, cultural project. It is a celebration of the efforts of our beloved pope and a testimony to all that is good and worthy of praise regarding the Catholic faith and the gift of femininity in today's world. If we are to nurture and strengthen the culture of life, we must advance into this untried millennium with the Spirit of the New Pentecost and Our Lady. Humanity must continue to cross over this "threshold of hope" with bold vigor. Women, supported by the Church, can experience a personal flowering of their womanhood at this point in time and come to a deeper maturity as models of light, as Christ is the Light. As women advance in this way, they are better able to bring forth the gift of the fruitfulness of their lives and successfully collaborate in the realization of a civilization of love.

How do we offer ourselves totally in love? The imitation of Mary provides a blessed answer. Through her, we are led to Jesus. Imitation of Jesus leads us to heaven, for with his whole being Jesus said "yes" to his Father's will. To please our heavenly Father in everything, to be conformed to his will for his glory, should be our heart's desire. This is the plan of the Most Holy Trinity for all humanity.

What a tremendous gift is Mary! Let us rejoice in the awareness that God created us also to be "gift" for each other at this time of new beginning. Let us follow the example of Mary, who is the full revelation of all that is included in the biblical word "woman":

> ... a revelation commensurate with the mystery of the Redemption. Mary means, in a sense, a going beyond the limit spoken of in the Book of Genesis (3:16) and a return to that "beginning" in which one finds the "woman" as she was intended to be in creation, and therefore in the eternal mind of God: in the bosom of the Most Holy Trinity. Mary is "the new beginning" of the dignity and vocation of women, of each and every woman.[30]

Women living at this time are crossing the threshold of a new millennium: a new beginning, rich with potential, one that is founded on the gift of the lives of many heroic women who were imbued with the spirit of the gospel, holding Mary as their guiding Star. Today we are called by our Holy Father to take Mary *still* as our model and receive her as the *Star of the New Evangelization*. Let us not hesitate in doing so!

In closing, for all that he has done to advance the true theology of women (indeed for all that has been done by his predecessors as well), let us say, "Thank you, Holy Father! The women of the world love you." We join with you in our hearts in your historic *Act of Entrustment* (of the world) *to the Blessed Virgin Mary,* as we pray:

To you, Dawn of Salvation, we commit our journey, through the new Millennium, so that with you as guide all people may know Christ, the light of the world and its only Savior, who reigns with the Father and the Holy Spirit for ever and ever. Amen.[31]

Contributors

Joanna Bogle
34 Barnard Gardens
New Malden, Surrey KT3 6QG
England

Dr. Ronda Chervin
Our Lady of Corpus Christi
P.O. Box 9785
Corpus Christi, Texas 78469
U.S.A.

Josette Croissant
Communante des Beatitudes
Le Sacre Coeur
La Cropte / BP 42
53170 Meslay Du Maine
France

Marika Gubasci
4 Leichardt Street
Waverley, N.S.W. 2024
Sydney, Australia

Kimberly Hahn
808 Belleview Blvd.
Steubenville, Ohio 43952
U.S.A.

Dr. Alice von Hildebrand
43 Calton Road #16-K
New Rochelle, New York, 10804
U.S.A.

Genevieve Kineke
Canticle Magazine
517 Middle Road
East Greenwich, Rhode Island 02818
U.S.A.

Chiara Lubich
Movimento dei Focolare
Via di Frascati, 306
00040 Rocca di Papa, Roma
Italy

Christine Anne Mugridge
Sacred Arts Communications
P.O. Box 937
Santa Rosa, California 95402
U.S.A.

Dr. Susan Muto
Epiphany Association
947 Tropical Avenue
Pittsburgh, Pennsylvania 15216-3031
U.S.A.

Maureen Roach
120 Enos Lane
Watsonville, California 95076
U.S.A.

Joy Shiroi
Quinta das Avencas
R. Cidadede Faro
Lote 2-Bloco, 41, r/cB
2775 Parede
Portugal

Mercedes Arzú Wilson
Family of the Americas
P.O. Box 1170
Dunkirk, Maryland 20754-3346
U.S.A.

Notes

Introduction

1. Pope John Paul II, Apostolic Letter *Mulieris Dignitatem* (On the dignity and vocation of women), March 25, 1988, n.1.
2. Pope John Paul II, Apostolic Exhortation to the Americas *Ecclesia in America,* January 22, 1997, n.45.
3. Pope John Paul II, *Mulieris Dignitatem,* March 25, 1988, n.1.

Part One

1. Pope John Paul II, *Mulieris Dignitatem,* August 15, 1988, n.5.
2. Pope John Paul II, Apostolic Letter *Tertio Millennio Adveniente* (On the coming of the third millennium), November 10, 1994, n.48.
3. Pope John Paul II, Encyclical Letter *Redemptoris Mater* (Mother of the Redeemer), March 25, 1987, n.28.
4. Pope John Paul II, *Mulieris Dignitatem,* August 15, 1988, n.5.
5. Pope John Paul II, Encyclical Letter *Redemptoris Mater* (Mother of the Redeemer), (March 25, 1987), n.8
6. Pope John Paul II, *Letter to Families,* February 2, 1994.
7. Pope John Paul II, General Audience, December 6, 1996.
8. Pope John Paul II, General Audience, December 6, 1996.

Chapter One

1. Pope John Paul II, *Mulieris Dignitatem,* n.2.
2. Pope John Paul II, *Mulieris Dignitatem,* n.4.
3. Pope John Paul II, *Mulieris Dignitatem,* n.4.
4. Pope John Paul II, *Mulieris Dignitatem,* n.5.
5. Pope John Paul II, *Mulieris Dignitatem,* n.7.
6. Pope John Paul II, as quoted in *L'Osservatore Romano,* August 20–21, 1984, 5.
7. Pope John Paul II, Speech to the Cardinals and Prelates of the Roman Curia, as quoted in *L'Osservatore Romano,* December 23, 1987.
8. Pope John Paul II, Address to Participants at the International Dialogue of Ecclesial Movements, as quoted in *L'Osservatore Romano,*

   March 2–3, 1987, 4.

9. Pope John Paul II, Address to Participants at the International Dialogue of Ecclesial Movements, 4.

10. Pope John Paul II, Apostolic Letter *To the Young Men and Women of the World on the Occasion of the International Year of the Youth,* March 31, 1985 (Vatican Polyglot Press, 1985), 4, 62–63.

11. Pope John Paul II, Speech to the Bishops of the United States, Los Angeles, September 16, 1987, as cited in *Teachings of John Paul II* (Vatican Publishing House, 1988), 566.

12. Pope John Paul II, *To the Youth,* Paris, June 1980, as cited in *Teachings of John Paul II,* 1628.

13. Pope John Paul II, *Mulieris Dignitatem,* August 15, 1988, n.56.

14. Portions of this chapter relied upon information from the following talk given by Chiara Lubich: Address to the National Conference on the Apostolic Letter *Mulieris Dignitatem,* sponsored by the Archdiocese of Spoleto and the Catholic University of the Sacred Heart, Roccaporena, Italy, June 1989.

Chapter Two

1. Ronda Chervin, *En Route to Eternity* (New York: Miriam Press, 1994).

2. Chervin, *En Route to Eternity;* see also, Ronda Chervin, *The Ingrafting* (New Hope, Ken.: Remnant of Israel, 1993).

3. Ronda Chervin, *Feminine, Free, and Faithful* (Oak Lawn, Ill.: CMJ, 2000).

4. Franciscan University of Steubenville makes available audio and videotapes of *Freed to Love* so that leaders all over can gather teams and work with groups. For information about *Freed to Love* in any of its forms call 1-800-437-8368 or 1-800-783-6357.

5. Ronda Chervin, *A Widow's Walk: Encouragement, Comfort, and Wisdom from the Widow-Saints* (Huntington, Ind.: Our Sunday Visitor Press, 1998).

6. In the fall of 1999, Ronda Chervin became a consecrated widow in the Society of Our Lady of the Most Holy Trinity [S.O.L.T.]. She is a full-time professor at Our Lady of Corpus Christi, in Corpus Christi, Texas.

Chapter Three

1. William Shakespeare, *Hamlet*, line 90.
2. Blaise Pascal, *Pensées,* A.J. Krailsheimer, trans. (Penguin Group, U.S.A., 1995), n.347.
3. Pascal, n.194.
4. Dom Prosper Gueranger, *Octave of the Nativity*, vol. 14, p. 205.
5. Dom Chautard, *The Soul of the Apostolate* (Rockford, Ill.: TAN, 1992).

Part Two

1. Pope John Paul II, Address, Rome, October 23, 1982.
2. Pope John Paul II, Insegnamenti, February 14, 1982.
3. Pope John Paul II, Insegnamenti, February 14, 1982.
4. Pope John Paul II, Address, Rome, October 23, 1982.
5. Pope John Paul II, *Letter to Women,* June 29, 1995, n.11.
6. Pope John Paul II, *Redemptoris Mater,* n.36.

Chapter Four

1. Pope John Paul II, *Letter to Women,* n.7.
2. Susan Muto, *Womanspirit: Reclaiming the Deep Feminine in Our Human Spirituality* (New York: Crossroad, 1991).
3. Pope John Paul II, *Mulieris Dignitatem,* August 15, 1998, n.29.
4. Pope John Paul II, Encyclical Letter *Dives in Misericordia* (Rich in mercy), November 30, 1980, n.13.
5. Pope John Paul II, Address to Members of the Diplomatic Corps, January 15, 1994.
6. Pope John Paul II, Apostolic Exhortation *Christifideles Laici* (The vocation and the mission of the lay faithful in the Church and in the world), December 30, 1988, n.49.
7. Pope John Paul II, *Christifideles Laici,* n.17.
8. Pope John Paul II, Encyclical Letter *Redemptoris Missio* (On the permanent validity of the Church's missionary mandate), December 7, 1990, n.86.

9. Susan Muto, *John of the Cross for Today: The Ascent* (Notre Dame, Ind.: Ave Maria Press, 1991).

10. Pope John Paul II, Apostolic Letter *Tertio Millennio Adveniente* (On the coming of the third millennium), November 10, 1994, n.16.

11. Pope John Paul II, Encyclical Letter *Evangelium Vitae* (The gospel of life), March 25, 1995, n.105.

Chapter Five

1. Pope John Paul II, *Original Unity of Man and Woman*, January 9, 1980, n.3.

2. Pope John Paul II, *Original Unity of Man and Woman*, n.4.

3. Pope John Paul II, *Original Unity of Man and Woman*.

4. Pope John Paul II, *Mulieris Dignitatem*, August 15, 1988, n.29.

5. Pope John Paul II, *Mulieris Dignitatem*.

6. Second Vatican Council, *The Council's Message to Women*, December 8, 1965; AAS 58 (1966), 13–14.

Part Three

1. Pope John Paul II, Homily, Rome, February 11, 1981.

2. Pope John Paul II, *Redemptoris Mater*, n.17.

Chapter Seven

1. Pope John Paul II, *Evangelium Vitae*, n.43, paragraph 5.

2. Pope John Paul II, *Evangelium Vitae*, n.44, paragraph 1.

3. Pope John Paul II, *Evangelium Vitae*, n.14, paragraph 1.

4. Pope Paul VI, Encyclical Letter *Humanae Vitae* (On the regulation of birth), July 25, 1968, n. 17, paragraph 1.

5. Pope John Paul II, *Evangelium Vitae*, n.91, paragraph 1.

6. Mother Teresa, *Mother's Message for the World Conference on Women in Beijing*, September 1995.

7. Pope John Paul II, Angelus, February 13, 1996.

Chapter Eight

1. As in any area of theology, time and space do not permit a detailed discussion about the variations of belief among Protestant denominations regarding the ordination of a pastor: How to define ordination, whether both men and women can be ordained, how much education should be required before ordination, or even if there is such a thing as ordination.

2. Pope John Paul II, *Mulieris Dignitatem*, August 15, 1988, n. 26.

3. Pope John Paul II, *Letter to Women*, n.12.

4. Pope John Paul II, *Mulieris Dignitatem*, August 15, 1988, n.16.

5. How did a nice pastor's wife like me end up in a place like the Catholic Church, you ask? For more details on our journey of faith into the Catholic Church, see our book *Rome Sweet Home* (San Francisco: Ignatius Press, 1997).

6. Pope John Paul II, *Ordinatio Sacerdotalis* (On reserving priestly ordination to men alone), May 22, 1994, n.4.

7. Pope John Paul II, *Mulieris Dignitatem*, August 15, 1988, n.26.

8. Pope John Paul II, *Mulieris Dignitatem*, August 15, 1988, n.5.

9. Pope John Paul II, *Mulieris Dignitatem*, August 15, 1988, n.5.

10. Pope John Paul II, *Mulieris Dignitatem*, August 15, 1988, n.20.

11. Second Vatican Council, Dogmatic Constitution on the Church, *Lumen Gentium*, November 21, 1964, n.36.

12. Pope John Paul II, *Letter to Women*, n.10.

13. G.K. Chesterton, *Brave New Family* (San Francisco: Ignatius Press, 1990). See the article, "The Emancipation of Domesticity," p. 113.

14. Pope John Paul II, *Mulieris Dignitatem*, August 15, 1988, n.27.

15. Pope John Paul II, *Ordinatio Sacerdotales*, n.3, citing the Congregation for the Doctrine of the Faith, Declaration *Inter Insigniores*, n.6.

16. Pope John Paul II, *Letter to Women*, n.11.

17. Pope John Paul II, *Ordinatio Sacerdotales*, n.3, citing the Congregation for the Doctrine of the Faith, Declaration *Inter Insigniores*, n.6.

18. Pope John Paul II, *Mulieris Dignitatem*, August 15, 1988, n.27.

19. Many of these Bible studies and talks are available on tape through Saint Joseph Communications.

20. Scott and I have co-authored a testimonial that details the story of our

conversions. If you are interested in reading about our journey of faith into the Catholic Church, it is discussed in our book *Rome Sweet Home.* I have also co-authored a book on home education with Mary Hasson called *Catholic Education: Homeward Bound.* I've also been a contributing author in *The Fabric of Our Lives, Catholic for a Reason Volume I* (on baptism), available from Emmaus Road Publishing, 827 N. Fourth St., Steubenville, OH 43952; *Catholic for a Reason Volume II* (on Mary and the Rosary), and *Millennial Insurance* (on family preparedness for the new millennium), available from Missionaries of Faith, 162 S. Rancho Santa Fe Rd., Suite E-100, Encinitas, CA 92024; (888) 41-FAITH. In 1993, Scott and I helped found the Coming Home Network International (P.O. Box 4100, Steubenville, OH 43952) for welcoming new Catholics, especially those who were previously involved in Protestant ministry. In 1998, I helped establish LUMEN—Lay Union of Missionaries Evangelizing the Nations (LUMEN, 808 Belleview Blvd., Steubenville, OH 43952; (740) 283-1016), which encourages lay Catholics to be involved in missionary outreach; and I serve the Board of NACHE—the National Association of Catholic Home Educators (NACHE, 6102 Saints Hill Ln., Broad Run, VA 20137; (540) 349-4314), which assists and networks Catholic home-schoolers all over the world. More opportunities seem to be available regularly in Catholic TV and radio. Future publishing projects include the following, God willing: a five-year parish Bible study program; a book on the Church's view of openness to life called *Life-Giving Love;* a book on Proverbs 31—a vision for being a Catholic wife and mom; and a book for Catholic families' prayer for missions. (These are my projects—my husband's list is much longer!)

Chapter Nine

1. Pope John Paul II, *Mulieris Dignitatem,* August 15, 1988, n.31.

Part Four

1. Pope John Paul II, *Redemptoris Mater,* n.14.
2. Pope John Paul II, *Redemptoris Mater,* n.15.
3. Pope John Paul II, *Redemptoris Mater,* n.36.

Chapter Eleven

1. Cardinal Léon Joseph Suenens, *A New Pentecost?* (New York: Seabury Press, Portuguese Edition, 1975), 97–98.
2. Caryll Houselander, *The Reed of God* (London: Sheed and Ward, 1944), 41–42.
3. Pope John Paul II, *Crossing the Threshold of Hope* (New York: Alfred A. Knopf, 1994), 216–17.
4. Pope John Paul II, *Tertio Millennio Adveniente,* n.16.

Chapter Twelve

1. Pope John Paul II, *Mulieris Dignitatem,* August 15, 1988, n.40.

Conclusion

1. *Fides et Ratio,* n.80, emphasis added.
2. Second Vatican Ecumenical Council, Pastoral Constitution on the Church in the Modern World, *Gaudium et Spes,* December 7, 1965, n.22, as cited in Pope John Paul II, Encyclical Letter *Redemptor Hominis* (Redeemer of man), March 4, 1979, n.8.
3. Pope John Paul II, Angelus, June 18, 1995, citing *Gaudium et Spes,* n.24.
4. Pope John Paul II, World Day of Peace Message, January 1, 1995.
5. Pope John Paul II, *Crossing the Threshold of Hope,* 221-22.
6. Pope John Paul II, Address, San Francisco, September 18, 1987.
7. Pope John Paul II, Homily, Los Angeles, September 15, 1987.

8. Pope John Paul II, Address, Rome, July 13, 1994.

9. Pope John Paul II, Insegnamenti, March 25, 1982.

10. Pope John Paul II, Homily, Rome, February 11, 1981.

11. Pope John Paul II, *Redemptoris Mater,* n.46.

12. Pope John Paul II, *Redemptoris Mater,* n.46.

13. Pope John Paul II, Angelus, June 25, 1995.

14. For a collection of teachings on this subject, read Pope John Paul II, *Theology of the Body—Human Lore in the Divine Plan* (Boston: Pauline Books and Media, 1997).

15. Pope John Paul II, World Day of Peace Message, January 1, 1995.

16. Pope John Paul II, World Day of Peace Message, January 1, 1995.

17. Pope John Paul II, World Day of Peace Message, January 1, 1995.

18. Fides et Ratio, n.2.

19. Pope John Paul II, World Day of Peace Message, January 1, 1995.

20. Pope John Paul II, Apostolic Letter Proclaiming Saint Bridget of Sweden, Saint Catherine of Sienna, and Saint Teresa Benedicta of the Cross Co-Patronesses of Europe, n.3.

21. Pope John Paul II, Apostolic Letter Proclaiming Saint Bridget of Sweden, Saint Catherine of Sienna, and Saint Teresa Benedicta of the Cross Co-Patronesses of Europe, n.3.

22. Pope John Paul II, Angelus, July 23, 1995.

23. Pope John Paul II, Angelus, June 25, 1995.

24. Luigi Accattoli, *When a Pope Asks Forgiveness* (Boston: Pauline Books and Media, 1998), 106.

25. Pope John Paul II, *Letter to Women.*

26. Pope John Paul II, *Letter to Women.*

27. Accattoli, 112.

28. Pope John Paul II, Angelus, June 18, 1995.

29. Pope John Paul II, *Evangelium Vitae,* n.90.

30. Pope John Paul II, *Mulieris Dignitatem,* August 15, 1988, n.11.

31. Pope John Paul II, *Act of Entrustment to the Blessed Virgin Mary,* Saint Peter's Basilica, Rome, October 8, 2000.